UNDERSTAND

What Jesus Wants You To Know - And Why

By Paul Tubach, Jr.

UNDERSTAND

"UNDERSTAND" by Paul B. Tubach, Jr. is licensed under a Creative Commons Attribution-NonCommercial-NoDerivatives 4.0 International License

You are free to copy, share and redistribute the material in any medium, format or language as long as the text and content is not altered or misconstrued. Freely it was received… freely it is given. The licensor cannot revoke these freedoms as long as you follow these license terms:

- **Attribution** — You must give appropriate credit, provide a link to the website, and indicate if any changes were made. You may do so in any reasonable manner, but not in any way that suggests the author endorses you or your use. "Attribute this work" as: Paul Tubach, Jr., www.newearthministries.org.
- **NonCommercial** — You may not use the material for commercial purposes, i.e. not for any private, corporate, nonprofit or otherwise financial gain.
- **NoDerivatives** — If you remix, transform or build upon the material, you may not distribute the modified material. The creation or development of any derivatives, secondary workbooks or manuals from this book is reserved solely by the author.
- **No additional restrictions** — You may not apply legal terms or technological measures that legally restrict others from doing anything the license permits.

Paperback ISBN 978-1-949892-20-8
Library of Congress Control Number - pending
Produced in the United States of America
New Earth Ministries

Scriptures taken from the New King James Version. Copyright © 1982 by Thomas Nelson. Used by permission. All rights reserved.

Books and other materials are available online through
www.newearthministries.org.

March 2018

Table of Contents

Introduction	xiii
Understanding 101	1
Sojourners in a Strange Land	3
The Divine Conversation	6
Understand The Word	9
Understand 17 Words	10
Understand The Message	15
We are Salt and Light	18
Hear and Understand	20
The Enemy's Plan	28
Infinite Oneness	35
Seeds of Life	36
The Kingdom of Oneness	42
The Alternate Reality	47
What is Truth	50
Consistency of Truth	52
Peace and Truth	52
Promises of Truth	52
Alternate Reality – Oldness Again	53
"The Yearning"	58
The Divine Spark	64
Why Do You Strive?	69
According To Grace	75
Reserved or Preserved	75
Hades and Death	77
New Earth Doctrine	78
Where is Understanding	81
Understand This…	89
To Help Us Understand	97
The Intellect of Man	102

No Root Within Us	104
Understanding Kingdom Principles	108
Heavenly Test: Truth in Action	112
The Mind of Christ	125
Thinking Like Jesus	129
The One Thing	135
The Inner Witness	137
Change Is The Reason Why	145
To Change – Becoming New	148
The Transfiguration	150
The Light of Glory	159
Two More Scriptures	165
The Glory of Jesus Christ	169
Temples and Tabernacles	172
Seeds of Truth and Glory	181
Glory Revealed in Metaphors	184
Who Am I Lord	190
Transition	193
Transitional Places	200
Transition Tales	205
Transition Safety	208
Trans To Trans	209
Now Therefore	210
The Third Person	214
The Mystery of Man	217
What On Earth Are We Doing Here	224
Two Schools of Thought	226
Thorough Thinking Through	231
The Dianoia Way	233
Understand Oneness	248
The Big Picture	249

The Image Bearer Series

2. Listen – How To Hear God's Voice – better
3. Image – The Revelation Of God Himself
4. Dominion – Our Heavenly Mandate To Occupy Earth
5. Understand – What Jesus Wants You To Know – and Why
6. Commission – Created On Purpose For A Purpose
7. Gateways – Manifesting Heaven In The Midst Of Chaos
8. Here – The Kingdom Of Heaven Is

The Image Bearer Series is based upon Genesis 1:26-28: "Let us make man in Our image, according to Our likeness… and grant them dominion."

"Image" explains 'who' the Lord of Heaven and Earth is, "Understand" explains 'why' we are here, "Commission" explains 'what' man is and 'how' we were created by the Lord, "Dominion" explains 'what' we are supposed to be doing, "Gateways" explains 'how' we are to accomplish our earthly mission, and "Here" explains our eternal destination is actually – Earth.

Many tools were given to mankind that enables us to accomplish our mission objective to have dominion over the kingdom of darkness – and we need to comprehend this truth: earth is our 'Here' – and our 'when' is now! How God created us – and why – is directly related to our sanctification and accomplishing our multifaceted mission for being on earth.

Why are you here – and what's your purpose in life? These books will answer those questions.

When I began writing in August 2012, four drafts were completed within a year, then on Sept. 27, 2013, the Lord spoke to me and said: "You are My writer. Now write!" and then the Spirit directed me to finish draft #4 which became the initial book, "*Regenesis: A Sojourn To Remember Who We Are*," released in August 2014. Next, the Spirit directed me to work on draft #3 (in reverse order) and then, on October 24, the Spirit told me, "That is not one book with seven chapters – those are seven books." Thus, I have been writing the Image Bearer series under His anointing by hearing His voice and writing what I am directed to write.

Regenesis helped us discover man's true identity, as spiritual beings that are having a human experience, who were created good and upright by God "in His Own image according to His likeness" (Gen. 1:26-27), whereby we have been blessed with many wonderful grace attributes by the Lord to accomplish all that He purposed for man… since the beginning.

Yet for most of us, we've forgotten who we are… and we've forgotten what we are supposed to be doing. Regenesis reminds us who we are, and now, the Image Bearer series is reminding us what we are supposed to do, how we should do it – and more importantly "why" we are doing it.

The Image Bearer series builds upon that knowledge of truth that mankind was created good so as to become what we were created for: to bear His image and imitate Jesus in every respect according to His earthly example – and operate as His heavenly ambassadors for earth.

The heavenly pattern for mankind is: imitate Jesus.
The earthly pattern for this world is: become like heaven.

Who you are is not based upon what you do; "what you do" is based upon "who you are." We get our identity from Jesus. This realigned perspective regarding "who" we are … is to reorient the applecart of faith pointing in the right direction, to focus on Jesus, and to accomplish our primary mission: have dominion on earth – in the name of Jesus.

The numeric order in which the Spirit directed these books: 1,2,8,3,5,4,6,7 was not linear in the least. Let the Spirit guide you in the order He wants you to read them; however, learning how to "Hear God's Voice" is always mission critical to get started on His path for anyone.

On October 24, 2015, the Lord told me to put these books on the internet for free. This was unexpected, and then the Lord whispered to me, "Can you make money on My words? Freely you have received… freely give."

When the Lord tells you what to do, He will also give you His authority, with power and provision, to do all that He commands. We need to embrace this perspective regarding our life on earth in order to understand and comprehend who we are and what we are supposed to be doing. There is much joy and peace living in this manner, and yet… we all make this choice daily to live according to His purpose for His glory – or to live according to our best laid plans. If I can do it – so can you.

Jesus did it, and therefore – "As He is, so are we in this world" (1 John 4:17). I hope you enjoy the Image Bearer series. Grace and peace be yours in abundance.

It's all about Jesus – and God gets the glory!!

Glossary of Terms and Definitions

These are some keys to help navigate and understand the scriptures.

Heaven – God's throne, God's home and the permanent place where God's glory dwells
heaven – the spiritual reality of God's kingdom and Christ's presence upon earth
Glory – the fullness of God's presence; the fullness of all God is
Shekinah Glory – the manifest presence of God's Spirit
Christ – the manifest expression of God in Jesus, and regenerate (born anew) men
Jesus – the manifested Living God; Lord of heaven and earth; Lord of Glory; Lord of Hosts
Host – army (a very important term omitted in the NIV and some other versions)
Host of heaven – angels; sons of God and our heavenly brethren (Rev. 19:10)
Host of earth – sons of men, becoming sons of God in the regeneration
Man – the generic term for male and female to connote mankind, humanity, etc.
Earth – the planet; one of three permanent places within the kingdom of God
Hell – the absence of God; one of three permanent places within the kingdom of God; the pit
World – temporary realm on earth under the dominion and operational control of Satan
Satan – Prince of "this world" (formerly known as Lucifer before he rebelled and fell to earth)
Sin – the operating system of this world in opposition to God's sovereignty; separation from God; things done that cause separation
Spirit – the operating system on earth under the Lord's dominion; the Holy Spirit; God's Spirit
Grace – attributes of God's character that are freely given to man

Light – a metaphor implying God's truth
Darkness – a metaphor implying evil – and sinful lies of "this world"
Wickedness – taking credit for what God has done
Evil – using God's glory and power to accomplish your personal agenda
Paradigm – the operating systems of sin or "by the Spirit" on earth
Paradise – the earthly realm in oneness with God apart from sin
Dwelling – a temporary place to live
Abode – a permanent place to live (of existence)
Rest – the permanent state of being where God's presence abides (in your heart and in heaven)
Kingdom of God – all places under the authority of Jesus
Kingdom of heaven – a term used exclusively in the gospel of
    Matthew to describe the kingdom of God as it pertains to
    earth under the Lordship of Jesus Christ

- Life – the source from which all creation exists, and is made alive, as coming from God through Christ Jesus, who is "the Life" and the "author and finisher" of faith (John 14:6; Heb. 12:2)
- Living – those persons spiritually alive with life, who no longer operate in the shadow of Death while sojourning in earthen vessels that will eventually perish for lack of life
- Alive – the spiritual state of being in existence from God's perspective, even apart from the body, and abiding eternally in communion with God's Presence and Spirit
- Dead – the spiritual state of being in existence from God's perspective, but temporarily separated from Him; the eventual disposition of the earthen body without life
- Death – the spiritual state of being permanently and eternally separated from God; the temporary holding place of unregenerate dead that wait there until the judgment

Introduction

Faith is the most important part of our salvation *in Christ*, yet "understanding" is the most important part of our faith-walk relationship *with Christ*. Jesus asked His disciples many times "Do you not understand?" as words challenging them into deeper understanding regarding spiritual things pertaining to the kingdom of God.

We've been taught what to believe… but now we also need to understand "why"!

There are 17 different Greek words in the New Testament translated "understand." Consider the number of times Jesus said these words: faith (26x), love (43x), and understand (71x) – and we can see just how important this topic was for Jesus as He taught His disciples to understand – and for you and me to understand as well.

Having been thoroughly persuaded and convinced to believe the truth that Jesus is Lord, through faith, you are saved. Being born again, however, is the next step in the renewal process to be changed, transformed, know kingdom principles and understand how the kingdom of God operates.

Jesus said "You must be born *anew from above to perceive* the kingdom of God" (John 3:3) as a spiritual reality that surrounds you – right now. This spiritual event of "becoming anew from above" is the work of the Holy Spirit to change you, transform you and conform you into the likeness of Jesus Christ.

We are here to imitate Christ. By living in relationship with Him, and by doing His will on earth, we establish the kingdom of heaven in our midst.

As disciples, we may understand… yet we must also perceive. We were created for a kingdom purpose, and we must comprehend this to make sense of this as sojourners on earth. There are two ways of going about life on earth: the way of death or the way of life. The only way anyone is able to discern the difference between the two is to listen to the Voice of Truth – and be guided in the way of the Spirit to gain understanding.

Jesus doesn't need believers that just believe – He wants disciples that understand!

Understanding 101

> "But where can wisdom be found? And where is the place of understanding?" (Job 28:12).

If you could ask God one question... what would it be? What if God answered your question, but you didn't understand the answer... now what? Greetings, everyone... and welcome to planet earth!

God wants to talk to everyone – including you. And God has been talking to everyone, including you, since you were born, but somewhere along the way you stopped listening to hear His voice.

> "Who has put wisdom in the mind? Or who has given understanding to the heart?" (Job 38:36).

Wisdom and understanding come from God. In order to understand life on earth and God's messages to us, we need to see and understand things from God's perspective. Man has tried to understand and comprehend life on earth from man's perspective for thousands of years without any long-lasting positive results; so, what if you could ask God to explain everything from His perspective in a way that it makes sense to you? Now what?

Well, the first thing we discover is that our thoughts and our words are not the same as His thoughts and His words, and this is why our ways are inconsistent – and oftentimes in conflict – with His ways. We may be using the same words, but the pattern language of this world that is being spoken among men is not the pattern language spoken by God in heaven. The words may be the same, but the terminology is fundamentally different; hence, many on earth do not understand the messages we get from God unless the pattern language of heaven is decoded for us so that we may comprehend what is being said. And this is why the Divine conversation is oftentimes misunderstood! We listen for it, we may hear it, but we do not understand it.

> "Therefore I speak to them in parables, because seeing they do not see, and hearing they do not hear, nor do they understand. And in them the prophecy of Isaiah is fulfilled, which says: 'Hearing you will hear and shall not understand, and seeing you will see and not perceive" (Matt. 13:13, 14).

So, why did Jesus speak to us using parables rather than speaking plainly? Because the truth of God's kingdom is made known only to those who are diligently seeking His truth, that is, Jesus Christ; and when such a person begins the journey back toward God to understand God's ways, who diligently seeks to know and understand God's truth, the Lord says: whomever seeks to know… more understanding will be given to them (Matt. 13:11-13; Luke 8:18), but God will not give His wisdom and understanding to casual admirers or passive spectators because God is seeking worshippers – in spirit and in truth.

God's truth is not hidden *from* us – it is hidden *for* us to seek and find.

Three of the most important aspects of hearing are: understanding, changing and following – so that we may enter into newness in God's kingdom… through truth, change and oneness. These are the basic concepts within all "Image Bearer" books whereby understanding is the most important topic, yet this is impossible unless we can hear the voice of the Messenger, Jesus Christ.

> "My sheep hear My voice, and I know them, and they follow Me" (John 10:27).

When we hear the voice of Jesus, several things are expected of us: we will seek to understand the message, we will respond in truth, we will convert (be changed through sanctification), and we will follow Him as our Lord (become His disciples). Our salvation is dependent upon hearing the Messenger and assembling the truth of His message in our mind in such a way that, having been thoroughly persuaded and convinced, faith compels us to obey the Lord Jesus, follow Him and do all that He commands. Any break in this process is a potential rupture of the salvation promise we have with Christ Jesus. This is His Way – and there is no other way whereby men can be saved.

Sojourners in a Strange Land

If you traveled to a different country and you wanted to understand the messages spoken to you, then you will probably seek and find a translator to translate the pattern language of that country into your language. In this regard, heaven is no different. In order to understand the spiritual language of heaven, then you must begin speaking this language "through the Spirit." In other words, the Holy Spirit is our heaven-to-earth communications translator to help us understand the messages from Jesus. Ok, so how do we talk to the Holy Spirit? Well, we don't! The Holy Spirit intercedes on our behalf to hear messages from the Messenger who then guides us with wisdom to understanding His message. We do not talk or pray to the Holy Spirit; we pray to Jesus and our divine conversation is with Him "through" the Spirit. Much like a translator communicates words between two persons of different countries, likewise, the Holy Spirit communicates the heavenly language to us so that all men may understand God's message – in spirit and in truth.

> "But God has revealed them to us *through His Spirit*. For the Spirit searches all things, yes, the deep things of God" (1 Cor. 2:10).

Do you want to understand your life on earth from God's perspective? Well, if you do, then that is what the content of this book is all about: understanding God, understanding the deep things of God, understanding life on earth, and understanding His messages to us – from God's perspective.

God wants us to understand, so He communicates to us in a unique way that His children will be able to hear: through the Spirit.[1] Why in this manner? Why not speak to us using our pattern language? Because the pattern language that we speak, which is of this world, is based upon a lie and is inconsistent with the spiritual language of heaven, which is based upon Truth. We are the sons of men, aka the host of earth, but every one of us has been taken captive to the thoughts and pattern language of this world which stands in rebellion to God and is opposed to (anti) Christ. This worldly system cannot speak nor can it comprehend the spiritual language of heaven, so we must incline our ears and listen to the whispered voice of the interpreter, the Holy Spirit, in order to hear *and* understand the message.

Make no mistake about it… everyone is able to hear the message, including principalities and powers in this world that are seated in opposition to Christ, yet everyone on earth has been blinded by sin and, therefore, is unable to understand the message – apart from the Spirit's enabling. Everyone hears the words – and the sound thereof, but they cannot understand the message because the pattern language of this world that everyone has been taught to understand – is violently opposed to Jesus, whereby the message is often misinterpreted and maligned. And for this reason, the Spirit prevents the culture of this world from hearing, understanding or perceiving divine wisdom and truth because they would use it recklessly… like pearls thrown before swine.

> "And He said, "Go, and tell this people: 'Keep on hearing, but do not understand; Keep on seeing, but do not perceive" (Isa. 6:9).

> "They do not know nor understand; for He has shut their eyes, so that they cannot see, and their hearts, so that they cannot understand" (Isa. 44:18).

And this is why this world is opposed to (anti) Christ, because Jesus is the message and the Messenger who came to us to teach us

---

[1] For more information, read "Listen: How To Hear God's Voice" in the Image Bearer series by the author.

how to live according to the spiritual pattern that was given to us – and to help us understand. In order to hear and understand the message, the Lord gave us the opportunity to be spiritually "born anew" behind enemy lines so that we may more fully understand and comprehend the message of hope and redemption… and be saved.

Once we are saved *and* born again, and we are listening to and following Jesus, then we can get back to our primary mission on earth: have dominion over the kingdom of darkness (this world).

There are many people sitting in church every Sunday who believe in Jesus as our Savior who came to earth to save us, but they likewise have heard His words but did not understand the message for one main reason: they were not born anew by the Spirit. Being saved and being born again (anew) are two entirely different concepts in the salvation experience. Jesus said:

> "You cannot *understand* (*oida*)[2] the kingdom of
> God unless you are born anew" (John 3:3).

Being born anew means you should be able to understand the kingdom of God and know how it operates. Being born anew enables you to comprehend the mysteries of the kingdom. Being born again is not admission into the fraternal order of an elevated form of Christianity; being born anew means you have been called out, set apart and activated for radical grace and radical love as demonstrated by Jesus your Lord and your God – to change this world from darkness into light with the truth of the Gospel: Jesus is Lord.

> "Jesus answered, "Most assuredly, I say to you,
> unless one is born of water and the Spirit, he cannot
> enter the kingdom of God" (John 3:5).

---

[2] Most Bibles translate '*oida*' as "see" and also as "tell" in verse 8, but is better translated as perceive, understand.

Everyone on this earth has been born of water into the kingdom of darkness and has become enslaved to sin through doubt and unbelief by the prince of darkness. This is the spiritual reality that is upon the earth even now; however, the Lord created a way for us to disregard that spiritual reality and embrace the kingdom of light by being born anew by the Spirit so that we may enter the kingdom of God – and do the will of God.

Apart from being born anew by the Spirit of God, you will never hear and understand the pattern language of heaven or the spiritual reality of heaven that already exists upon the earth. Period! Nor will you be able to read the word of God to understand the message or comprehend the mysteries of God's kingdom. Everyone who is born of water upon this earth has learned the pattern language of this world, but unless you are born anew by the Spirit, no one can understand the spiritual language of heaven – nor can you live according to its' heavenly pattern. We are sojourners who have been taken captive to sin behind enemy lines (this world) by the prince of darkness (Satan) and we have been taught many lies about God, including such things as there are many ways to get to heaven and no one can hear God's voice. Balderdash! Jesus is the only way! And Jesus never promised us heaven… He promised us entrance into the kingdom of God.

Everyone can hear the message because God is everywhere and He is speaking to everyone all the time, but the Spirit brings understanding to our mind only when we are diligently seeking Jesus and pursuing a personal relationship with Him. And this is why the Holy Spirit guides us to the Door (John 10), so that we may enter in and have a divine personal relationship with Jesus Christ, whereby the Divine conversation may begin again – in newness.

The Divine Conversation

What does it mean "to understand"? What is the most important thing to know when a person is seeking to understand? A common language? A unified theory? How about truth absolute?

If you were to put a multitude of people in one room and asked them to define their answers based upon their knowledge and understanding, their perspective would yield an unlimited number of answers. Our perspective regarding these questions, as well as the big picture regarding life on earth, represents a "paradigm" that determines our understanding which influences our operation in day-to-day matters, but what if I told you that our worldly paradigm and understanding is inconsistent with God's perspective? What would be your first step to begin the journey to understand the heavenly paradigm from God's perspective? Purchase a book or video?

The most important thing is to have a willing heart that yearns to hear and understand God's words… and to love Him with the fullness of your attention and affection.

What is the big picture regarding man upon the earth? And what is the meaning of life? Did God create man or did he evolve? How were the cosmos formed? Does God exist and, by extension then, what is God? These are incredibly great questions to ask, but the answers are irrelevant without God's understanding. A thousand more questions will result in vanity, futility and a chasing after wind, which Solomon also experienced… even after the Lord blessed him with wisdom and understanding beyond measure. Solomon had everything, but he lacked the one thing needed to help him comprehend the mysteries of God's kingdom (which will be explained in a little while).

Why is man on the earth? If you believe in the physical reality of man from an evolutionary perspective, then there is no rationale to explain "why" because he is merely the highest evolved organism… whereby any person will perceive himself as either more evolved or less evolved than another person based upon their own standard of comparison (which is why mankind spends more time tearing down each other rather than the heavenly pattern of building up and edifying one another in love). Man's numerous opinions about life in general – are totally irrelevant to the truth found within the kingdom of God.

> Solomon said, "I applied my heart to know, to search and seek out wisdom and the reason of things, to know the wickedness of folly, even of foolishness and madness" (Eccl. 7:25).
>
> However… "Wisdom rests in the heart of him who has understanding, but what is in the heart of fools is made known" (Prov. 14:33).

Is there a simple answer that helps us understand what God wants from us? Yes, and you have already read it, but there are some who will continue to read with rebellious hearts…

> "… whose minds the god of this age has blinded, who do not believe, lest the light of the gospel of the glory of Christ, who is the image of God, should shine on them" (2 Cor. 4:4).

We need the mind of Christ!

Understand The Word

Many preachers and teachers tell us we need to believe the Word of God and stand upon the Word of truth so that we can walk in the truth of Christ, yet these phrases are typically wrapped around the written Word to imply obedience to a written document, i.e. the Bible. We have been taught these past four centuries, since the written word became available to the common man, to read the word, know the word, study the word and believe the word, and yet the Apostles preached this: accept the truth found in the teachings of Jesus Christ. Matthew, Mark, Luke, John and Paul all had "their" gospel, but they all received their gospels from the teachings of Jesus Christ as the Holy Spirit revealed truth to them and gave them "understanding."

Since the advent of the New Thought movement, with various scientology and unitarian theologies that sound like Christian doctrine (which focus on the self improvement of man without the grace of God that gives all glory to God), there has been a reactive response by many Christian denominations to teach against any human understanding that comes from the mind of man. Emphasis is placed upon "confess with your mouth and believe in your heart" thus bypassing the intellect of man altogether, as if we can turn off the mind that is tandem-connected to our heart in the oneness of our soul. "Trust your heart" is what I was taught, but I prefer to trust in Jesus with the oneness of my "heart and mind" i.e. my soul. They also said, "The mind is rational" and cannot be trusted with spiritual truth, but this is contrary to the teachings of Christ.

What did Jesus say about believing the truth with our heart or mind? Jesus taught us that hearing God's voice that leads us into spiritual understanding comes from the operation of the *mind with the heart* in unified oneness (Matt. 13:15). In order for us to attain this understanding that comes to us through the Holy Spirit whereby we are being born anew and transformed by the renewing of our mind, it is mission critical for us to understand the terminology Jesus used as well as the implied meaning Jesus meant.

The Greek language is very expressive and explicit when using specific words and terms to convey meaning and intent. For instance, there are eight words for doubt, four words for love, eight words for wash and at least seventeen words for understand, so let's examine various words that are used in the New Testament that convey the meaning and intent of Christ's message.

Understand 17 Words

A mind that lacks understanding is perhaps the greatest purveyor of doubt and unbelief. There are seventeen Greek words in the scriptures that are translated "understanding" and even more that describe knowing, knowledge, perception and comprehension:[3]

- 'Suniemi' (4920) to put together mentally, to comprehend, be wise, to consider, to unite perception with what is perceived (Luke 24:45; Matt. 13:15)
- 'Noieo' (3539) from 3563-nous, to comprehend, to perceive with the mind (as distinct from perception by feeling); think, exercise the intellect, understand (Matt. 15:17; 16:9, 11; 24:15; John 12:40; Rom. 1:20; Eph. 3:4; Mark 7:18; 8:17)
- 'Ginosko' (1097) to know or understand in the abstract, in the process of knowing; to come to know by experience or observation; to know (absolutely) by gaining knowledge (the truth), but less personal or intimate as 'oida' (Matt. 26:10; John 8:27)
- 'Epistamai' (1987) to know of or be acquainted with; to know well; to understand or comprehend (Mark 14:68; James 4:4; Jude 10)
- 'Nous' (3563) the intellect, i.e. the mind, seat of reflective consciousness, comprising the faculties of perception and understanding, and those of feeling, judging and

---

[3] All words found resulting from a study on UNDERSTAND in Strong's Concordance and Vines Expository.

determining[4] (Luke 24:45; Rom. 1:28; 14:5; 1 Cor. 14:14, 15 (twice), 19; Eph. 4:17; Phil. 4:7; Col. 2:18; 1 Tim. 6:5; 2 Tim. 3:8; Titus 1:15; Rev. 3:18; 19:7). Having been born anew, "this new nature belongs to every believer by reason of the new birth (Rom. 7:23, 25)"[5]

- 'Dianoia' (1271) understanding, a thorough thinking through, the exercise of the mind; deep thought, meditation (Eph. 1:18; 4:18; 1 John 5:20). *We are told to love the Lord with all our heart, soul and 'dianoia'* (Matt. 22:37; Mark 12:30; Luke 10:27). Other references include (Eph. 2:3; Col. 1:21; Heb. 8:10; 10:16; 1 Pet. 1:13; and esp. 2 Pet. 3:1). "Imagination" (Luke 1:51).
- 'Katalambano' (2638) to apprehend, to possess as one's own; to attain, obtain, appropriate; to comprehend (Acts 4:13; 10:34; 25;25; Rom. 9:30; Eph. 3:18; Phil. 3:12, 13; 1 Cor. 9:24)
- 'Piazo' (4084) to take hold of (squeeze gently), to lay hand on; to seize, to apprehend (Christ; John 7:30, 32, 43; 10:39; 11:57)
- 'Epiginosko' (1921) to know, to gain a full knowledge of; to become fully acquainted with, fully perceive; observe, acknowledge, discern (Mark 5:30; Luke 1:22; 5:22; Acts 19:34)
- 'Akouo'(191) to hear, not just the sensational perception of hearing the sound, but to understand the message by hearing *and* perceiving (Rom. 10:16; 1 Thess. 2:13); (1 Cor. 14:2) "no one hears" – no one understands what they heard because the words come as a mystery; (John 12:38) "who has believed our report" – i.e. heard and not understood)
- 'Phren' (5424) the thoughts in the mind, to have in mind, to think in a certain way; the cognitive faculties; it implies moral interest or reflection, not mere unreasoning opinion; in three places it is translated soul (Acts 14:2; Phil. 1:27; Heb. 12:3).

---

[4] Vines, word study on MIND.
[5] Ibid.

- 'Oida' or 'Eido' (1492) to know completely and absolutely; to behold, see, perceive; to know by perception, to understand perfectly (John 3:3, 8; 1 Cor. 13:2; 14:16); "You have not known Him (*ginosko*- begun to know), but I know Him (*oida*- know Him perfectly)" (John 8:55); "Do you not understand this parable (*oida*)" How then will you understand (*ginosko*) all the parables" (Mark 4:13).
- 'Gnorizo' (1107) to know, to make known (Luke 2:15; John 15:15; Phil. 1:22)
- 'Ennoia' (1771) thoughtfulness, i.e. moral understanding; intent (Heb. 4:12; 1 Pet. 4:1)
- 'Parakoloutheo' (3877) to follow closely, fully know, perfect understanding (Mark 16:17; Luke 1:3; 2 Tim. 3:10)
- 'Sunesis' (4907) a mental putting together (from 4920); intelligence; understanding; (Gnosis (1108) denotes knowledge by itself and apprehension of truths; Sophia (4678) denotes wisdom as exhibited in action by power of reasoning; Sunesis denotes critical, apprehending the hearing of things; Phronesis (5428) practical, suggesting lines of action)
- 'Mathano' (3129) to ascertain and understand (Acts 23:27), and is also the root for 'methetes-3101' – "disciple" as one who applies the knowledge of Christ to imitate Him
- Other terms used to convey understanding are: 4441 (Acts 23:34), 2154 (1 Cor. 14:9), 1425 (2 Pet. 3:16) some things hard to be understood

In contrast, there are negative terms as well:

- 'Agnoeo' (50) to be ignorant, not to know; to not understand (1 Cor. 14:38; Heb. 5:2; 2 Pet. 2:12)
- 'Asunetos' (801) unintelligent, stupid, without understanding (Matt. 15:16; Mk 7:18)
- 'Dipsuche' (1374) double minded; literally, two-souled (James 1:8; 4:8)

There are many other terms that also apply to knowing and understanding with the mind as well, and the Strong's numbers for them are as follows: 4993, 5426, 1011, 1014, 5427 (spiritually minded; Rom. 8:6 (2x),

We will examine various passages in scripture to help shed light on this "understanding" dilemma throughout this book. For example, on the road to Emmaus, Jesus met with two disciples soon after His resurrection and, unbeknownst to them as He walked with them, He began to teach them about the Christ.[6]

> "And He opened (*dianoigo*) their understanding (*nous*), that they might comprehend (*suniemi*) the Scriptures" (Luke 24:45).

The Lord Jesus "opened their understanding," referring to the complete opening '*dianoigo*' of the mind '*nous*,' so that "they might comprehend" '*suniemi*' the scriptures in their mind. Literally, it reads: "He opened up of them the mind to comprehend the scriptures." '*Dianoigo*' means "thoroughly open" and herein constitutes a complete and thorough opening of the mind by the Holy Spirit which cannot be closed. In other words, unless the Spirit of Christ thoroughly and completely opens your mind to understand the truth, then comprehension of the scriptures is limited, if not nearly impossible. The natural mind cannot comprehend spiritual truth, which is why the Spirit's opening of the mind as a facilitative function of being born anew – is imperative. The mind must be opened by the Spirit before understanding and perception can occur – but we must be willing for our mind to be opened! We cannot be standing between two ways. This is not an intellectual exercise; this is a work of grace.

Of the seventeen words translated "understand," five different words are utilized in 1 Corinthians chapter 14: v.2 (191), v.9 (2154), vs.14, 15, 15, 19 (3563 – nous/mind), v.16 (1492 – perceive) and vs.20, 20 (5424). We often focus on the main topic of tongues and interpretations in this passage, but it is equally important for us to focus on understanding the "why" as much as

---

[6] These four paragraphs are modified excerpts from "Regenesis" by the author.

the "what." Let us consider this so we may glean more from this wonderful message.

> "Therefore let him who speaks in a tongue pray that he may interpret. ^{14} For if I pray in a tongue, my spirit prays, but my *understanding* (3563-mind) is unfruitful. ^{15} What is the conclusion then? I will pray with the spirit, and I will also pray with the *understanding* (mind). I will sing with the spirit, and I will also sing with the *understanding* (mind). ^{16} Otherwise, if you bless with the spirit, how will he who occupies the place of the uninformed say "Amen" at your giving of thanks, since he does not *understand* (1492-perceive, comprehend) what you say?" (1 Cor. 14:13-16).

We need to understand 'with our mind' what is happening around us. It is not enough to just know. If we do not understand, then how is it possible for us to comprehend and perceive spiritual things? Exactly! It is impossible to understand, comprehend or perceive anything apart from the Spirit. To the naturally inclined mind of man, all spiritual manifestations will appear bizarre, crazy, incredulous and utterly foolish because they must be spiritually discerned by our spiritually enlightened mind according to the Spirit. If your church forbids tongues or the manifestation of spiritual gifts, then there is probably a good reason why: the Spirit is not welcome to operate in that manner. The Spirit does not make us do anything against our will. If the Holy Spirit is there, then the gifts will be operational, each distributed as the Spirit wills. If the gifts are not manifested, then the Spirit is either not there (which is spiritually impossible), or is being hindered by a controlling spirit.

Simply stated… apart from the birthing anew by the Holy Spirit, the spiritual reality that surrounds us will not make sense, nor will we be able to understand the gospel message from Jesus in the scriptures – because we lack the pattern language of heaven to comprehend the meaning and intent of the message.

Understand The Message

> Jesus said, "The time is fulfilled, and the kingdom of God is at hand. Repent, and believe in the gospel" (Mark 1:15).

The message of the kingdom of heaven that Jesus kept teaching us over and over is: understand the message and believe in the Messenger. In order for us to fully understand and comprehend the gospel, we need to understand: who Jesus is[7], who we are[8] and what our purpose on earth is.

Why is man on the earth? This is an excellent question and one of the main points of this book, which I believe has much to do with our first command from God: have dominion over the earth (Gen. 1:16, 28). And yet, it seems like there is more going on than that alone. People have been born and have perished for thousands of years – perhaps as many as 60 billion people over 6,000 years through 300 generations of man… and what seems to be the whole point of it? We are born, grow up, work to pay bills, create kids, work harder to support the family, live life, and after all this… the body dies and goes back to the earth from whence it came. Then what?

We have been told about the promise of eternal life with God in heaven after we die; however, is that explanation good enough to explain "why" man was put upon the earth in the first place as we endure many things and move forward in the midst of much adversity? "Who are we" and "why" are we doing "what" we are doing? There are a multitude of theories to explain the mystery of man upon the earth, and while this book proposes a slightly different theory, we may eventually find the answer… but we need to keep seeking truth with understanding in order to find it – from God's perspective, through the Spirit.

---

[7] Read "Image: The Revelation of God Himself" by the author.
[8] Read "Regenesis" by the author.

> "Ask, and it will be given to you; seek, and you will find; knock, and it will be opened to you. For everyone who asks receives, and he who seeks finds, and to him who knocks it will be opened" (Matt. 7:7, 8).

Truth is the key to the quest for the answers we seek, and once we know the truth, then understanding is given to us as a means to comprehend all truth and, especially, deep truth… specifically wisdom hidden within the mysteries of God.

Understanding who we are is only part of the equation; understanding *who we are to God* is supremely more important!

Man was created by God for a Divine purpose – and we need to comprehend this truth. Man was made, created, then commissioned by God to have dominion over the earth, then formed of the earth and then sent on a mission by God according to His eternal purposes. This sounds well and good, but it still doesn't help us comprehend "why"? What is God's eternal purpose regarding man upon the earth? Do we have any idea what we will be doing in the hereafter?

It seems we were sent to recover something which was lost or stolen, but somewhere along this journey man forgot what the mission is because now it seems we are operating without directions and without tools to do whatever we were intended to accomplish… or at least no one seems to know or remember based upon any wisdom having been passed down from prior generations. We are sheep following other sheep that don't know the reason "why."

When little children begin asking their parents questions to help them understand the world and how it operates, they keep asking, "why, why, why" questions – whereby most parents eventually succumb to this endless barrage with the "because" answer – and their quest to understand ends in frustration… and thus, another generation maintains the status quo.

Yes, we have the Holy Bible with enough scriptures to explain "why" and enough wisdom to change the world many times over; however, it seems we are being taught just enough truth in order to be complacent in our understanding of God and His eternal purposes for man. For starters, man was never promised heaven; Jesus never promised it, the Apostles never preached it and the Creeds don't teach it.[9] So, if we are expecting something that was never promised, then what else have we been taught that is inconsistent with God's purpose for mankind? Well... that is why the Lord told me to write what I hear.

The best chance we have to understand man's purpose on earth is to embrace the "dominion mandate" and follow Christ, but what do I mean by follow Christ? Isn't following Christ what the church has been teaching for nearly 2,000 years, yet without much success in making the world a better place to live? Truly, following Jesus Christ is the key to gain understanding... because Jesus came to show us the way and manner we were intended to live! Jesus said:

> "I am the way, the truth, and the life. No one comes to the Father except through Me" (John 14:6).

God knows that we thoroughly forgot what we are supposed to be doing on planet earth, so God came to earth and manifested Himself as Jesus, the Christ of God,[10] in order to teach us the original manner in which we were created to live upon the earth. This is incredibly important for us to comprehend: Jesus came to teach us and show us, in tangible ways and by His example – how to walk in "the Way." His focus on teaching us kingdom truth wasn't to tell us what we were doing wrong, but rather... how to live rightly in proper relationship with God Almighty.

This is the key to truth, knowledge, understanding and wisdom that helps us to walk in the Way of Christ: follow Jesus Christ! Say and do what He said and did. Live according to His example.

---

[9] Read, "Here: The Kingdom of Heaven Is" by the author.
[10] Read, "Image: The Revelation of God Himself" by the author.

Sounds simple enough: key in on Jesus only! … but it doesn't appear anyone has a clue because it seems there is still a piece missing from the puzzle. Even though we know Jesus is the key, what are we missing?

The Spirit, the Spirit, the Spirit!!!

Jesus is the Key – and the Spirit is the missing piece to comprehending the kingdom of God upon the earth. This is how man can live according to God's purposes and thus… to know what and understand why.

Are you intrigued thus far? Do you want to know more? Are you compelled to seek the truth?

We are Salt and Light

When Jesus referred to us as "the salt of the earth" and as "the light of the world" (Matt. 5:13, 14), He was communicating kingdom truth to help us comprehend who we are, and yet, Jesus spoke to us in metaphors and parables that many of us have difficulty comprehending, including myself.

In the Parable of the Sower, Jesus characterized us as being like, or having, four types of soil material in our field (i.e. our heart) that responds to the seed (which is the word of God) sown into us, but then moments later Jesus seems to change the terms and refers to Himself as the Sower, "the field is the world, the good seeds are the sons of the kingdom" (Matt. 13:38) and tares were sown by the devil. How can seed represent the word of God and also mankind, and the field represent our heart and the world? Jesus is sowing seed and so is the devil. See what I mean…

There may be a consistent thread within these parables that is veiled from our understanding, so let's look at salt and light as metaphors for mankind to see if we can shed any light on the matter.

Jesus referred to people as salt and light as two elements within nature that cannot be changed without altering their nature. If salt loses its saltiness, then it ceases to act like salt and becomes worthless; when the nature of salt has been altered or changed, it "ceases to be" salt. The word Jesus used to describe salt that "*lost*" its' flavor is '*moraino*' (G3471) and literally means, "to become insipid." [11] 'What do you call insipid, salt-less salt? Well, I'm not sure there is even a name for such a thing, but it is rendered worthless in value from God's perspective because it no longer has the essential nature to influence or flavor the world with God's truth.

When light is present, it disperses darkness. Darkness is defined as the absence of light, but light cannot be defined as the absence of darkness; light is light – and the nature of light cannot be changed… nor can it hidden under a basket. Light cannot be hidden anywhere because it is not hide-able and can never be extinguished by trying to contain it under or within something.

However, we can invite darkness into our life and partner with darkness and allow it to become dominate within us, and this is what Christ meant when He said…

> "The lamp of the body is the eye. If therefore your eye is good, your whole body will be full of light. [23] But if your eye is bad, your whole body will be full of darkness. If therefore the light that is in you is darkness, how great is that darkness!" (Matt. 6:22-24).

In this situation, we must repent from allowing sin and darkness from infiltrating our soul – and empty out the darkness that we invited into our earthen vessel whereby we partnered with evil.

Jesus said we are salt and light – and these pertain to our spiritual nature, but if our nature has been altered or changed to become saltlessness and darkness, then we have become insipidly

---

[11] Strong's Concordance.

worthless in regard to the kingdom of God.

Jesus is "the light of the World" and He told us "we are the light of the world" as a means of teaching us how to become like Him in every regard. Got it? We have a divine nature in the similitude of His Divine Nature, having been created in His image according to His likeness, so that we may think, say and do the same things Jesus did while He was teaching us the way to live and move according to His '*charakter*' at work within us… as holy, consecrated and sanctified (*hagios*) vessels according to His work being done to us – and for us – by the Holy Spirit in us.

Mystery solved!

Hear and Understand

        "Hear and Understand" (Matt. 15:10)

The primary mission of Jesus upon the earth was simple: teach them to understand the way. It was not that the disciples whom the Father chose to walk with Jesus were not intellectually up to the task, but time and again, we see Jesus asking the disciples, "Have you understood all these things?" (Matt. 13:51). Invariably, their answer was always a resounding "Yes," but within moments, another teaching or test of their understanding would be brought to them by Jesus – and the same result ensued: "How is it you still do not understand?"

What, then, do you understand about Jesus? Do you believe that He is the Son of God? How wonderful, because even demons believe – and tremble (James 2:19). Do you know that Jesus came to take away your sin? Great, but does your sin remain and do you keep sinning? Did Jesus rise from the dead and will He also raise true believers in the resurrection on the last day? Absolutely – but what do you mean by "true believers?" Are you a disciple of Jesus, or just a passive spectator and casual believer?

Herein lies the problem within Christian theology: just because we know about Jesus, doesn't mean we have a "true believer" personal relationship with Him. If you read this and have begun to take offense, then answer this question for yourself: describe your relationship with Jesus.

It is better to ponder and deeply consider this question – than to simply rush past its significance.

Describe your personal relationship with Jesus (other than Jesus being your Savior)? What was the last thing you heard Him say to you? The Apostle Paul had a way of asking and re-asking his question until the listener came to the same conclusion through personal self examination; is your relationship intimate – or shallow and superficial? Ok, do you want to know Jesus more?

If you want to know Jesus deeper and more intimately –you cannot be content with superficial knowing that lacks the essence of being a true believer and disciple of Jesus Christ.

How did you come to the knowledge of the truth? Was it by the hearing of the ears? Great, because that is how most of us got started on the path of faith that leads to righteousness, but do you continue to hear from the Lord on a regular basis? Do you even bother to listen or are you content in your knowledge of who you think Jesus is? You heard Jesus call your name as He invited you to have a personal relationship through the Door of faith, which is the "hearing of faith" (Gal. 3:2), but how have you continued to listen to hear His voice? How, indeed… because your salvation is dependent upon it!

> "My sheep hear My voice, and I know them, and they follow Me" (John 10:27).

Many claim to have a personal relationship with Jesus, but if you cannot describe this relationship or if you cannot remember that last thing He said to you or you cannot recall having had a personal encounter with Him, then is there enough evidence to prove that a divine relationship with Jesus exists?

Jesus came to teach us the way and to show us how to understand the kingdom of God. Within a broad scope, Jesus taught us the principles of the kingdom (Matt. 4:17) and then He began to teach us the mysteries of the kingdom in parables, but only those with spiritual insight and understanding could comprehend these teachings. Jesus wanted the multitudes to believe, but He spoke in terms that only the diligent who truly desire to seek and find truth will come to know and be able to understand it. Jesus wants all of us to believe and understand so that we thoroughly comprehend kingdom truth and, thus, are able to apply kingdom knowledge with spiritual understanding, combined with wisdom and maturity, to change the world according to the will of the Father.

We were sent to change the world. "You are the salt of the earth" (Matt. 5:13); "You are the light of the world" (v.14). This is 'who' you really are. You were sent here to 'season' the earth with the saltiness of kingdom truth that resides within you and you are to bring the light of this truth into the darkest corners of the earth. We are sons of light, and sons of truth, and sons of righteousness. It is for this reason that we were sent here and it is for this reason that we must remember who we are and why we were sent. Without the knowledge of this truth, we will never be able to understand, nor will we be able to comprehend the spiritual manifestations that are coming soon. But before we can do anything, we must be born anew by the Spirit, because apart from the Spirit of God, we can know nothing – and understand even less.

We live in a spiritual universe, but the lie of the enemy has taught us we live in a physical and material universe that we must strive to spiritually attain and ascend, yet nothing could be farther from the truth. You and I are spiritual beings having a human experience; we live in a spiritual reality that is known to us when our spiritual senses have been enjoined with truth and understanding. We sense there are multitudes of things happening around us all the time, but we do not understand for one reason: our hardened, weighty hearts do not want to search for hidden truth.

However, the nature of the kingdom is this: God has hidden the truth within us and He wants us to search for it and find it. The pearl of great price (Jesus, the truth) was hidden in a field (the world) and the Lord is searching to and fro for seekers of truth with their spirit who desire to know the Lord Jesus and imitate Him as the truest form of spiritual worship (John 4:23, 24; Rom. 12:1, 2).

The Lord wants us to seek the truth and find it so that we can become like Him. Trust me when I say that this is not heresy or blasphemy. The Lord wants us to become like Him, not as God, but to be like Him according to His attributes, thoughts and ways. Why else would He create us as His image according to His likeness, as *elohims* in the likeness of *Elohim*, if He didn't want us to become like him? Not just a likeness of Him, but to imitate Him in such a manner as to look and sound and think and live like Him in every regard except for one: we are not Divine.

We need to understand. Period.

For too long we have embraced the romantic superficial knowledge of the kingdom as "lowly sinners saved by grace;" however, the Lord wants us to rise up and ascend in spiritual maturity to bear spiritual fruit worthy of the kingdom – and to fill the earth with the atmosphere of heaven that is within us *and* flowing through us.

If the kingdom of heaven is not operational within you, then you are of little earthly good. The kingdom of God is already within you because God, who made everything and is everywhere and is in everything, is already in you and has already revealed Himself to you through the evidence found within all creation (the inner witness) – but – do you believe this? Indeed, the kingdom of God is already within you (Luke 17:21; Eccl. 3:11), but that does not mean you are going to heaven; it merely means that you are without excuse. Everything belongs to God already, but heaven awaits those who willfully seek Christ and desire to act like Him, and thus, become children begotten of the Father through faith in Jesus Christ.

Do you honor and imitate your earthly father? Great! How much more so you should honor your heavenly Father. If this is your desire, then imitate Christ!

You are the salt of the earth. You were sent to flavor the earth with the salty truth of Jesus Christ abiding within you, but if you are not living like a child of God and you are not standing together with Christ to do the Lord's will, then you are in danger of being cast out and trampled underfoot.[12] Make no mistake about it – either you are standing with Christ to become like Him by listening to His voice and obediently following Him as His disciple, and are being conformed into His image and His likeness to do the will of the Father, *and* you are avoiding sinful passions and desires and the cares of this world because the Spirit is at work within you – or you are doing the works of the evil one and your saltlessness salt will be thrown out.

God does not need more salt – He wants to have a personal relationship with you! If you are not willing or do not want to have, or desire to maintain, a deeper relationship with Jesus, then you still have no earthly idea why you were sent here. We are dual citizens of heaven and earth – and now is the time to show and prove where, and to whom, your allegiance resides. There is no second chance to get this right the first time. This **_is_** your second chance to live according to righteousness – or get thrown into outer darkness for all eternity.

Life on earth is a test to prove your allegiance to Jesus – and to be sanctified by the Spirit of grace.

We were residents of heaven "in Christ", but there was a cataclysm in heaven and seeds of doubt were scattered everywhere by the enemy (Satan). These doubting thoughts created fear and a loss of

---

[12] Read "Where Do We Go From Here" in "Here: the Kingdom of Heaven Is" learn about Hades.

trust within the children of God, so our loving and merciful Father sent us to earth to learn two of many lessons: to remember who you are – and remember the Lord! Do we desire to maintain a deep personal relationship that is established upon love and thereby trust Him at His word – or not? Do we desire to live according to His covenant agreements – or not? Do we desire to do His will according to His plan in the kingdom – or not? I can assure you, that if this seems like a simple request to follow, then you do not understand what is at stake, because millions of souls are perishing every single day without any hope because they lack understanding. God does not owe you anything! Everyone has been invited to come to the knowledge of the truth, gain understanding, and then live accordingly – but not everyone has accepted the invitation.

This is the meaning of the Parable of the Wheat and Tares (Matt. 13:24). Jesus sowed good seed in the kingdom of heaven (which are those who live according to the truth), but during the night while men slept, the enemy came and sowed weed seed (doubt) that also sprouted (into tares).

We live within a spiritual reality where the mind of man is the battleground between these two kingdoms (light and darkness, good and evil). On earth as it is in heaven, Jesus sowed good seeds of truth in us, but while we slept (in heaven as it now is upon the earth), our love and trust relationship with the Lord became corrupted by seeds of doubt and distrust. The enemy has very little imagination – and we can see him pulling the same routine with Eve in the Garden, and with each of us, over and over again. He sows seeds of doubt, and then he sows seeds of distrust in God's covenant words of truth for us. He gets us to doubt God's truth and then he distorts the truth so that we believe a lie – whereby we make a decision to act independently of Him and take reprehensible actions known as sin to do things we were told not to do. It was we who broke trust with God, and it was we who caused the separation known as sin that has negatively impacted our oneness with God. Where it was intended we grow truth, we allowed seeds of doubt to be cast in our field of faith and grow –

and because we were unable to withstand the onslaught of this cunning adversary and accuser of the brethren, Jesus Christ came to show us the way back home – because only Jesus knows the way.

Jesus came to testify to the truth (John 18:37), He overcame the enemy, He conquered sin and death, He came to show us the way back to the Father, and He came to restore us to the life we had before the cataclysm happened.

The power of God can be known by the veracity of His words. God does not speak a word casually! When He says it, then it shall be… unlike men, who must all give an account one day for every careless and casually spoken word.

> "But I say to you that for every idle word men may speak, they will give account of it in the day of judgment" (Matt. 12:36).

> "Are you still without understanding? The things that proceed out of the mouth come from the heart, and they defile a man" (Matt. 15:16, 18).

We live in a spiritual world and we will be judged by word and deed, not just deeds alone, but by words also, because words proceeding forth from the heart according to our intellect – are as important to the Father as they are to us. Anyone who speaks with lies, falsehood, guile, deceit, trickery, guilt and/or manipulation, a spirit of control, or any disingenuous means of flattery to acquire dishonest gain, are considered by the Lord as "an offense" and a threshold that others trip over. Truth and honesty are non-negotiable principles in God's kingdom.

You were one of the ones who fell asleep, as was I, and we allowed the enemy to sow seeds of doubt, distrust, discord, misunderstanding, unbelief, fear and every spiritual ailment within our soul. God protects us, but we also have a responsibility to remain alert, keep watch, be diligent and stay vigilant to guard the good seed and keep it (tereo-5083; Matt. 19:17) from corruption and defilement – by not participating in all things that offend (v.18; 13:41); either through our own deliberate actions or by imitating the actions of others, we carelessly allowed the enemy to challenge our beliefs and then change our understanding.

There is much understanding that is needed today, perhaps now more than ever before, because we live in a world full of words and messages and minute-by-minute news reports. There is an enormous amount of "word-data" that comes at us from every angle and most of it is presented in such a manner to manipulate us and get us to think in a way we were not thinking before. When we begin to doubt something, or we begin to adopt a spirit of distrust, then who do you think is behind the message? Yes, the enemy!

Every day we see ads in print, in television commercials, on billboards, in magazines, and on mobile devices and computers that are enticing us to want and desire something we do not have by pulling at our emotional strings to manipulate our minds into thinking about having – and to take action. Have you ever wondered why these ads and marketing campaigns are enticing you to do something beyond your capability? Well, think about it. You are being enticed by the cares of this world to adopt a world of careless words that prevents you from finding the hidden truth of God in all things… in every way similar to Satan's temptation of Adam and Eve.

We are no different today than when Jesus walked upon the earth with His disciples. The disciples were taught by the Lord daily and Jesus showed them the truth of the kingdom, but time and time again, they did not understand or comprehend. They were so accustomed to believing the reality around them that they were unable to understand kingdom truth – even when God Almighty stood in front of them. They had been indoctrinated into a religious system of institutional beliefs that were fundamentally hostile to the kingdom of God, so much so, that their hardened hearts were not able to accept Divine truth.

Jesus is today as much alive as He was then, and we also have the voice of the Holy Spirit who speaks to us to enlighten us with words of truth from Jesus, but, sadly, we prefer status quo. Much like the disciples, we are often amazed and perplexed when the supernatural happens, but according to the reality of the kingdom, these are spirit-normal occurrences. And these miraculous events should be a part of our everyday life – if only we had the faith of a mustard seed – ***and the understanding to go along with it***!

We need understanding! And we need it fast!

The spiritual reality of the kingdom is accelerating rapidly and the times and seasons are accelerating with them. And likewise, so also are the attacks of the enemy.

The Enemy's Plan

What exactly happened in the rebellion in heaven is a mystery hidden within the scriptures. There may come a time when we know, but in all fairness, we can assume what happened by looking at the MO of the enemy, which hasn't changed one bit.

One morning, as I was meditating upon the word of the Lord, I asked him, "Lord, why did you send us from heaven to earth?" I wondered why God could not have fixed the problem in heaven, rather than send us here where blind lead the blind. And the Lord replied, "To remove all seeds of doubt." From this word, the Lord has brought understanding to me so that we may understand the problem, as well as prepare in advance for the eminent attacks of the enemy.

Do you know how a gardener nurtures a garden? They remove weeds from the garden; and with each successive year, as the Lord continues to plow furrows of truth in our mind, weeds and weed seeds of doubt are increasingly removed until they are eliminated. We must believe!

Eve doubted the word that was spoken to her (yes, she heard it in the oneness of Adam before she was built from one of Adam's ribs) and this doubt was exacerbated by a lie from Satan who deceived her into denying the truthfulness of God's word.

Likewise, Jesus often asked His disciples, "Why do you doubt?" Doubt is the single greatest enemy to faith abiding in truth; it attacks a covenant trust that is easily broken by deceptive lies resulting in doubt and unbelief, but these covenant-breakers are easily ensnared by the dragnet of faith when confronted by truth… and believing in the truth.

Lucifer was blinded by pride to covet God's glory and thus, once iniquity was found in him, he rebelled against God. Having been blinded by sin, Lucifer proceeded to cast seeds of doubt in the minds of many angels in heaven and the kingdom of God was corrupted, everything that is, except the love of God. In this moment, the Father implemented a plan to regenerate all things whereby a new heaven and a new earth would be established with one exception: the presence of evil and all doubt that leads to sin and unbelief that culminates in death must be eradicated.

We are a covenant people; always have been – and always will be. We are a people who live according to a covenant agreement with God, as spiritual beings who resided in His presence in heaven before the foundation of the world (Eph. 1:4), and we will always be a covenant people – if – we remain faithful, trust in the Lord implicitly, and do not doubt. The enemy cast seeds of doubt in angels in heaven – and then was cast down to earth where he continues to sow seeds of doubt in men. The darkness that was removed from heaven is now upon earth, whereby the host of earth (sons of men) were sent into the darkness to invade earth as living lights with the truth of heaven within them. We are regime changers who are redeeming stolen kingdom property. If you are not walking in the light of this truth, then you are probably perishing – without understanding. Either you are standing together with Jesus and you are doing what He tells you, or your actions alone will judge you and condemn you to outer darkness. There are no two ways to look at this spiritual reality.

Even as God has sown good seed (children of truth on this earth), the deceiver has sown evil seed (children of disobedience). And there is only one way to tell if good or evil seed is being manifested by you: look at the fruit being produced.

Earth is the place where we are being tested and proofed to determine if we are standing together in allegiance with Christ – or we are aligned to the "prince of this world." If the Spirit is not in you, then you are not Christ's (Rom. 8:9). Earth is the place of sanctification where the refiner's fire is intended to burn away chaff from wheat and remove dross from earthen vessels; this is the working of the Holy Spirit to sanctify us and prepare us for the regeneration of all things. Regardless of whether good or evil seed is at work in you, the Holy Spirit is able to convert us by the knowledge of the truth and empower us to walk in righteousness, holiness and obedience to the truth. "For all have sinned and fallen short of the glory of God" and we are all without excuse, so this text should not be used as a license to hunt evildoers because our battle is not against flesh and blood "but against principalities, against powers, against the rulers of the darkness of this age, against spiritual hosts of wickedness in the heavenly places" (Eph. 6:12). The dragnet of faith according to the Spirit is sufficient alone to separate the chaff from wheat; He separates things new from the old things based upon your decision to act (Matt. 5:37; 13:52).

Our mission is simple: speak the truth, live according to the truth, declare "Our God Reigns" and have dominion over darkness upon the earth. It is this truth that sets people free from doubt and unbelief! And this is done as a working of the Spirit within us – to hear, believe, understand, convert, follow Jesus and enter into His salvation.

The kingdom of God is a spiritual kingdom based upon words. When God speaks… so it is. The *"ratio and oratio"* of His intellect made and created the universe with a Divine thought followed by His utterance (word). His Word created worlds, and covenants, and kingdoms, and in Christ all things stand together with Him – and *through Him all things consist and exist for Him.* And this includes you and me. The comprehensive importance of God's Utterance, His spoken word through Jesus Christ, is the very thing that holds everything together, especially us.

God's kingdom is a kingdom based upon His word. He says it… and it happens. When God speaks a word, then it will happen because His word never returns void; it *always* accomplishes what is intended. This is why it is so essential to believe every word of God, because it is truth, the whole truth and nothing but truth! Without this foundational understanding, we are unable to trust in anything, including the veracity of His word.

I have never subscribed to being a fundamentalist Christian who stands on every word of scripture. Rather, I stand on the truth contained within every word from God – and I believe it wholeheartedly.

> "It is written, 'Man shall not live by bread alone, but by every word that proceeds from the mouth of God.'" (Matt. 4:4).

During the past 70 years, the church has taught the inerrancy of scripture and to reverence His words contained within Holy Script, but, it seems, the Bible as the Word of God (capital W) has now become as much a religious icon as the golden calf; we prefer to read His Word rather than hear His word (utterance) that proceeds from His mouth. When we exalt anything higher than God Himself, then it has become an idol, and now it seems we worship the written word above the spoken word. Anathema!

Much to our shame, and to Satan's delight, when we refuse to hear His utterance (the Voice of the Spirit) by preferring to read the word in script, we are, in one sense, exchanging the truth for a lie. What do I mean? When we do not believe that God speaks today, or when we do not believe that He will speak to us, or we undermine the divine communication by saying we cannot hear His voice, or if we trivialize the word that we hear, or we claim He does not speak through our situation or circumstance which we then brush off as coincidence – we have traded the truth for a lie.

God can speak to us through an infinite number of ways, but know this… that He prefers to speak to us by the small still voice of the Holy Spirit when we quiet ourselves down long enough to hear His whisper. God has no intention of competing against the background chatter of a busy, self-willed life devoted to building our own kingdoms. He will continue to speak, just as He always has – and always will, as a small still voice within your (heart and mind) soul.

The enemy will do whatever things possible to prevent us from hearing His voice – and then he will do whatever things possible to cause us to doubt it, and worse even, to deny that we ever heard it! So, what things can we learn from the enemy to thwart his plans?

The Scriptures give us an outline of our enemy's strategy and, lacking imagination, he will continue to use this strategy.

1. Satan compromised his divine relationship with God by choosing to doubt
2. He entered into sin and continues to walk in sin and denial
3. He attacked the veracity of God's word (by doubting the truth)
4. He denigrated the truth of God's word (by denying its inerrancy)
5. He impugned the integrity of God (by inferring Him to be a liar)
6. He exalted his opinion above the sanctity of God's word
7. He set up a counterfeit kingdom to receive God's glory for himself
8. His goal is to cause everyone to doubt the word of truth and stumble into sin

Satan used this strategy to tempt and deceive Adam and Eve; He will attack us with lies and deceit to make us feel insecure, inferior and insignificant… and it doesn't seem like it takes much to get us to doubt the truth of God and freefall into sin. So, how do we avert this strategy?

1. Walk according to the Spirit of truth and you will not gratify the desires of the flesh
2. Maintain the divine relationship with Jesus through daily devotions, listening to hear His voice every day by reposing in stillness, meditation and prayer to know Him more
3. Reverence the Lord Jesus in His holiness and declare His sovereignty over all creation
4. Defend the truth and declare it whenever lies are uttered
5. Maintain the Lord's honor and integrity (who abides within you) by living a life according to truth and righteousness
6. Die to self daily and do not give the enemy a foothold to compromise you with seeds of doubt. If you sin, repent immediately, receive His forgiveness, and move on.
7. Proclaim Jesus Lord of all, worship the Lord in righteousness and truth, declare your allegiance to Jesus and devote your life to building His kingdom upon the earth
8. Tell other people about the good news of the kingdom that has come to earth – and the hope that is living in you

Now, with this in mind, let us return to our earlier quest to know and understand – and consider that an alternate reality exists upon the earth (the kingdom of darkness) and how Jesus came to vanquish this kingdom to help us return to the original way we were intended to live – in Spirit and Presence in Oneness with Jesus.

> "My people are destroyed for lack of knowledge" (Hosea 4:6)

> "The fear of the LORD is the beginning of wisdom, and the knowledge of the *Holy One* [*Jesus*] is understanding" (Prov. 9:10)

Infinite Oneness

> "Hear O Israel, the Lord our God, the Lord is One" (Deut. 6:5).

Understanding God in Oneness will require us to perceive His infinite nature. God began the creation and regeneration story with one thing: the thought of His intellect. He thought everything into being and Jesus spoke everything into existence – and through the manifested Word of God, all things were created by Him, through Him and for Him, that is, Jesus Christ, and He is the eternally existent One Who has been revealed to all men by the utterance of His Word, so that "all are without excuse."

During the days in which Christ lived upon the earth, He used the term "seed" in a literal manner, as something that can be known by what it grows up to become, yet I would like us to think of "seed" within a microscopic realm so we can understand God within the fullest extent of oneness as humanly possible.

God is Oneness. In Him all things consist. Within Him – is everything.

God is everywhere, infinite, eternally existent all the time, and everything – is within Him.

God is infinite! So then, it stands to reason, that our ability to understand Him is limited, yet our ability to express Him according to our thoughts, ideas, imaginations and actions – is infinite. We can have infinite thoughts and infinite understandings about who God is whereby God is not diminished one bit by what we say or what we think or what we do. God does not change, so it is impossible for us to change who He is by what we think about Him – but we *can* change how other people understand Him, and herein lies the problem when man chooses to talk about God with limited truth without any understanding; we tarnish the integrity of His character by expressing things about Him without understanding the essence and substance of who He is.

We choose what and how we think – and how to live according to what we think – which is based upon whatever truth we believe. On one side of the equation – is understanding by God's grace and truth within the prescriptive and predetermined will of God; on the other side is free will as the 'permissive and restrictive' will of self (or ego). We either choose to live in truth with grace and understanding according to the will of God or we choose to live according to free will in self-determination, but life eternal only resides within the Oneness side of truth.

The Father represents the highest goodness – and He wants us to live according to His standard of truth. God is big – *and* – He also exists in the microscopic details of life itself.

Seeds of Life

Jesus taught us many parables about the kingdom of God being like a seed. The seed is so easy to relate to, and at the same time, the root remains somewhat mysterious. Try watching a root emerge from a seed (patiently, as I have done) and you will get a small glimpse into eternity.

Jesus referred to believers as the seed of Abraham, and Christ refers to Himself as the Seed of David, and in both instances the word 'seed' is singular, not plural. We often think of seed from a human perspective as sperm originating from a man to fertilize the egg in a woman, and there is no contradiction of my belief in this regard either, but I want us to see the sperm and egg within the context of creation and God's oneness in microscopic detail.

The sperm and egg have DNA codes of information about both parents, and when they come together, the DNA codes are **united in oneness** to "create" a new living being. This new person is not two blended persons into one, but rather, two **becoming one in oneness** to beget 'one' in newness. This new one has a unique DNA code unlike any other human being and the DNA code of this new person can be stretched to the moon and back – seven times. Our God is infinite – and He often chooses to express Himself within infinite and often inexpressible ways. Understanding the vastness of our DNA is incredible, but there is one thing far surpassing this scientific discovery: what God actually thinks about us.

It says, "His thoughts of us are as numerous as the sands on the shore" and His many thoughts of us are good always and that we are His delight, not because of what we have or have not done, but because of how He made us – to be like Him in every regard (except His Divinity).

Everything that God creates has His fingerprint on it – and in it. Everything that exists is able to testify who the Owner is. If you think you are the owner of your own body, then think again. You began as a fertilized egg from your mother – as a single cell. Period! Just one cell! This is who you are and yet you have two people to acknowledge for this miracle within nature. Within this one cell are four elements: your father's DNA, your mother's DNA, the substance of minerals and elements from God's creation (nature), and the essence of God's glory which He places within everything that He creates. All things exist and have been created for His glory, not yours, so that in all things, God gets the glory!, not you or me. You are merely a steward of what has been given to you by God through the united oneness of two others.

So here you are as a one-cell being. You are a soul. . infinite in two dimensions. You may not seem like much at this point, being about $1/1200^{th}$ of a centimeter in size (.004 inches in diameter and just barely big enough to be seen without the aid of a microscope), yet you have all the DNA coding you need to become a human being – and the glory of God is in you as well. If nothing else happens beyond this point, the miracle of God's glory can still be seen, as a small seed *united in infinite oneness*, yet when this cell divides, not only is the DNA equally divided, but God's glory inhabits this new cell as well. His glory resides in every cell of your body and there is not one aspect of who you are that God does not know about. So intimately known to God are you that He knows the very number of hairs upon your head (even if that number is zero), and He knitted you together in your mother's womb, but the real question we need to seek and understand is this:

How well do you know God?

God is infinite, and God is everywhere, and there is not any place where God does not exist, except in the pit of separation reserved for those who reject Jesus and do evil. God is in you; however, just because God is in you does not mean that you are in God. God has a *dwelling place* in you; however, **God wants to have an abode in you where He can abide forever**.

This next concept is mission critical to comprehend: your temporary dwelling (house) needs to be "converted" into a permanent abode that hosts God's Presence and Spirit.

> "Heaven is My throne, and earth is My footstool. ***What*** house [tabernacle] will you build for Me? says the Lord, or ***what*** is the place of My rest?" (Acts 7:49).

> "***What*** is man that you are mindful of him"?
> A: Regenerate man becomes God's resting place!
> "***What*** house will you build for Me? says the Lord."
> A: Disciples of Jesus will build a permanent abode – on a solid rock foundation of truth!
> "***What*** is the place of My rest?
> A: God's rest is a place of permanent abiding

God's rest within us provides true spiritual contentment and peace for the soul according to the manner in which we were created, which nothing in this world is able to duplicate. Our place of rest is where God abides permanently, where all work has ceased in completion, where all hostility has been reconciled in peace and where all striving has been exchanged in joy.

> "For the kingdom of God is not eating and drinking, but righteousness and peace and joy in the Holy Spirit" (Rom. 14:17).

You are one member of the "host of earth," and you were created for the purpose of becoming a living tabernacle for the Lord… to host His Presence and Spirit; therefore, in order for you to live in eternity with *Elohim* (God in Oneness), then you must be united "in Christ" and become of one mind "with Christ" and make a permanent abode (*mone*-G3438, house, dwelling, tabernacle) in your heart for Jesus and the Father to abide *with* you.

> "[2] In My Father's house are many *mansions* (*mone*); if it were not so, I would have told you." "[23] Jesus said, "If anyone loves Me, he will keep My word; and My Father will love him, and *We* will come to him and make *Our* home (*mone*) *with* him" (John 14:2, 23).

Just because a person believes in Jesus doesn't mean a permanent abode was established in you. Therefore, make a permanent abode *within* you so God can manifest His glory and grace *through* you. This is the way and the truth of Christ – resulting in life eternal in the kingdom of God.

There is only one person who knows the way to the Father: Jesus Christ. This way is hidden and known only to Jesus (John 14:6) and the Holy Spirit (John 10:3; 16:13). There are many religions that teach about the path to heaven and eternal enlightenment, but these are false theologies; Jesus only is the Way. The Father and Son are living in Oneness, united in Oneness, in *Elohim* Oneness, and if Jesus is in you, then Jesus will lead you to the Father – but herein is the covenantal condition of faith: you must hear His voice, follow, understand, and obey Jesus. There is no other way!

> "Teach me to do Your will, for You are my God; Your Spirit is good. Lead me in the land of uprightness" (Psa. 143:10).

The glory of God is in every seed, including the single cell in which you began life upon earth. This cell divided, but the glory of the Lord remains in Oneness. Just as matter can neither be created or destroyed, neither can God's glory; and one more thing: *size matters not in the eternal realm of an infinite kingdom.* His glory is His and His glory will always be His and His glory is in all things and "all things are in Him." The abundance of many things is merely an illusion; all things are His, He delights in His things (including you) and His glory resides in all things because they are His – until such time when rebellious disobedient souls, by choosing to reject Jesus, judge themselves unworthy of His grace and eternal life, then – His glory returns to Him and those glory-less branches are removed from the vine to await the judgment fire.

Now consider this: if you remain attached to the vine of His glory, His glory will always remain with you. If Christ abides within you and the Holy Spirit dwells within you, then your salvation is secure, and the Father will receive you into His glory to unite your glory into oneness with the glory of His Son.

> "Abide in Me, and I in you. As the branch cannot bear fruit of itself, unless it abides in the vine, neither can you, unless you abide in Me. [5] "I am the vine, you are the branches. He who abides in Me, and I in him, bears much fruit; *for without Me you can do nothing*" (John 15:4, 5).

You have a light that was placed within you; this is not the light of love or hope or peace or any other Hallmark greeting card metaphors – the light is God's glory and truth. Just as Jesus is the Light of the world, being "the true light as having come from the Father," so also we are the light of the world, also having come from the Father in the name of Jesus. The light of God's glory was placed within us (i.e. our spirit) for the entire world to see because we were created as image bearers "in His image according to His likeness" to let this light shine as a testimony before all men – and as a testimony against the kingdom of darkness upon the earth as well.

We exist as earthen vessels "to be" a dwelling place for His glory and to reflect the awesome, wonderful and glorious character of the One who created us, Jesus Christ, who is the expressed image

(Heb. 1:3; *charakter*) and perfect representation of the Father's glory and goodness. And this is why we were created: to represent and reflect His glory in all we think, say and do. His magnificent glory is in us and we were created as earthen tabernacles to host His Presence; however, we are not to focus on "us" because His glory and His story *is not about who you are…* it is all about the Lord of Glory who dwells within you. You are a sanctified vessel to host His Presence. The focus is Jesus!

We can choose to live according to His standard – or we can compare ourselves against a lower standard, even that of our own, which is established by using others or self as the example. This creates such a low standard whereby excellence can never be achieved because excellence can only be achieved when compared against the standard God established, namely, Jesus Christ.

Consider how we determine what a good cup of coffee (or tea) is. Do we determine quality based upon all the other elements that are on the shelf for comparison purposes – or do we base our choice upon the highest standard of quality? If you are comparing your standard of coffee to, let us say for example, Starbucks, then your standard for coffee will never exceed that level of quality, but if you compare all quality to a supremely high unattainable standard, then you will always be striving to achieve excellence surpassing all other coffee manufacturers. The same is true in all walks of life, including humans.

God has a standard whereby man was established to walk therein – by imitating Jesus Christ. And Jesus came to show us the manner in which we were created to live, according to His standard. Can we achieve this standard? Yes and no. We cannot achieve this standard by living according to the flesh, but when we live according to the Spirit of life, then we can achieve this standard just like Jesus did, just like Enoch did, and just like Elijah did.

Yet our ignorance of God is truly astounding. When we choose to make the knowledge of God unattainable by any measure, so that we limit our understanding with inexcusable ignorance, we subtly choose to remain complacent in mediocrity – but that is not how God made us. We were designed with destiny in mind to live in eternity where we will know all things with a mind that has three million years worth of memory storage capacity. Our mind, soul and free will are going to remain with us as "who we are" when we enter into the next phase of eternity, so let me ask you this: how little do you see yourself? Do you still see yourself as "just a human being" or do you want to begin the journey to understand "who you are" as "greater than" according to the God Who Is – versus – the god you want.

Many years ago, as I was meditating about the character of God and His glory, I had two dreams back-to-back. In the first dream, I was with one sister who allowed me to stop what I was doing to write a message the Lord had given me, but in the second dream, another sister sought to interrupt my thoughts to espouse her religious opinions. So, which of these sisters was more sensitive to receiving and walking in God's glory?

Whenever we encounter someone who tries to limit or diminish God's glory in any respect, then our spirit-man will rise up within us to either come against it – or simply walk away, because you cannot argue with or contradict someone whose mind is limited, finite and completely made up '*diakrino*' according to their own understanding. The "God" standard for understanding Him is really big and is based upon His truth, not yours – nor anyone else's.

The Kingdom of Oneness

We know that God made all things, and in all things – God exists. And we know that Jesus created all things, and that in Him – all things consist (Col. 1:16-17). God is everywhere – and so is Jesus.

A friend of mine was telling me a story about how a man from Papua New Guinea came to the knowledge of Christ; He simply said, "You cannot get away from this person Jesus whom you serve." How right He is! So, let me take this one step further. God is everywhere, and God is in you and God has decided to express His glory by manifesting His glory in the seed of life itself (within you), so where do you think the kingdom of God is? Since Jesus told us the kingdom of God is within you, then this is to be taken literally.

> "The kingdom of God is within you" (Luke 17:21).

God is everywhere – and He exists in the unity of Oneness – in Oneness. This is a huge concept to consider, which will be discussed as we move along, but first, we need to establish some fundamental ideas to grasp the totality of truth… beginning with truth itself.

The first thing we need to understand is that there is one truth and only one truth, but there is a counterfeit truth in "this world" that stands in opposition to Jesus Christ. This counterfeit truth is the operating system of the "alternate reality" within "this world" that keeps people blinded by sin from ever seeing God's truth and understanding the big picture. There are many who, having believed in this alternate truth, have also come to a counterfeit understanding as it relates to mankind and what happens to them when they die. In the counterfeit reality, nearly everyone except the most evil and vile men on earth get to go to heaven because it is based upon one element of God's truth, that God loves everyone – which is true, but the counterfeit understanding rejects the very tenet this truth is based upon which results in true understanding: Jesus is the Truth (John 14:6) and Jesus is Lord (1 Cor. 12:3).

It is impossible to reject Jesus as Lord and expect all the privileges associated with life eternal because (this is the truth) you cannot claim God as your Father unless you have declared Jesus Lord of your life. The rules of adoption into the kingdom of God state this as rule number one: you must declare Jesus is Lord and profess your allegiance to Him.

> "For you are all sons of God through faith in Christ Jesus" (Gal. 3:26).

> "For through Him we both have access by one
> Spirit to the Father" (Eph. 2:18).

The second rule of adoption whereby you are given the tools of understanding to live as a citizen of God's kingdom is – you must be born *anew from above* by the Spirit of God.

> "Most assuredly, I say to you, unless one is born again, he cannot *understand* the kingdom of God" (John 3:3).

> "The Spirit Himself bears witness with our spirit that we are children of God" (Rom. 8:6).

Truly I tell you… it doesn't matter what you think, feel, believe or understand… because if you have based your entire life upon a truth that is not regarded as Truth in the kingdom of God, then you have been deceived to believe in the counterfeit truth within the alternate reality that promises you only one thing: eternal life in hell (it's in the fine print).

> "Jesus answered, "You say rightly that I am a king. For this cause I was born, and for this cause I have come into the world, that I should bear witness to the truth. *Everyone who is of the truth hears My voice*." (John 18:37).

> "My sheep hear My voice, and I know them, and they follow Me" (John 10:27).

The third rule of adoption that leads to life eternal is: you must be able to hear the voice of Jesus and obediently do what He says.

Any deviation from these three rules of adoption is inconsistent with the truth of God's kingdom!

Before anyone continues reading in a noble effort to gain understanding about life and spiritual things without being *in agreement with and living in full compliance with* these three rules of adoption – is utter foolishness. This book is about understanding how the kingdom of God operates so that you may become as you were originally designed and destined to be – sons and daughters of God. God has an incredible plan for you – ***but it is based upon His truth***, not yours or anyone else's.

Recently, I had a chance encounter with a cashier at a state park and we began talking about life and faith – and then I asked her if she was born again. The puzzled expression on her face took me by surprise. She was an active member of a mainline Protestant denomination but had never heard anything about being "born again." Listen, my friends, being a member of any church is not the standard for salvation by which you will be judged because Christianity is not a membership roster with lists of members from each denomination; Christianity is a way of life that lives according to faith in Jesus Christ as His disciple that follows His example – according to the truth He taught – that operates in obedience by hearing His voice and doing what He says… whereby you abide in oneness with Jesus the Lord.

He is the True Vine – and you must remain as a branch attached to His Vine and no other vine (or else your branch will be cut off and thrown into the fire and burned).

Yet multitudes have attached themselves to the vine of the alternate reality without knowing it.

The Alternate Reality

> If the reality you understand no longer makes sense,
> then return to the last place when it did.

There are two realities upon this earth: the Lord's truth and the lies of "this world."

Before we can even begin to discuss the spiritual reality that surrounds us even now, we need to understand *why* so many people are oblivious to the things of God and, therefore, are reluctant to hear any words of wisdom regarding the truth of God. These people have no concept whatsoever to say one way or the other if this wisdom or any other wisdom is true (or not) because they have no knowledge of the truth. They believe what they want to believe and this, then, is the first false premise within the alternate reality that people choose to believe: 1) truth is relative and subjective. If a persons' reality is based upon a lie, then their sole basis for living is based upon this lie; either they must confront it somehow or find rigorous ways in which to defend the lie which they are living. And this, my friend, is "the world" in which we are living in; it is based upon a lie and a deceitful, false supposition that is marketed as "a type of truth." The lie that is upon "the earth" is a counterfeit truth that was put here by Satan, the Devil, the father of lies since long before man got here... we merely stumbled into it. The Father of truth is God, who gives truth willingly and without measure to anyone who asks for it, and seeks to find it, and knocks upon truth's door for it to be opened unto them.

The second false premise: 2) this is normal and everyone is doing it. We have been behind enemy lines for so long that no one remembers what living according to God's truth is really like. This is not new – nor is it normal – nor is everyone doing it; and even though everyone has been doing it this way for centuries... is no longer a justifiable and defensible reason to continue doing it. A dysfunctional family has no clue what "functional" family values are until someone gets ahold of the truth to realize "dysfunctional" isn't normal; those changed by the truth are immediately ostracized by their own family because they cannot cope with truth – and because they fear change. When truth becomes the governing force in your life, changes will occur within you, but don't expect others to embrace it as easily as you did; they must defend the lie they are living in order to protect the status quo! Situation normal – all fouled up!

This is just my opinion, but the reason children are constantly asking the "why mommy" and "why daddy" questions while they are in the formative stage of understanding the world they observe is because it is inconsistent with the spiritual reality that they vaguely remember (while residing in Christ) as their original operating system of heaven. Children behave like cherubs… and then they are taught how to grow up and to conform to many family traditions and the patterns of this world; they observe hypocrisies, often forsaking their childlike nature in the process, but they are never fully convinced by the answers they get when they seek to understand "why" this or "why" that happens. It doesn't make sense, so they throw temper tantrums and then begin to act like little demons. Why? Because they are being taught to adopt the lies of this world that is radically opposed to the light of truth within them. They are salt and light, but they are being taught to adopt the counterfeit reality and become part of an ungodly spiritual pattern that is worldly and, thus, contrary to their spiritual nature within them.

> "But if your eye is bad, your whole body will be full of darkness. If therefore the light that is in you is darkness, how great is that darkness!" (Matt. 6:23)

"Essentially, by clinging to the bad, we have neutralized the good within us by making ourselves of "no reputation" (*kenoo*-G2758) meaning, "to abase, neutralize; make void; make of none effect; to neutralize the positive effects and renders them neutral; making negative is not within the definition of the word."[13] (See 1 Cor.

---

[13] Strong's Concordance.

1:17; Rom. 4:14; Phil. 2:7)[14] Man is not inherently bad, nor is he a negative component within the kingdom of God, nor was he ever given a sinful nature; however, we have been taught to believe many foolish things since we were young by parents, grandparents, neighbors, friends, teachers and clergy as well. We adopted these lies and partnered with them, and because these were added into our earthen vessel, they can and must be poured out!" [15] The new birth and renewing by the Spirit within us is dependent upon this voluntary emptying.

One of the principles I adopted when raising my children was to accept what they see and hear – even if it doesn't make sense… because we live within a spiritual reality that adults have been trained (more like indoctrinated) to reject (no, you didn't see an angel; no, there is not a boogey-man (aka demon) hiding in the closet; no, that is just your wild imagination… which implies the idea had to come into their mind from somewhere). Children are born with spiritual eyes that have yet to be dimmed by doubt and unbelief, and because I was able to keep an open mind, they were free to share many events with me about things they saw and heard – and even dreamed about. Dare to live in a place without "no" and live in the place called "yes and amen."

Having the nature and character qualities to believe like little children is what Jesus wants us to have! They were born with the light of truth – yet without the compromise of many lies.

> Jesus said, "Assuredly, I say to you, unless you are

---

[14] *Kenoo* (G2758) was used in Phil. 2:7 to describe Jesus "who made Himself of no reputation" wherewith some theologians have interpreted as "He emptied Himself" which is utterly preposterous. Jesus is the fullness of the Godhead bodily and did not need to empty Himself of anything, most especially iniquity or sin, nor did He empty Himself of His glory or Divine Nature. His life was poured out (Psa. 22) as an offering to satisfy (fulfill) the Old Covenant requirement of sacrificial offerings for sin – and then Christ rendered that covenant obsolete.

[15] Excerpt from "Gateways" (in the introduction) in the Image Bearer series by the author.

converted and become as little children, you will by no means enter the kingdom of heaven" (Matt. 18:3).

"You are the light of the world. A city that is set on a hill cannot be hidden. Nor do they light a lamp and put it under a basket, but on a lampstand, and it gives light to all who are in the house. *Let your light so shine before men, that they may see your good works and glorify your Father in heaven*" (Matt. 5:14-16).

The light is in you! Period!!! Jesus said, "You are the light of the world." End of discussion! Since we have partnered with evil and adopted many lies from the enemy to do things which our conscience cautioned against, we desperately must remember who we are and pour out any darkness from our lives. Darkness cannot overtake light… light can only be obscured. Do not forfeit your birthright as a child in God's kingdom by continuing to live with evil and darkness within you… pour it out! Repent… and return to the Light of Truth: Jesus Christ. *Kabash* the darkness! Dedicate your earthen vessel to the Lord and make it right and holy before the Lord – and stand before Him in your emptiness, brokenness and despair with a willing heart to be consecrated and restored to Him – in newness again.

Who you were and who you are – is not as important to God as who you are becoming – now!

What is Truth

God's truth is consistent, reliable and absolute! He means what He says, and there are consequences for not believing His truth and walking according to the truth. But, some will argue, much like Pontius Pilate did when he questioned Jesus, "What is truth?" Is truth subjective? These are fair questions which are impossible to support or defend unless there are some axiomatic principles and laws which govern the cosmos that are unchangeable, immutable and absolute.

God's spiritual reality operates according to these principles and principle number one is: 1) Jesus is the Truth. ***Truth is not a good opinion; Truth is a Person***! How do we know this truth is absolute? Because everything that Jesus ever said has been proven to be absolutely true. Jesus said, "I am the way, the truth and the life" (John 14:6). Jesus is the Truth of God and Jesus came as a witness to the truth (John 18:37; see above)... and this is why the alternate reality of "this world" rejects the Truth of God:

> "... the Spirit of truth, whom the world cannot receive, because it neither sees Him nor knows Him; but you know Him, for He dwells with you and will be in you" (John 14:17).

There are not two truths on the earth; there is only one truth and "an other" counterfeit truth in the alternate reality that portends to be based upon truth but in actuality is based upon a lie to support the alternate reality. This lie must employ deceitful practices with cunning guile in order to deceive and promote this deception whereby the standards and principles that support this lie are always changing. A lie will always need to defend itself, but truth needs no defense:

- You do not need to defend truth. Simply let it out and truth will defend itself.
- "If you always tell the truth, then you do not need to remember anything." (Mark Twain)
- How can you tell the truth from a lie? The truth never changes.

People who say a great many things but are constantly changing their opinion or position have adopted the lie as their fundamental and first principle... and the words they speak will always advance an ideology or agenda, primarily, their own.

The best description for this deceitful aberration of truth is to call it "darkness." Light is light. Darkness is the absence of light;

however, light is not the absence of darkness because light is the "standard" whereby light cannot be diminished, stopped, hidden or contained… which is why Jesus is the Light of the world. Jesus is the standard regarding truth.

Consistency of Truth

Another fundamental truism of truth is that it never changes… nor does it need to. Truth is consistent in all places everywhere, it is consistent across all periods of time and space, and it is consistent within all cultures. Truth has a high standard by which everything can be measured against, but a lie has an inconsistent, lower standard that allows for comparative analysis between various things to render a value judgment. Truth is uniformly and equally applied to everyone, but a lie will create subjective criteria to impose different values that apply to specific persons and things.

Peace and Truth

One of the primary litmus tests to determine the origin and presence of truth is to observe the evidence of peace within the ripples of the wake as it passes by. Truth does not create division; truth creates unity and oneness within the truth, but truth will often create division between ideas that contradict and, thus, are in conflict (anti) to the truth. Peace will always create a safe harbor within truth, whereas conflict and discord will always be waiting on the docks to confront anyone who anchors to a lie. Truth is pro – lies are cons.

Promises of Truth

It is estimated that there are around 7,400 promises within the scriptures that God has made for man. Many of these promises are conditional (if-then) based upon our acceptance to His covenantal agreement with us and, thus, it is up to us to honor our end of the agreement in order to claim these promises. The terms and conditions of these promises are never compromised nor are they disregarded by God; these promises are based upon an agreement in truth that will never be ignored, but the promises based upon the lie are unconditional, subjective, and often results in withholding the reward based upon a technicality or minor infraction. A promise based upon truth is always valid, but the promise based upon a lie will routinely pull the carpet out from under us; truth will readily invite us to "trade up" to a "better than" condition while a lie will invariably trick us into accepting a compromised or "less than agreed upon" option or solution that keeps us unsatisfied, unhappy and unfulfilled.

Alternate Reality – Oldness Again

In a word… we have believed an alternate truth with many rationalizations that creates a false reality to explain "this world" … which prevents us from understanding "the kingdom of God" and hinders us from comprehending the spiritual reality that is upon this earth and living according to God's truth.

One day, I had a chance encounter (and divine appointment) with "JB" in Myrtle Beach. We chatted about the books we were writing and he explained his being about "the last second" on earth in order to describe what happens to the body and the soul upon the death of the body. Many of us have been taught the soul leaves the body when we die, so then, where does it go? Most people will say to heaven because we do not like the other possible option, and this is the reason why this earthly reality does not make sense to us, because we (as a soul) do not go anywhere; it is the body that leaves the soul… and we remain in the third option. Allow me to explain…

The Lord God brought "*us*" together, in oneness as a soul (with body and spirit) for a Divine purpose according to His plan for the earth – and He breathed a spirit with life into us (on the earth) because we are "the host of earth" (Gen. 2:1). We are in the place that the Lord God created for us – *and created us for*, and this is where we are supposed to remain: on the earth. The physical body we were given was to accomplish this phase of His plan of creation "on the earth" in advance of the next part of His eternal plan: the regeneration of all things becoming (*anothen*) *new* again on the new earth!

The bottom line is this: the soul does not leave the body to go anywhere, but rather, the body leaves the soul and returns to the earth from whence we came, and the spirit with life that was breathed into us will return to God who gave it (Eccl. 12:7). Then, in the regeneration of all things, our new resurrection body will come down to us "from out of heaven" whereby we will be joined once again (restored) to Jesus – who is "the Resurrection and the Life."

Our soul never goes anywhere… because earth *is* our rightful place and proper habitation where we belong. The word "*habitation*" (*oiketerion*-G3613; *residence*) in Jude 6 and 2 Cor. 5:2 occurs only twice in the scriptures, which refers to the former home of angels that did not keep their "first estate, proper domain" residence which was in heaven, but had to leave their *habitation* on account of disobedience and rebellion. Angels have a proper domain (in heaven)… and the proper domain for humans – is earth; however, rebellion toward God will cause us to lose our proper domain on earth just like the angels lost theirs in heaven. Is this making sense? The reason it may not make sense is because we have been taught doctrines about heaven as our only eternal destination by men that have created "religions" within the alternate reality.

Christian theology has also adopted an escape-pod mentality for the soul whereby we are jettisoned off planet earth to enter into heaven, but this heaven-only understanding is not supported by scripture. Our eternal destination is Paradise on the new earth because earth is our proper domain. The true spiritual reality that surrounds us, yet is ignored by the pulpit of man, is why the good and glorious things of God never seem to get accomplished on earth. We keep waiting for the good to happen to us after we pass from this life into the next in heaven, but the goodness of God is already in us, as is heaven – and we were sent here to manifest the glory of God that dwells within us – here and now! Saints of God – it's time to manifest the glory of heaven that was hidden in us – and let it out!

We have been tricked by Satan to seek the glory and pleasures of paradise on earth during this life – and then hope for paradise in heaven in the hereafter rather than releasing the atmosphere of heaven onto the earth even now (thus, having dominion over Satan's kingdom). By enjoying paradise on earth now – which prevents us from doing God's will to establish the kingdom of heaven HERE, we are forfeiting Paradise on earth in the hereafter. This inverted human understanding of eternal life results from centuries of religious doctrine to comprehend life on earth from man's perspective rather than from God's perspective, which is why the greater things of God never get accomplished on the earth. We believed the lie and compromised God's truth!

We have been tricked into believing an alternate reality (paradigm) within a grand illusion that prevents us from doing God's will and releasing heaven upon the earth because we believed the lies of the enemy that keeps us separated from God and in bondage to sin. And the biggest lie of all is also the greatest illusion on earth. *We can never be separated from the love of God.*

> "For I am persuaded that neither death nor life, nor angels nor principalities nor powers, nor things present nor things to come, [39] nor height nor depth, nor any other created thing, shall be able to separate us from the love of God which is in Christ Jesus our Lord" (Rom. 8:38, 39).

However, when we see this life as a continuation of the life we had "in Christ" before the foundation of the world (Eph. 1:4) and we are on earth to accomplish His will for the earth, by grace through faith, then we will enter the eternal life phase on earth that we will experience *with* Jesus as the faithful and obedient sheep of His pasture during our next generation of this life *with* Christ in the Garden of God: in Paradise – on the new earth! Our perspective regarding this life on earth must become radically changed – by His truth. Simply put…the earthen-vessel phase of our personal relationship in Christ upon the earth is temporary, but our response to Him in this life will determine our eternal outcome *with* Him.

You are a spiritual being that is eternal that is having a human experience for one season of eternity upon the earth. The reality of heaven and hell is already upon the earth, such that you will determine which reality you are going to live in for all eternity according to the way and manner of life you lived. Just like the angels that are in heaven, they had a choice… but one-third were swept away by believing in a false promise by Satan and they lost their rightful place in heaven; and humanity is being given the same choice as well. We will always remain on earth, yet *you* shall determine which kingdom reality you are going to live in (heaven or hell), and this decision is an experiential choice based upon the life you are living now which is based upon Who you give the glory of your life to – and how you lived according to what you believed (which is called faith).

Just as our earthen vessel was given to us, so also this earthen vessel is taken from us at death and given over to corruption. The spirit that the Lord God gave us was given to help the soul of man complete this earthly sojourn and to help us (in our weakness, that is, the body of flesh), under the guidance and tutoring of the Holy Spirit, to return to Him who created us in the beginning. (This is only step number one; having dominion is step two.) When we die, the body returns to the earth and the spirit returns to God – and the soul waits. For lack of a better way to put this: the soul waits on earth within the dual reality of heaven and hell within "a place" that is already upon the earth awaiting the day of Christ and final judgment of all souls by Jesus Christ Himself. What is the name of this place? [16] We will get to that answer in a moment, but we must first realize that the faithful who have "put on Christ" will be preserved "*in Christ*" until the day of Christ, whereby "His sheep" will be raised into newness in the resurrection and be given a "resurrection" body that comes down to us "from out of heaven" in order to rule and reign *with Christ* upon the earth for eternity.

Everyone was created to be and become a unique expression of God's glory on the earth as He lives within each of us and

---

[16] Excerpt from "Here: The Kingdom of Heaven Is" section titled "Where Do We Go From Here."

expresses Himself through us; however, if we do not give Him all the glory for the life we are living (because it is His *'zoe'* life that was given to us), then we must give an account for our disobedience… and such a soul will complete the remainder of its existence in hellish torment.

Perhaps the greatest trick of the enemy is to convince us to worry less about where our soul goes when the body leaves rather than what happens to disobedient souls for all eternity. By creating an upside-down, inside-out false perspective of reality and eternity, the enemy has tricked us to focus our attention upon seeking heaven rather than Jesus Himself. The enemy even placates these fears by convincing us though many worldly religions that everyone goes to heaven when we die – when there is no scriptural evidence to support this.[17]

It seems this current generation spends more time and effort running away from agonizing challenges and problems than they do seeking Jesus for the solution.

We were created as souls with *'zoe'* life in us, then God formed the dust of the physical reality of earth around our spiritual reality and we became manifest as an earthen vessel (aka body, house, tent, garment, tabernacle) upon the earth, then the Lord God breathed into this earthen form "the spirit of life" (our spirit with life, or perhaps life-giving spirit), and thus we (our soul with body and spirit) became a living soul (Gen. 2:7).

We were created in the image of Jesus according to His likeness for this purpose. Just as there is only one God *and* His Spirit, we are only one person *with* our spirit. For this brief time, while we live upon the earth for one season of eternity, we are experiencing this life within a manifested life form called "the body of flesh;" however, the soul within us needs to be spiritually born anew by the Spirit of God in order to enter into the next phase of our earthly destiny. We need to comprehend God's reality of newness

---

[17] Excerpt from "Here: The Kingdom of Heaven Is" by the author.

through the new birth whereby the Lord gives us (our soul) a new heart and a new spirit (Ezek. 36:26, 27) and then His Holy Spirit becomes enjoined (partnered) *with* our new spirit to complete the remainder of this earthly sojourn as heavenly ambassadors of Jesus to usher in a regime change on this earth – in this life that continues into the next life – i.e. life eternal upon the new earth.

We truly are the host of earth and our souls are inextricably connected to this planet within both the spiritual and the physical realities of heaven and earth to operate in oneness of heart and mind to build one kingdom or the "other" on earth. This is the big picture of the kingdom of God, but the message of the kingdom is even larger than this.

What Could I Convey…

What words could I write to help others know the truth – and to inquire and know God more? One morning, this thought came to me… "If I could tell people one thing about the spiritual reality that is all around them to get them started on their journey to know the truth, what is the arrow that can be put in the bulls-eye to pierce through the darkness that obscures their vision?" What one thing could I tell everyone so they would understand? What "one thing"… do we all have in common that is universally true for everyone that, this one thing alone, would be the arrow that pierces the darkness? So, I meditated on this matter day and night and awoke the next morning with this word:

"The Yearning"

What is it about man and his life upon this planet that keeps him unsatisfied? This is not just the need to have more, but also the insatiable need to know more and to become more. This is a quest-driven search that we can neither turn off nor explain "why" mankind is seemingly compelled to strive for more, as if we are all competing for an invisible prize. Even if it remains beyond our reach at the moment, the thought of attaining this goal, and to have and possess it, is often translated into art, poems and songs to reach an unreachable star. Indeed, there is more – much, much more –

that remains unknown than is currently known to us, and yet, God has given us all that we will ever need, including a divine nature in the likeness of His, to rise above the *koinos* things and to walk in the *megas* things.[18]

There is nothing that man cannot accomplish; the Lord even said, "Truly, nothing that they propose will be too difficult to accomplish which they have imagined to do" (Gen. 11:6), and nowadays, we can live underwater in submarines and in orbiting space stations without air in the surrounding environment, as well as travel through air in cylindrical aluminum tubes all over the earth, but it seems our primary purpose for being on earth has become forgotten over time and lost within the pages of history. If I were to tell you what "the one thing" is, you undoubtedly will say, "Oh yeah, that's right" and keep reading more words, sentences, pages and books to gloss over these very important words. You've already read them and listened to them thousands of times before, so hearing them or reading them again will probably not have the same impact as when you first heard them. Do you remember your first anything… your first toy, dolly, flower or smile? How about your first kiss? Probably not, but the first of everything in our life makes an impact crater upon our soul that our heart will never ever forget… even if our mind can't remember long after the event has passed. The cellular capacity of our mind has the capability of storing three million years worth of data, and yet, the one thing that keeps us unsatisfied and seeking more of anything "to become satisfied" has already been experienced by us not long ago. It is identifiably known when we hear it yet is unquantifiable to prove to anyone else that we heard it. What is it? It is the quiet, still, whispered voice of God saying, "Beloved, I love you." It is buried deep within the consciousness of our soul and we know it to be true because Love left an impact crater upon our soul and we want more of it. Every single culture throughout human history has had some expression of worship toward a god they cannot see or touch… but they can hear Him and they know He's real. They

---

[18] Greek words meaning: koinos-common, megas-greater.

have looked into the heavens at stars and even built enormous structures to help them make contact with this Voice for one reason: to hear the message again. Everyone has been born with the knowledge that God exists whereby atheism and godlessness must be taught; however, I am suggesting to you that we have all heard His voice and we know that He does exist, and yet, our search has often taken us on many pathways away from Him whereby we have believed many lies and false opinions about the reality of the Voice.

> "Truly, this only I have found: that God made man upright, but they have sought out many schemes" (Eccl. 7:29).

How do I know that everyone has experienced this voice? Because we were created by God with the spiritual ability to hear His voice and to be guided by the hearing of His voice. We can't see Him or touch Him, *but we can all hear Him!*

From the age of about 19 months, Helen Keller became deaf, blind and without the sense of smell as a result of Scarlet Fever. Sometime afterward, when she was able to engage in conversation, "she was told of God and His love in sending Christ to die on the cross." She responded... "I always knew He was there, but I didn't know His name." [19]

This is the one thing that we all have in common; we have all heard God's voice.

This is the bulls-eye that I was trying to describe earlier. The Voice is proof that an even greater reality extends beyond our visible physical reality, and mankind has been yearning to find the source of the Voice since the beginning of time. History is one means of recording our experiences in order to keep track of all our failed attempts to hear the voice again without repeating historic attempts which failed. We worshipped this god, but it didn't work; we erected monolithic stones and massive monuments, but they

---

[19] Willmington's Guide To The Bible, p. 591.1.A.1.

didn't help us hear the voice again either; we built this civilization to serve a god, but it collapsed; we invaded and captured one nation to possess the knowledge and resources they had, only to be invaded and captured by another nation; we established religions which were replaced by other religions, and built places to study philosophy, math, science and architecture by reading a multitude of books, of which there is no end – most of which have vanished over time.

We keep yearning in every season and sector of life to create and attain more upon more in each generation of man, and yet, the one thing we so desperately seek… has been living inside of us the entire time. The Lord is our First Love and the Voice planted a memory of "I love you" in our soul and mankind is driven to hear it once again. We strive to experience many new things in order to hear the Voice of truth tell us what our soul desires to hear more than anything else… "I love you." The Voice that we yearn to hear in order to attain that which our soul desperately craves in order to be satisfied and made whole once again… is already living within us. The search to climb higher mountains and explore greater depths, to peer into the cosmos and seek the place where the Divine resides… has been hidden within our heart to seek and find. The search for the truth of God, the truth about God and the experiential truth regarding the spiritual reality that surrounds us is in neither up nor down…

… *the journey is in*!

> "I have seen the God-given task with which the sons of men are to be occupied. [11] He has made everything beautiful in its time. Also *He has put eternity in their hearts*, except that no one can find out the work that God does from beginning to end" (Eccl. 3:10, 11).

These words by the second-wisest man to ever live upon the earth, King Solomon, spent his entire life seeking wisdom to know the answers regarding "why" man is upon the earth. His search, he summarized, and life in general, was vanity and "a chasing after wind" as something that cannot be qualified, verified, ascertained or comprehended by man. His search ended in frustration, and much like all previous searches throughout history that have recorded their failed attempts to seek the Voice which was lost, Solomon wrote Ecclesiastes whereby he gave us the answer he missed… simply by looking for the missing piece that he was unable to find.

He searched out everything and experienced everything in this earthly life that might possibly satisfy him and thus, help him attain contentment in his soul; he had great riches beyond measure, many beautiful wives, spectacular buildings, a fortified kingdom, exquisite pets, luxurious furnishings, exotic gardens and servants to take care of every human need imaginable – and even a glorious temple built so that he could hear the Voice and make a tangible connection to Him – and yet, he never found what his quest compelled him to seek and find. So, what is the missing piece that Solomon never wrote about?

>The Spirit of God in man – is the missing piece.

>And apart from the Spirit of God – we are nothing.

>"Or do you think that the Scripture says in vain,
>"The Spirit who dwells in us yearns jealously?"
>(James 4:5).

The Spirit of God, who is already within every human being living upon the planet, continues to speak the words of God with fresh newness and vitality to everyone every day; unfortunately, every one of us (at some point in time) has turned off our willingness to hear the Voice that speaks daily to us the truth from heaven that helps us comprehend what our soul desires to know more than anything else… "Beloved, I love you… come home to Me."

Home, in this context, is not place-based, but rather, relationship-based (as in, the Prodigal Son who returns to his waiting Father).

The tangible proof that everyone has been searching for – *is the search itself*, which is proof enough to authenticate the reality of God and His spiritual kingdom that surrounds us. The manifest proof that God exists… is the glory hidden within us! The message by Jesus which He communicated on many levels testified to us that the spiritual reality that surrounds us can only be discerned by the Holy Spirit's birthing anew ***within us*** (John 3:3-8). We cannot see, know, understand or comprehend the spiritual reality that surrounds us apart from us yielding our control into the formative hands of the Holy Spirit… and to hear His Voice. Once we begin to hear His voice again, then something remarkable begins to happen…

We remember the Voice from long ago that whispers to us…

"Beloved… I love you."

"I am your First Love. Return to Me."

The reason why none of this makes any sense to some people is because we have listened to a great many opinions by people who stopped listening long ago to explain a mystery that was hidden within every person. Like Solomon, they vainly tried to find the answers apart from the Holy Spirit and created numerous theologies to explain why the world is the way it is – without inquiring God's perspective on it. Thirty-seven times Solomon referenced God, but not once ever mentioned "the Lord" or "the Spirit of God," which seems to me… you can be given great wisdom and understanding *from* God, yet not have a personal relationship *with* God. His yearning to understand life, apart from the Spirit of God, truly ended in vanity and futility.

Therefore, Jesus came to teach us about the Spirit of God so that we may, once again, hear the Voice of truth that speaks words of grace and lovingkindness to us. God does not hate us because…. God is love. The holiness of our heavenly Father cannot entertain anything less than pure and precious holy thoughts toward us… which are more numerous than grains of sand along the seashore.

Our heavenly Father's loving thoughts toward us are good always, and without partiality or favoritism, and will always lovingly call out to us every day we are alive upon the earth to "Come home" until we breathe our last breath. At that moment, our journey on earth with God Who is dwelling within us ends – and then we must stand before the judgment seat of Christ to give an account of this life we lived. Did we love the Father as He loved us? Did we love one another as Jesus taught us? Did we listen to the Voice calling out to us or did we disregard it to focus on our plans and agendas? Did we surrender our sovereignty and our life into the Lordship of Jesus Christ without whom, and apart from having a personal relationship with Jesus, we cannot claim God as our heavenly Father? Did we live life as disciples of Jesus or did we live like passive admirers and spectators for fifty minutes every Sunday? Jesus said…

> "My sheep hear My voice, and I know them, and they follow Me" (John 10:27).

Every person on this planet has heard His voice, even if they have not heard the message or the good news of the gospel. The yearning to seek God and hear His voice is universal to mankind, and it is the Voice of the Spirit that resonates within everyone – to hear and understand.

> "Nevertheless the solid foundation of God stands, having this seal: "The Lord knows those who are His," and, "Let everyone who names the name of Christ depart from iniquity" (2 Tim. 2:19).

The Divine Spark

The life-giving Spirit of God was breathed into every one of us, and thus… we are all without excuse (Gen. 2:7; Rom. 1:20). When I began my sojourn "to remember who we are" in August 2012, I was perplexed and seemingly obsessed by the thought of "the Divine Spark." I did not know what it was, or how I became obsessed by this thought to search it out, so I began researching and studying the scriptures and writing about it for four solid months. All I could discern at that time was this: something inside of me – is guiding me to search, seek and find the most important piece that was missing from my life.

Now, four years later, with much wisdom and spiritual understanding in the truth, I believe the divine spark is given to every one of us once we became a living (human) being (at conception), and this spark (the life-giving Spirit of God) resides within everyone one without exception. God placed a remnant of Himself (His Spirit and His glory) within every one of us so that we may always know that He is always with us *and* speaking to us – so that we might yearn to come home again.

When we consider our creation as individuals, as becoming a new creation through the united oneness of two cells from two human beings to form a new person, this alone is miraculous; however, the true miracle of creation occurred by the overshadowing of the Holy Spirit over the womb to conceive. When these two cells became untied in oneness – within this instantaneous moment, a divine spark was released by the Divine Spark… and the glory of God became manifest in creation within this new person. Our soul, with spirit, and now a body placed upon us as like a garment, became yet another expression of His glory upon the earth. Our soul "sinks into"[20] the physical framework of a one-cell organism to become who we are today.

Life began before conception… because Jesus is the Life… and our origin is always and eternally found in Him.

We existed as a soul "in Christ" before the foundation of the world, yet in this instantaneous miraculous moment, our soul was imparted into an earthen vessel by the Holy Spirit… and we became a living *'nephesh'* soul. We came to earth by the overshadowing of the Holy Spirit, having been sent by the Father, to manifest a human form as another member of the host of earth

---

[20] The term "to sink into" is the implied meaning of *'enduo'* (G1746) i.e. to be clothed or "to get into" our eternal habitation clothing (2 Cor. 5:3).

to do all the Lord's will upon the earth. And in this regard, we are truly just like Jesus Christ, who was sent by the Father, conceived by the Holy Spirit, and was manifested upon the earth for one purpose: the be a light in the darkness and a witness to the truth.

Everything that Jesus did and everything that was ever recorded about Jesus was written so that we may thoroughly understand and comprehend man's ordination upon the earth – according to His Divine example – in order to teach us who we are and what we are supposed to be doing. Who we are is another unique manifestation of Who Jesus is – being revealed through you, to do all that Jesus commands by the hearing of His voice. Christ in you… is all that ever mattered.

> "You are the light of the world" (Matt. 5:14).

God is in us. God is with us. God is for us. You are not alone.

Unfortunately, there have been a great many humanistic voices that have taught us the exact opposite, which is why we keep searching the whole world over in hope of finding God in order to restore our relationship with Him, and by doing a great many pious religious works in our attempt to appease Him, but little did we know or understand at the time… is this said by Jesus:

> "And lo, I am with you always, even to the end of the age." Amen." (Matt. 18:20).

Jesus is God, and He came from heaven to earth, and adorned flesh, to teach us to remember, to help us hear the Voice again, and to tangibly demonstrate how to live according to the Spirit that He placed within us. Jesus is the message and the Messenger who speaks the words of God to each and every one of us – every day – ***through the Holy Spirit*** who dwells within our heart. This is His eternal gift to us that was sown into us… that the Spirit may guide us as we seek and find Jesus, the Pearl of Great Price, who is waiting for us to find Him within our heart.

We don't need more of God… we need to yield more of our will to the Lord God who is within us already…

The journey we are on – that restores our relationship with the Father – is not that far a journey after all. Seek Jesus – and follow Him because…

>It's all about Jesus – and God gets the glory!!

The key to finding the missing piece is to hear the Holy Spirit's voice once again – and allow the Spirit to guide you in the Way. Only the Spirit knows the way to Jesus because the Holy Spirit is the Doorkeeper that guides us up to and through the Door called Jesus who then becomes our Teacher, and leads us in the Way as our Lord, Master, Sovereign and Savior (John 10).

By Grace, God is doing it all – in us, with us, to us and through us – all we need to do is listen to the Voice that guides us as we surrender our will into the Lordship of Jesus Christ.

Now that you know what your soul has been searching for, and where the missing piece is, what are you prepared to do in order to be restored to God as your heavenly Father and to hear Him call you "Beloved. Enter into the joy of your Lord" (Matt. 19:17; Matt. 25:21-23). Are you interested in talking with the Lord? Do you desire to have a conversation with Him?

True peace and spiritual contentment will not happen in this life during this season of eternity on earth; the peace and joy that surpasses all understanding in the hereafter is infinitely more than we are able to comprehend.

>"Eye has not seen, nor ear heard, nor have entered into the heart of man the things which God has prepared for those who love Him" (1 Cor.2:9)

The best part about this wonderfully new relationship with your Lord and Savior, Jesus Christ, is you do not have to pay anything or attend a special meeting or travel to a holy place or buy someone else's manuals and teachings in order to experience the God of Glory in this moment right now as you sit reading these words. God is in you and His Spirit is speaking into your mind right now, so open your heart to hear His voice – and let the Lord speak truth to you. Yet man has created various religions in order to take things away from you that God has freely given to you, most especially… understanding! The gospel (Good News) of Jesus Christ is simple: repent, believe, trust in God, and live by the Spirit. Man's messages are over-complicated and onerous, but the message of Jesus is simple: ***hear My voice and follow Me***! Let the Spirit guide you into all truth and allow the grace of God to minister to your soul as you become a new creation in the sight of your heavenly Father – through faith in Christ Jesus.

Are you yearning to hear again – in newness – what God spoke to you long ago? The most wonderful part of the Divine conversation is that He will remind you and help you remember all the wonderful things that He spoke to you before you began to listen to and believe the multitude of many lies by people who stopped listening to the Voice in generations both past and present.

Yearn to hear the voice of Yahweh… again.

Yearn to remember.

He hears *all* our thoughts, so, get quiet before Him – and turn your attention and the fullness of affection toward Him; He is already within you and He can hear all your thoughts. Let your words be few… and be ready to hear the Voice your soul has been desperate to hear - again.

There is only one way to comprehend the meaning of life and to discover your purpose on earth, which is why we need to remember, acknowledge, understand and comprehend "why" from God's perspective rather than "why" from mans' limited understanding. Seek Jesus – and follow Him – and yearn to remember.

Why Do You Strive?

One of the very first words I heard the Lord say to me was, "Why do you strive?" It took me many years to understand what He was saying to me and the impact this had upon me was not fully comprehended until I began my sojourn thirty years later. His message to me was… "stop striving; abide in Me; rest in My presence; let Me help you; don't do this on your own; you can't earn grace; you can't earn My favor by works; nothing you do will make Me love you more than I already do."

Well, I was a very determined, well disciplined and highly motivated individual born into a strict German Catholic Marine Corps family that were brought up to have an excellent work ethic and to be the best you can be. I was tenacious in my efforts to excel and exceed all expectations… including my own. In everything I did, striving to be the best and striving to do the best was at the core of my character. When the Lord asked me, "Why do you strive?" He knew exactly what needed to change inside me in order to resume our conversation that I walked away from early on in my youth. I was striving… but going in the wrong direction. The Lord had a purpose for me, but to put it bluntly, I had to "sit down, shut up and get (self) out of the way" and surrender my heart-throne to Jesus as Lord of my life. My old man had to die… completely die, and become born anew by the Spirit of God dwelling in me.

We are all striving and yearning. This is a good thing – and this is a God thing, because we were all created to yearn for better things and to be restored to God by the hearing of His voice, and yet, Jesus taught us to strive for only one thing:

> "Strive to enter through the narrow gate, for many, I say to you, will seek to enter and will not be able" (Luke 13:24).

Striving, in this sense, involves more than just making it to the gate. Believers strive to find the gate (Matt. 7:14)… yet disciples struggle to enter the gate! There are multitudes of scripture messages that Jesus taught us concerning entering into the kingdom of heaven through the narrow gate; however, the church teaches a contradictory message that the gate is wide because all who call upon the Lord will be saved. The word "strive" is '*agonizomai*' (G75) and means, "to struggle, to compete for a prize, to contend with an adversary." [21] This word summarizes our struggle on this earth as we have dominion in His name while our adversary seeks to destroy the message of grace and truth that is being manifested in us and through us. This struggle is not easily won by simply flicking a wrist, or making a verbal profession, or signing a membership roster, or attending the Sunday morning fraternal order of any denomination. Folks, we are in a spiritual battle on this earth and our adversary has been deceiving us with many lies and eating the church's lunch to keep us captive to sin and controlled by sin for one purpose: to deceive us, obliterate us – and maintain possession of "this world." We must overcome the lies of the enemy and strive to enter through the straight and narrow gate, but in order to do this… we must know the truth and be obedient to the truth.

When Pilate questioned Jesus before He was sentenced to crucifixion, he asked Him, "Are you the king of the Jews?" Christ's response is earth-shattering:

> "Jesus answered, "My kingdom is not of this world. If My kingdom were of this world, My servants would fight [*agonizomai*], so that I should not be delivered to the Jews; but now My kingdom is not from here" (John 18:36).

> "Pilate therefore said to Him, "Are You a king then?" Jesus answered, "You say rightly that I am a king. For this cause I was born, and for this cause I have come into the world, **_that I should bear witness to the truth. Everyone who is of the truth hears My voice_**" (John 18:37).

---

[21] Strong's Concordance.

Jesus has been speaking to us, through the Spirit, and the words from Jesus that we hear is the Voice of the Spirit! Everyone "who is of the truth" hears the Voice, and the yearning that we yearn for... is to hear His voice – again!

> "My sheep hear My voice, and I know them, and they follow Me" (John 10:27).

The striving we are supposed to be doing on this earth is not based upon personal ambition but rather... on attaining that to which we have been called to do for the Lord. We need to yearn to do the Lord's will and to fight His fight that He purposed for us and planted within us to accomplish, which is... to establish the kingdom of heaven on earth in the presence of His enemies – that is, in front of all principalities and powers seated in heavenly places in "this world." We were sent to take the fight to Satan, not flee from him when he attacks us; we were sent to advance and overtake the enemy by the truth of the gospel and the word of our testimony being armed only with grace, our witness and the empowering of the Holy Spirit dwelling within weak earthen vessels. And this is why we "agonize" and are instructed to be fervent in prayer...

> "Epaphras, who is one of you, a bondservant of Christ, greets you, always *laboring fervently* [*agonizomai*] for you in prayers, that you may stand perfect and complete in all the will of God" (Col. 4:12).

We are to stand perfect and complete... as faithful witnesses to complete the task set before us and take back (redeem) what the enemy has stolen from God – and from us! Our battle is not against flesh and blood, but against the rulers of darkness upon the earth (Eph. 6:12); however, our enemy has tricked us to wage combat against one another over trivial disputes regarding baptisms, resurrections, end times, race, religion, communion, and worship rather than striving with the Lord "to *fight* [*agonizomai*] the good *fight* [*agon*-G73] of faith" (1 Tim. 6:12) and deliver the dominion of "this world" into His hands. Unlike the Jews who did not comprehend the day of the Lord's visitation to them, the Lord instructed His disciples to engage in spiritual battle, remain faithful, and in doing so, we will enter through the narrow gate to receive the crown of life (1 Cor. 9:25).

We do not just strive to enter the gate – we struggle fervently to do the Lord's will and, therefore thus… are invited to enter through the narrow gate by being faithful in this struggle by doing the Lord's will – as we carry our cross. Our reward is not for believing in Jesus – but by doing His will!

This, my friends, is something worth living for– because it is something worth fighting for and dying for!

There is an alternate reality upon the earth that is based upon a lie – and the church needs to get back to its primary mission to teach the truth and make disciples of all nations (people groups).

We are not on earth to live, die and populate heaven, as some of our doctrines seem to indicate; if God wanted spirit-babies, then there are easier ways of creating them other than sending them to earth and putting us into earth suits. One day, I encountered two LDS missionaries and began asking them this question: why are you on earth? They replied, "We are here to receive a body because God has a body, and when we die we will return home to Him in glorified resurrection bodies." So I pressed the issue: why are you on earth? And then their doctrines started coming out, so I asked them again in order to help them understand the core reason why we are here. Then they asked me for my opinion (and thus, their minds were open for a moment to receive truth they were seeking): God is in heaven and Satan opposes the kingdom of God on earth, so he wages war in the heavens and on earth for worldwide domination… wherein man is the battleground… we are the conquest *and* the prize! We were sent to have dominion over Satan's domination and redeem the earth.

But man forgot who he was and what his purpose on earth is. We need to remember!

We are being tested by the Lord to determine which kingdom we prefer. This body is our life support vehicle *and* the means whereby we are being sanctified – either to walk in the truth and live… or to walk in rebellion and disobedience to die in death. Saints… you are being tested to prove your allegiance to the Lord – either you are training your body to walk in obedience and righteousness as a consecrated holy vessel unto the Lord Jesus – or you are using your body to walk in sin and gratify the carnal cravings of the flesh. The flesh was created with weakness to be subject to the Lord – or to sin. The flesh is merely a vehicle to test our resolve and to choose His Way or any other. Where have you placed your trust?

We are here for a reason – we are here for God's good pleasure and it has everything to do with our eternal purpose: have dominion on earth. [22] We are in a spiritual fight: light against darkness, good against evil, order against chaos, and truth against the lie of "this world" that is in opposition to (anti) Christ.

According To Grace

John chapter 14 is the roadmap to discerning what happens to us when the body dies; however, many words which have multiple meanings are often translated in such a way so as to convey a meaning that may be inconsistent with the truth of Who Jesus is and what heaven is. Now that we know Jesus as Lord Almighty and God Most High,[23] and that the kingdom of heaven includes the spiritual reality of Christ dwelling within you, then by grace through faith, perhaps we should reexamine the original text to see what the Apostle John meant when he wrote these words by Jesus Christ the Lord.

> "Because I live, you will live also. [20] At that day you will know that I am in My Father, and *you in Me, and I in you*" (John 14:19b-20).

---

[22] Read "Dominion" in the "Image Bearer" series.
[23] Read "Image: The Revelation of God Himself" by the author.

Where does the soul go upon the death of this earthly body of flesh? It doesn't go anywhere. This is the hardest truth to try and comprehend, so allow me much latitude and grace to explain...

If Christ is in you, then the *Spirit of life* in Christ Jesus is also in you and you are being renewed according to the image of Him who created you. Since Christ is in you, then His life is in you – and you have already passed from death into life; whatever happens to your mortal body from now on is inconsequential to the work of God being revealed in you and through you.

Since Christ is in you, and the Spirit is dwelling within you to work (manifest) the works of God, and you are living as a disciple of Jesus Christ, then "you are in Christ." You do not go anywhere because ... you *are* already there. You *are* both now and forevermore – "in Christ."

The reality of heaven is already within you because the life of Christ is in you. You *already are*, not according to who you are... but according to He who dwells within you; *you are*! When Jesus is in you, then "you [are] in Me, and *I* [*am*] in you" (John 14:20 paraphrased).

The key to comprehending our present day and eternal reality is found in the relationship of "the One" who calls us unto Himself and bids us "come." Once you are there, in Christ – abiding in Presence and Spirit with Christ Jesus, there is no longer another place for you to go – or be. You already are! You are in *I Am*! And you are with *I Am* in you! Isn't that amazing!!!

Once we have entered into this divine relationship with Christ, we must remain with Him. If we have truly entered into such a deep and abiding relationship with the Creator of the universe, then we would never even consider the alternative of walking out of so great a love as His... but that is what some people actually do. Jesus tells us to "remain" and "abide" *in* Him so that He can carry us the rest of the way.

It seems "to carry us" the rest of the way is an odd phrase, so let me explain it as entering into Christ who is "the Resurrection and the Life." Once we have entered into oneness with Christ, then His Life and His Resurrection are within us also, and with this being true, then we have been rendered anew and alive again in the kingdom of God. It is no longer you who live… it is now Christ's '*zoe*' life living in you to make you alive again (Gal. 2:20; Luke 15:24). And since Christ is "the Resurrection" and "the Resurrection" is within us, then we are raised up (resurrected) in Christ by the Spirit into "the resurrection of life" (John 5:29).

Christians spend more time trying to get to heaven rather than living "out of" the heaven that already exists within them.

Heaven and the eternal reality is an *understanding* – and also – a *standing in*! Heaven is the Presence of Jesus. Since you are in Christ, then you are already home with Jesus "in Christ"… who is dwelling within your heart through faith. Stop striving to do something in order to go somewhere – just BE. ABIDE in Christ! Live according to His grace and live out of His Presence that is abiding within you!

> "No one has ascended to heaven but He who came down from heaven, *that is,* the Son of Man who is in heaven" (John 3:13).

> "He is not the God of the dead, but the God of the living" (Mark 12:27)

Reserved or Preserved

There are only two kinds of people of the earth: saved or unsaved. Either you believe *in* Jesus and are preserved in Christ for the day of resurrection – or you are reserved in darkness until the day of judgment. The regenerate soul ceases from all work and waits to enter into "His rest," but the unregenerate soul enters into a place of silence and darkness reserved for judgment.

> "For if God did not spare the angels who sinned, but cast them down to hell and delivered them into chains of darkness, to be *reserved for judgment*;"...
> "And the angels who did not keep their proper domain, but left their own abode, He has *reserved* in everlasting chains under darkness for the judgment of the great day" (2 Pet. 2:4; Jude 1:6);
> "But the heavens and the earth *which are now* ***preserved*** by the same word, are **reserved** for fire until the day of judgment and perdition of ungodly men" (2 Pet. 3:7).

Souls who are dead to Christ are delivered "into chains of darkness" and *reserved* "in everlasting chains under darkness" until the great day of judgment – the day of Jesus Christ (Phil. 1:6).

Greek translation: "οἱ δὲ (but the) νῦν (now) οὐρανοὶ (heavens) καὶ (and) ἡ (the) γῆ (earth) τῷ (by) αὐτῷ (same) λόγῳ (word) τεθησαυρισμένοι (A2having been stored up, preserved) εἰσὶν (A1are) πυρὶ (**B2**fire-4442) τηρούμενοι (**B1**being kept, reserved) εἰς (in) ἡμέραν (a day) κρίσεως (of judgment) καὶ (and) ἀπωλείας (destruction) τῶν (of) ἀσεβῶν (impious) ἀνθρώπων (men)" (2 Pet. 3:7).

The word translated as fire is πυρ, (pur - G4442), but the actual word that we see is πυρὶ with an extra letter added; unfortunately, this word is not categorized in Strong's Concordance. A similar word in Rev. 2:18 is used regarding the eyes of the Lord as "a flame of fire" φλόγα πυρός which has two extra letters added onto πυρ and, likewise, is not categorized in Strong's. Does this make any sense? Or perhaps we should ask – does this make any difference? I am neither a Greek scholar nor an expert with tenses, nouns, pronouns and sentence structure, but it seems fairly obvious this scripture verse needs more refinement in light of man's eternal reality upon earth, rather than heaven as our eternal destination, which may explain why Peter is the only person who references the earth being destroyed by fire, but this is perhaps based upon the mistranslation of certain words that may have produced another meaning entirely.

Yet somehow, the church has adopted a doctrine that teaches us the earth that Jesus created will be completely destroyed by "god the destroyer," when in fact... it is only "this world" that will be destroyed. Our enemy, the destroyer and accuser of the brethren, doesn't care if everything becomes toast because he knows that he will burn in hellish torment for all eternity anyway... and he will take as many souls as will deny Jesus with him.

Hades and Death

There is a place in between heaven and hell where all departed souls go to wait, whereby some are waiting "in Christ" and some are waiting "in chains of darkness." It is well outside the scope of this book to understand where our soul goes after our body dies, so I invite readers to read "Here: the Kingdom of Heaven Is" (chapter 6) to learn more about what happens to us after the body dies and where our soul goes to wait. So, until then, consider these bullet points:

- Jesus never promised us life eternal in heaven, the Apostles never preached it and our Creeds don't teach it
- The term "men go to heaven" *is not found* in any of the 692 scriptures with heaven in it
- There are three groups of earth-born residents that are in heaven, but can you guess which five people only whom the Bible mentions as being in heaven?
- Hades (G86-*hades*) is not Hell (G1067-*gehena*)
- Jesus spoke as many times about Hades as He did Hell (11x each), but the pulpit is silent concerning the place called Hades, as well as the place called Death
- There are at least fourteen specific places within the kingdom of God that are referenced in the Bible, and each "place" is designated for specific people according to their deeds done on earth
- Jesus said, "I go to prepare a place for you" (John 14:3)
- Heaven is place-based, reality-based *and* especially relationship-based

- Man's physical reality represents just one season of his eternity on earth

New Earth Doctrine

But the Voice of Truth is telling me a different story. There is more going on in the spiritual reality than we are aware of because we were commissioned to do more – and we were created by our Creator to "be" more. Jesus came to us and showed us the "greater than" reality of our life in Him so that we may have a share in God's eternal glory through faith in Him... but somewhere along the way, we stopped our diligent search to seek and understand how the kingdom of God operates – and thus, no longer became interested in "why." Heaven, it seems, was good enough for the church age – even though multitudes will perish on account of a false heaven theology because we were never promised heaven – we were promised Paradise on earth!

The church needs a heart transplant and an intellectual paradigm shift in order to prepare in advance for the kingdom age which is already upon us now. The institutional church has adopted many false theories and operational ideas from other world views simply because it was reluctant to perceive the physical reality of earth from God's perspective – and to hear the Voice of the Spirit without interpreting His words through a heaven-only lens with many preconceived notions, including the rapture. In short – we need to perceive the big picture from God's perspective – and live accordingly.

Evolutionists explain the appearance of man on the earth as an organism that achieved the highest level of complexity and intelligence, and then proceed to place him within a descending and devolving spiral within entropy, as if to say – we are the best at this moment in evolutionary science – that can easily be wiped out by a virus or something else yet unknown to us. Man cannot become "greater than" because the *scientific world view* doesn't support it.

Religious doctrines explain man from his initial appearance in the

Garden of Eden who was placed there by the hand of the Lord God Himself to tend His garden. This romantic story is often ridiculed by the scientific world as fanciful, naïve and unsophisticated, and yet, only the Bible has been able to explain the events on earth within a logical, consistent manner that includes a spiritual perspective beyond our "capability of knowing" whereby we may ascend higher than and become "greater than" we currently are at this moment. This *religious doctrinal view*, however, cannot explain "why" all worldly events are happening because it only perceives truth from man's perspective regarding what is happening to man on earth, which is somehow and somewhere in the midst of heaven itself.

And then we have other man-centric world views, the false-religion world view, the mother-earth world view and many other emotional appeals to join some type of feel-good movement that gratifies our soul within the physical reality around us by trading our eternal birthright for carnal-gratification stew, and yet, our soul yearns for something more, even eternally more… that is far deeper than we can verbally explain with words.

But listen to the Voice of Truth, and pay careful attention to what the Spirit is saying to you. You are a soul that is eternal (Psa. 22:26; 23:6; **49:7-9**; Eccl. 12:7; Dan. 12:2, 3; Matt. 25:46; John 10:28; 17:2, 3; 1 John 2:25; 5:11-13); you are a spiritual being that is having a human experience on earth within one season of eternity. You existed "in Christ before the foundation of the world" (Eph. 1:4), and you were sent to earth on a mission to fulfill your dominion mandate and perform the will of God while you are being sanctified unto "greater works" right here and now, whereby your faithfulness and deeds in righteousness will be rewarded in (and on) the new earth in the regeneration at the end of the ages – when all things become new again. You were, you are becoming – and you will be – new again. This is the big picture to explain "why" man is on the earth in a manner that helps us to understand and comprehend what our purpose in life is, as well as the meaning of life. We need to stop selling ourselves short!

In one sense, evolutionists and religious doctrinalists share the same shortcoming: they stop short in their explanation to understand "why" man is the way he is… and "why" he is on the earth.

The world view doesn't believe in "what" nor do they care to know "why"; the religious view knows the "what" in doctrinal detail but cannot explain "why" we believe what we are told to believe that determines how we are supposed to act; the man-centric view is indifferent to "what" and "why" as long as it feels good while doing the things it cannot explain; however, the new earth view explains "why" we believe "what" we believe… and "all these things which are added unto it" as we love God, love one another in meekness, imitate Jesus our Lord and our God, worship the Lord in spirit and in truth… and listen to the Voice of Truth as we prepare for our next season of eternity on the new earth.

> "Thus says the Lord: "Heaven is My throne, And earth is My footstool. Where is the house that you will build Me? And where is the place of My rest? (Isa. 66:1; Acts 7:49).

> "For behold, I create new heavens and a new earth; and the former shall not be remembered or come to mind" (Isa. 65:17; see also Rev. 21:1).

There is infinitely more going on than we have been taught and this is why I have been called to write what I hear. And there is a "greater than" truth regarding man's ordination upon the earth, but we will never be able to understand who we are or what is happening unless we can hear the Voice of truth… and understand the message.

Where is Understanding

Where does our understanding come from? This is an ancient question that philosophers, scientists and theologians have been pursuing for centuries in order to make sense of our world within the cosmos – and the reason for man upon the earth. These perspectives represent the three major camps of understanding as coming from: man, observational study (science) and the word of the Lord. Man's efforts to explain the mysteries of life, wherein many theories abound that appear to make sense, but as I have come to find out, the understanding we have and the conclusions we arrive at do not come to us in a box with nice packaging and a bow; the universe is messy and mysterious and oftentimes does not make sense, which is why faith is so important. It bypasses the understanding of man's feeble attempts to comprehend the vast expanse of an infinite universe to humbly admit we do not have all the answers and then… to trust in the One who ordered everything into being.

> "Trust in the LORD with all your heart, *and lean not on your own understanding*; [6] in all your ways acknowledge Him, and He shall direct your paths" (Prov. 3:5-6).

My journey in this life thus far has sought to understand and comprehend the reason for everything, and to perceive the truth hidden behind the truth within the mystery. My quest has been relentless, as I have endured many face-plants on the road of life with forehead bruises from walking into walls of unanswered questions, but I have never fallen out of the arms of my loving Savior who repeatedly rescues me from my own worst enemy: my mind.

It is here within all of us that the battle lines of faith and understanding have been drawn to demarcate the boundary of a pleasant pasture with Jesus that keeps us safe from the many cares of "this world" and the multitude of many voices that tend to rob us of love, joy peace… most especially peace. Our mind is the place where we come to know and understand spiritual reality from personal experience and this perspective forms the basis for our world view – i.e. the reasons why things happen, but this I have learned thus far: I will never be able to comprehend everything… and the only thing that remains trustworthy and true is my trust in Jesus my Lord. Keep it simple. Love Jesus! And trust Jesus, who knows the way back to the Father.

If you were asked to demonstrate just how much you love Jesus, your heart might be filled to overflowing with many emotions; however, if our love for God could measured by our trust in Him to provide for _all_ our needs, then what would this look like?

If the Lord asked you to do something for Him, some of us would do it unquestionably; however, if the thing that He asked you to accomplish was monumental in scope yet came without any plan or guidelines for the future, would you "let go and let God" trust Him implicitly? My own personal experience in regard to trusting the Lord happened in this manner, and continues to unfold as I journal these words, because trusting in the Lord is a never ending journey of discovery; I never really know what I will find out about God – or myself – in the process.

On September 27, 2013, the Lord spoke to me while I was in prayer and said, "You are My writer. Now write." During the next 15 minutes, the Holy Spirit gave me a supernatural download of information with understanding regarding how these writings will become a source of understanding for others in many nations. I was overjoyed because the cry of my heart was to be used by the Lord in full-time ministry, and writing is what I had already been doing for 18 months while I was unemployed, yet now, I was given a calling to write for Him and this joy was enormously fulfilling and exhilarating.

As I continued to write, I kept looking for a full-time job to support the writing, but I sensed after five months that this showed a lack of faith and trust, so I stopped seeking work on Feb. 21, 2014. Do not be misconstrued by my actions; I love to work and was taught to work hard, but after having been invited to dozens of interviews, the job always went to another candidate. After a while it became clear to me that – even after I scored a near-perfect interview – the Lord was turning the hearts of those on the interview panel away from me to give favor to other candidates.

Meanwhile, my finances dried up on November 1, 2013 and I was no longer able to pay the mortgage or monthly credit card bills, and quite expectedly, the barrage of phone calls day and night ensued. Since the Lord told me to write, then that was what I was supposed to do, but doing this without any plan or financial resources seemed fatalistic, at best. And then the Lord reminded me of a conversation we had earlier in the year, and it went like this:

Me: "Lord, I need money to pay the mortgage and the credit cards."
Lord: "I know."
Me: "I am not sure you understand. I am really out of money, I have been living on credit cards and they are maxed-out."
Lord: "I know."
So I pressed the Lord further: "Lord, the banks are calling to get their money and I need provision from You to pay the mortgage. I need Your help."
Lord: "Do you care more about the banks money than Me?"
Me: "But Lord, You don't understand… I need money."
So the Lord pressed me further: "Do you care more about the banks money – or ME?"

The Lord lovingly put me in my place. And then He told me, "Worry is idolatry." Anything that we focus on other than Him becomes a form of idolatry. What I learned from this encounter with the Lord is simple: He knows what we need, He cares… yet He desires us to seek Him above all else as we sojourn this life to learn what He has called us to do. Jesus is my focus. Period!

> "But seek first the kingdom of God and His righteousness, and all these things shall be added to you" (Matt. 6:33).

The Holy Spirit added to this understanding by telling me the Lord is in control and that I can trust Him without reservation, and by the way... everything in the universe belongs to Him. He not only owns the banks, and the money in the banks, but He also owns the land that the banks are on. Retirement accounts, 401(k), healthcare coverage, education, and world peace... everything in this world is being held together by Him, and in Him all things consist (Col. 1:17).

That, my friends, should have been the end of my doubt to challenge my trust in Him, yet it seems my trust in Jesus struggled (*agonizomai*) to release my grip on stuff – and my control of the situation. God creates the circumstances – and then the circumstances make the man.

One by one, my fingers were pried from my grip on stuff that I considered "mine." This is the illusion that we must all come to terms with: we are merely stewards and caretakers of His things and everything in this life is temporary... such that nothing is really "mine" after all. The Lord knows exactly what we need and the Father has promised to provide us with daily sustenance, but we tend to desire more and more, yet more never seems to be enough. Having and holding onto stuff is somewhat like a drug addiction that waits to make another purchase to feel the exhilaration and power of the purchase, until discontentment, sobriety or buyer's remorse sets in. The consumer is always looking for the best deal on the best product, and if you wait long enough, an even better product will be produced to render the previous purchase obsolete. In the realm of consumerism, there is no end to the buy-more process. This process does not apply to just household furnishings and clothes, but to everything including vehicles, RV's, houses, vacations and retirement property where you will one day build your dream home to live out your remaining days in peaceful bliss, that is, until you see an ad for another retirement community with a house on the lake with a boat dock and a golf course, with yada yada more.

What I have learned about this dream that we all want and chase after is: it is an illusion. You can search the whole world over for contentment (or substitute this word for joy, peace, love), but unless you take it with you, then you will never find it. The grand illusion of this world is to seek and have more stuff, but the kingdom of God instructs us to seek first the kingdom of God and His righteousness (which is Christ); the spiritual basis for living on earth is God-focused… seek the Lord first, and keep your eyes upon Him, then everything will be added unto that.

> "For what profit is it to a man if he gains the whole world, and loses his own soul? Or what will a man give in exchange for his soul? (Matt. 16:26).

Several months after I ran out of money, the mortgage company began calling and writing me notes of 'encouragement' to politely resume payments, and I received their encouragement mail daily. Then I inquired about getting a forbearance on my mortgage and the bank gave me 12 months mortgage and rent free to live in my house to get back on my feet. God provides!

Fast forward 24 months and I have learned to trust *"in"* the Lord in deeper, more meaningful ways… and to host His Presence. I had no income for 54 of the previous 64 months, I lost the house and all possessions, and despite my current conditions, I stopped accepting food stamps for a period of time, choosing to trust "in" the Lord for the meals He provides. Most of my family considered my current living irrational and illogical… but they as yet did not even know that I was living in my car at the time… in the middle of winter no less. These things are being shared with you with a three-fold purpose: to encourage you to trust the Lord because He lovingly cares for you, to be open to the Lord's guidance along the way… and don't let the fear of the unknown prevent you from doing marvelous deeds for God. And another thing: never say "It can't get any worse than this!" because it oftentimes does. Along this journey, I have helped encourage and inspire many homeless people that needed a helping hand or word of encouragement during dark moments, even sharing the scriptures with others through open car windows in a Walmart parking lot at 9 PM at night. When it comes to life on earth… it isn't *all about you* anyway.

Many of the homeless I've talked with have been rejected by their families, and our society does not have a place for them unless they fit into the system; however, I have witnessed their great faith and trust in the Lord despite their circumstances. One lady I helped seek shelter after dusk had the best response to my inquiry the next day: "Where do your finances come from?" I asked. She pointed up to heaven and replied, "I have unlimited credit! My Daddy takes care of me," whereby she told me story after story how God provided for her needs in unmistakably miraculous ways. Spirit normal!

> "I will lift up my eyes to the hills— from whence comes my help? [2] My help comes from the LORD, Who made heaven and earth" (Psa. 121:1, 2).

It is easy to trust the Lord, but to trust Him for subsistence living and daily nourishment is very difficult unless you know the Lord Jesus – personally and intimately! It is nearly impossible to live out of your understanding in such circumstances without having a love and trust relationship with the Lord, which brings me back to my earlier comment…

If your love for God could be measured by 'your trust in Him' to provide for all your needs, then what would your life look like?

Said somewhat differently – if all you had today was what you thanked Jesus for yesterday, what would you have?

Consider the Parable of the Rich Young Ruler. He was invited by Jesus to follow Him and become His disciple, but he went away sad because his wealth was significant, and we do not know what ever happened to him. When we trust in our own riches to get us through today, then our level of trust in the Lord to provide for our needs will become a threshold that we trip over. We oftentimes trust in our provision-making capabilities rather than in God our provider, and for this reason (among many) I have been on this sojourn to thoroughly comprehend the error of my ways: I always thought I was my provider and God was my helper (my co-pilot), but now I know experientially that my provision comes from *Jehovah Jireh*: God my Provider.

God is my Source and my Sustainer… in Whom I trust. Now read the back of a U.S. dollar bill.

Consider all the financial plans and investments you've made over the years; some were successful and others were abysmal. Regardless whether you win some or lose some, at the end of this life… you are either holding onto Jesus or you are left empty-handed. Acquiring riches is not evil or bad in itself, but if these become the focus of your life, then they have become a form of idolatry.

Making money and acquiring riches is a great thing and a God-ordained capability if these financial resources are used within kingdom operational procedures for kingdom purposes. Money is not the root of all evil… "the love of money is a root *of all kinds of evil*" (1 Tim. 6:10; also can be translated: a root *for* all kinds of evil).

We are here on earth as stewards and caretakers to tend "the Garden of God" and we will be held accountable to the Lord God on many levels for what we did and/or did not do. The scriptures are not restricted to the spiritual realities of heaven and earth; they specifically mention taking care of the physical reality of earth as well. Polluters – be advised!

Not everyone can, nor does the Lord expect them to, do what He has asked me to do. He called me according to His purpose to fulfill the works He predestined for me, and likewise, we must all seek the Lord to know what our individual assignments should be. The bottom line is this: imitate Christ! Ask Jesus what He wants you to do rather than listening to pastors and priests. Why settle for second-hand opinions? Ask Jesus! Then do whatever He tells you.

Some of us may get an interesting response from Jesus because some will obey unquestionably while others will seek a second opinion rather than listen to the Voice of the Spirit. Take for example the following persons with wild testimonies who listened and obeyed:

- Noah took 120 years to build an ark under constant ridicule by his neighbors
- Abraham was 75 years old when he took his entire family of 300+ people with herds on a 750-mile journey without knowing the destination (Gen. 12:1)
- Isaiah walked around nude for three years (Isa. 20:2-4)
- Ezekiel laid on his sides for 430 days and baked food using animal dung for fuel (Ezek. 4:12-15)
- Hosea married a prostitute (Hosea 1:2)
- John the Baptist was clothed with camel hair and ate bugs (Matt. 3:4)

The Lord may or may not call you into a wild ministry; however, to think that He cannot because He has not – has already become a garment of disobedience to the Lord. This world will tell you suffering in the name of Christ is illogical and irrational because it may lead to personal humiliation, when it fact… it leads to your sanctification – and the salvation of many other souls as well.

It doesn't matter how old you are or what your physical condition is; even if you are advanced in age, the Lord can use you if you are willing to say, "Here I am, send me." Sarah was 90 when she gave birth to Isaac; I was unemployed and financially broke at age 54 when the Lord called me to be His writer; the Apostle John was boiled in oil but did not start writing until he was exiled on Patmos at about age 75.

If the Lord is calling you to something – regardless of its significance or the logic-based irrationality of it – then do it! Trust Jesus. You *will* have a wild experience and a testimony to share…

Understand This…

> Life is not about you…
> Life is about He who dwells within you.

Man wants to understand. The Lord wants us to understand. So, the Lord sent us on a sojourn for us to listen, to hear and see, to remember, and then understand.

Sometimes, experience is the best teacher. We may think we know and oftentimes we profess to know more than we think, but the whole point of life is this: understand.

There are at least six types and ways to understand spiritual truth (the types: to know anecdotally, to believe intellectually, to know experientially, to understand completely, to comprehend thoroughly and perceive):

1. Obey – hear it, do it (like Abraham, without question, without waiting)
2. Seek the Lord (to find out the reason from Him)
3. To figure it out (truth revealed by diligent search)
4. To see what may come of it (tests that give answers)
5. To wait on it (preparation, alignment, timing)
6. To persevere and patiently endure (even in silence when the Lord is silent)
7. The end result is always: to give God all credit, praise, honor and glory

Man's greatest quest is to understand 'why' and then to understand 'how.' We can go round and round in our mind to try and make sense of it, but in the final analysis, we may still be chasing the shadow or the essence rather than the substance. Man has been trying to make sense of things from a human perspective for thousands of years, but now the time has come to see things from God's perspective and to begin this final journey: to comprehend.

There is only one way to transition from understanding to comprehension: we must let go of human instruction to listen for and learn spiritual lessons of divine instruction by the Spirit. We are not human beings in search of a spiritual experience, but rather, we are spiritual beings having a human experience, and now we need to see ourselves as living souls, living in partnership with our spirit that has been placed within human bodies for one purpose: to gain wisdom so as to attain comprehension.

Information is good, knowledge is wonderful, understanding is divine, but comprehension is for the glory of kings. Man typically "puts two things together to try and make sense of a matter," but the net result is merely human engineered knowledge that puffs up, lacking the true substance of intellectual wisdom that is born out of much deep thought and meditation. Man has always tried to resolve cosmic questions with the quick-fix-thought, but these solutions have only served to create more questions and problems than answers.

Revelation is the reward given by the Holy Spirit to Christ's disciples seeking wisdom and understanding; it is the result of a dedicated and diligent search with perseverance to push past all obstacles, setbacks, trials, tribulations, persecutions, and painful ordeals to seek first the kingdom of God and His Righteousness, i.e. Jesus Christ.

Jesus reveals Himself to His disciples through direct revelation and personal experience. The fullness of Love came to us because we lacked the human ability to come to Him. He appeared to us when we were blind, spoke to us when we were deaf and He presented Himself as The Way in order to lead us back into the truth when we became lost. We were hopelessly lost and clueless and falling apart, but in this moment, Jesus came to us and revealed Himself to us, and then it all began to make sense again. We forgot who we are – and we needed to remember. In one sense, we can say that we were lost and now we are found, but it would be more accurate to say we forgot He who dwells within us, we walked away from His presence that abides within us and now we have found Him – again – dwelling in our hearts all along. We went on a long journey to seek and find, but we went looking in all the wrong places; we desired to know the truth and understand why, but in the absence and knowledge of why, we focused on how. We have been on a journey to understand so that we may comprehend all things – oftentimes ending in futility. However, through the anointing of the Spirit, we know all things, but it is not until the Holy Spirit opens our mind and provides understanding that we are able to comprehend truth from a revelatory perspective. The knowledge of truth within understanding is far greater than man can even imagine; truth is exponential and limitless; in our quest to understand the infinite nature of truth, much like the moment a firework explodes, we understand thoroughly and completely where all Truth originates… if only for a brief moment.

If we want to know anything, or if we want to know something specific, then ask the One who is Truth Incarnate. There is no longer any need to keep searching for answers because all answers and all truth are found in the One. Do you think the lover of your soul would send you on a long journey to find a hidden treasure yet withhold maps with understanding to foil all attempts to uncover clues to find what you were sent to look for? Jesus himself is the Treasure; Jesus is the Pearl of great price; Jesus is the Truth in our quest to understand *and* comprehend all mysteries. And yes, mysteries were presented to us so that we might search for clues to find the hidden treasure… which He hid within us.

Man is much like an explorer seeking a new country, an adventurer seeking a new discovery, an inventor seeking a new innovation, a poet seeking a new poem, a photographer seeking a new sunrise every morning. Man has been looking and searching to find the missing clue for nearly 6,000 years, and just when it seems the ability to process information and truth exponentially, as well as to translate this truth into one universal language that all men may understand, it seems in our search to know "why" we have forgotten the most important truth to understand: who are you looking for? Why are we looking and searching? What is compelling us to keep searching and looking? Where will we go to find more truth? When will we know if we have come to the end of our search? How can anyone make sense of all of this knowledge and truth? How, indeed! Man is searching to know why – and he embarks on the journey to understand all the familiar pieces of what, when, where, and how; and yet, unless man understands Who the who is that he is searching for (and not 'who you are'), as the one missing piece that makes all things comprehensible, in Whom all things consist, then all the pieces that come together will remain a puzzled mystery without ever knowing even "why."

We are on a journey to understand.

We are sojourners who were sent from heaven to live on earth for one season in eternity to experience the fullness of "understand" in order to comprehend all things, namely, Christ in us – our hope of glory. Man was created by God and crowned with glory and honor; we do not have to earn it – we already have it; however, spiritual truth is not within us. We have been given many wonderful grace attributes by God, but the only way truth can be found in us – is when we allow Truth Incarnate to rule and reign in our hearts through faith. Spiritual truth does not come by way of casual observation – it can only be perceived by the working of the Holy Spirit within us to become born anew into the kingdom of God.

We don't have to search for truth or wisdom; the truth is within us on account of Christ in us. We need only to seek and find Jesus and then let revelation truth be found in us. We are not looking for hidden treasure that is impossible to find; the Treasure is already within us – we just have to open the door and be found in Him. You do not have to search the whole world over looking for love, joy, peace or happiness; these emotional gifts already reside within you – if you turn yourself over to them. However, you must search for heavenly and spiritual gifts which can only come to us as born anew citizens of the kingdom of God; eternal life already resides within you – and God has put eternity in our hearts… but will we have faith to believe in the Truth?

The substance of the entire universe as well as the mysteries of creation have all been placed within us, but we will never know or experience or understand any of this, nor will we ever be able to comprehend all mysteries until we do this one thing: convert!

We need to turn away from everything we have sought with our human effort and intellect, then abandon ourselves into the arms of a loving Savior who will rescue us from the merry-go-round of life to experience the fullness of life itself – true Love. When we turn around, we can expect to see only one thing: Jesus Christ. When you look into His arms and feel His embrace and hear His words calling you "My beloved," you will never want or desire anything else ever again. Truly, there will be no more need of anything. In Christ, the fullness of fullness resides in Him and we have all things in Christ who first loved us and gave Himself for us, so that we may understand and comprehend one of the mysteries of man: to hope in Christ alone. He is everything – and apart from Him, we are nothing. We can hope to stand in His presence and experience the divine wonder of knowing, but why settle for something less-than; why not enter into and stand in His presence to experience the fullness of the divine relationship washing over you again and again with uninterrupted love and affection. Why settle for second best when the highest best is freely given to us without measure? Why embrace second-hand understanding when the Lord of Glory wants us to enter into revelation whereby we comprehend all things. This is not a challenge – this is an open invitation to enter in. Anything less than this is simply: less than. Jesus wants us to know more, have more and experience more because He loves us with never-ending "more."

It is impossible to quantify or qualify the infinite riches that are found within the divine relationship. They are like streams of living water incessantly nourishing and washing over our mind with peace; they are like non-stop waves of emotion crashing upon the shores of our soul to fill our hearts with love and joy; they are like deep breaths that pant pounding surges of blood through our ecstatic bodies in His embrace; and they are like the power of a waterfall, a mighty whirlwind and a tsunami coming upon our spirit to empower us with grace upon grace to help us walk in glory and honor – His glory and His honor.

We have been given the dominion and we have been given us the keys of the kingdom. We have been invited to have "shares with" His kingdom and to partake of His inheritance. Verily, we have been promised much and will be rewarded with much… if only we would turn and believe.

Conversion is the key to understanding and revelation is the key to unlocking mysteries. Heaven has been thoroughly *'dianoigo'* open for the past 2,000 years, but we have slumbered in our knowledge of who we are and have forsaken our first love. We were never abandoned. He who loves us with a never-ending love placed Himself within us so that we would never lose our way. We forgot who we are and then we became confused, lost, disoriented, perplexed and frightened. We traded trust for fear and then faith for doubt and unbelief – and then we changed the meaning of love to search out evil instead. We changed the message and the meaning of the words; we substituted love for obligatory rules; we counterfeited the divine relationship and substituted in its place religious performance; we even changed our understanding as spiritual beings into human-doing-work-machines that run faster and faster until we, like terrorized sheep, leave the safety of the sheepfold to suffer physical ailments of worry, stress, depression and phobic attacks; we have compounded health-less unhealthiness with worrisome depression-alienation. And now we take pills to overcome our human condition so that we may continue in the rat-race to go faster, farther, higher – only to completely fall apart wondering – where did we go wrong? What is the meaning of life? Tell me there is more out there that is worth living for? Tell me one shred of truth in all of this frenzy that makes sense. Tell me what and tell me why. Why, why, why??? Where did we go wrong?

We can ask these questions over and over a thousand times, but in the final analysis, we stopped listening to the Voice of Truth, and we need to realize that we were asking the wrong question, which is not "why" but rather… Who will help us through it!

Much like Job, we can ask one 'why' or a thousand 'whys' and the answer remains the same. It was never about understanding why things are happening to us – it is about "Who" that is helping us get through it. We were never created, nor were we meant, to be alone. We were created as *'hagios'*–to live and to be – in divine intimate relationship with God. This is our purpose: to be hagios. This is our reason for living: hagios. Our purpose and our reason for living, as well as the meaning of life, is simply this: hagios. We are the reason "why" we were created. We were created as earthen vessels to host the presence of the Divine within us. We are tabernacles for the Spirit of God to dwell in our midst – in oneness with us – with oneness flowing through us.

Everything about who we are is predicated upon Who that is dwelling within us, hoping one day, that we might enter again into a divine relationship with Him, and to abide in Him so that the Father may also abide in us. In this we may know if the Father abides in us, when we have love for one another. In this perfect union orchestrated by love, we cease from striving – now we abide; we cease from contention – now we live in unity; we cease from worry and turmoil and stress – now we live in peace. Everything that we ever wanted is found in Him when we enter into His rest. "Abide in Me." This is not the temporary rest that comes when earthen bodies die apart from the divine relationship, which results in permanent death; this is the eternal rest that comes when we leave our way, truth and life outside the Door of Christ to take His yoke upon us, so that our old ways are crucified on the cross, with Christ, so that we are never able to climb again into that meagerly peasant existence to operate in the flesh any more. We are spiritual beings who were created to operate from our spirit according to the Spirit of life in Christ Jesus – but – we forgot who we are….

The time to know is now; the time to remember is upon us; this season of eternity in which we are living is coming to a close. This is not a fatalistic attempt to cause fear, but rather, this is a wake-up call to all who will listen – and hear. The truth is all around us and the truth is within us on account of Christ, but until we believe, this truth means absolutely nothing! It is a banging cymbal in the cacophony of materialistic modernity as it struggles to understand without any hope to comprehend the real answer that man so desperately craves: Jesus only! Hear Him! Seek Him and find Him, forsaking everything else and all other endeavors as worthless vanity. Seek to love Jesus and serve Him only. Listen to hear what He has to say – because, truly I tell you – there is no other way.

Nothing else makes sense. Nor does it even come close! It never has – and it never will.

Christ plus anything equals nothing, yet Christ plus nothing else equals everything!

The truth is within you since Christ is in you – but – will you believe? Trust, believe, have faith to live and love once again – in newness – through truth, change and oneness.

It is all about Jesus – and God gets the glory!!

And one more thing – life on earth is not about you.

It is about He who dwells within you!

What house are you building in your heart as a permanent abode for the Lord?

How do we begin this journey to remember and understand? By listening – and then by hearing. Jesus wants to tell us all about it and He wants to reveal everything to us at this time, including things past, present and future – but there isn't much time left in this age. We have been tricked to believe that the world has always been and that man has existed for hundreds of thousands of years, but in reality, the spirited soul in man has existed for only 5,775 years. There were expressions of man that existed as a naturally inclined brute, but these remnants were washed away in the flood, even though some traces remain. All things hidden and all mysteries obscured are about to be revealed in one final age to bring to closure, in the culmination of all things, in order for this season of eternity to close. The end is about to begin – again.

We need to understand – quickly. We need to understand what has happened in the past – and to recognize and understand what is happening now in this present time – so that we can understand what is about to happen for the remainder of eternity. Whether a thousand years remains, or not… eternity is about to begin – anew.

He who has ears to hear, let them hear.

The kingdom age of divine revelation and comprehension is about to begin.

To Help Us Understand

There has been much written about who Jesus is and why He came to earth. Why He came would proliferate an entire university of thought, but since Jesus came with a simple message, let us consider two simple reasons: to help us understand and to show us how to live.

The gospel is not complicated, so neither should our reasons to comprehend why Jesus came. Jesus is the light, who came to the darkness, and the darkness did not comprehend it. If there are any individuals, communities or people groups who do not understand who Jesus is and why He came, then they are living within a kingdom that they cannot comprehend nor acknowledge nor understand. This is not meant to create a dividing wall of hostility, but rather, it is an exhortation for us to take the light into the darkness so that others may understand also.

Jesus came as the Way, Truth and Life – to show us the way, testify to the truth and offer us eternal life. He gave us this opportunity to enter into this reality by turning, through conversion. Therefore, let us closely examine the conditions that predicate conversion to see 'why' Jesus wants us to understand first, turn second, and be healed third.

Jesus came to teach us the principles of the kingdom, and He demonstrated these principles in action as the working of the Holy Spirit within us – and then He showed us the Father so that we may understand the big picture. Jesus came in love, without condemnation, so that we may understand. Jesus came with signs and miracles that we may know and understand that He is the Messiah, but, now (this is the most important part) Jesus came in the power of the Spirit to help us understand that we are to walk according to the way of the Spirit with the empowering of the Spirit – in spirit and in truth. This was our original mission mandate, from the beginning, and this is still part of our mission mandate – to help all men believe the truth and understand.

> "However, we speak wisdom among those who are mature, yet not the wisdom of this age, nor of the rulers of this age, who are coming to nothing. [7] But we speak the wisdom of God in a mystery, the hidden *wisdom* which God ordained before the ages for our glory, [8] which none of the rulers of this age knew; for had they known, they would not have crucified the Lord of glory. [9] But as it is written: "Eye has not seen, nor ear heard, nor have entered into the heart of man the things which God has prepared for those who love Him." [10] But God has revealed them to us through His Spirit. For the Spirit searches all things, yes, the deep things of God" (1 Cor. 2:6-10).

This is one of the primary reasons Jesus came to earth: to help us understand and comprehend all things, not just the way, truth and life, not just redemption and salvation, nor just the taking away the sin of the world or the fulfillment of the scriptures; Jesus came as Understanding in order to help all men understand and come to the knowledge of the truth, through faith, trusting in nothing else except their experiential encounter of Christ abiding within us – our hope of glory.

Truth upon truth is vanity. Wisdom without understanding is vanity. Above all else, gain wisdom. Wisdom is supreme.

> "Wisdom is the principal thing; therefore get wisdom. And in all your getting, get understanding" (Prov. 4:7).

The word wisdom should, therefore, be directly related to understanding, but not the understanding that comes from endless information searches with a naturally inclined mind; this understanding comes from having our mind opened by the Spirit of truth in order to gain, not just the essence of truth, but the substance of wisdom and comprehension that results from a thorough *'dianoia'* understanding. Once we have experienced this understanding, then we are able to move beyond the basics of truth (which puffs up) to embrace the understanding that comes through the Spirit – to then perceive the deep things of God through revelation.

> "Can you search out the deep things of God? Can you find out the limits of the Almighty?" (Job 11:7).

> "But God has revealed them to us through His Spirit. For the Spirit searches all things, yes, the deep things of God" (1 Cor. 2:10).

The Father wants us to go deeper in truth to gain understanding. When we come to the fullness of this understanding, then we will speak with power and authority to act on Christ's behalf!

Christ alone – and nothing else!

How can we profess to know or understand anything unless we see deep truth and experience revelation that leads to understanding? Consider the perfect set-up that was orchestrated against Jesus: the woman caught in adultery. Jesus knew what was going through their minds when those men brought a woman before Him; they wanted Jesus to talk about the law and the consequences of sin, as a trap set against Him, but Jesus changed the conversation altogether. He put the kabash on the sin discussion by inviting any sinless man to cast the first stone. Jesus was teaching them, as well as you and me today, that His primary mission was not to condemn or convict us of sin or even judge us; Jesus came as Understanding to teach us the understanding residing within the big picture… and be merciful to one another. We do not come to this understanding by way of knowledge or information; rather, we enter into understanding through personal encounter and personal experiences that teach us the love of the Father as the highest form of understanding. All other truth and all other spiritual fruit are born upon this living tree of life.

Turn around – again and again. The Lord keeps turning us around again and again until we can see the big picture and hear the full gospel message of hope residing within the mystery, namely, Jesus Christ. If I have written one billion words, then let me share the most important 3,2,1: Jesus is Lord; Jesus only; love. The sooner we understand these truths and begin setting aside all of our mental machinations to attempt understanding God's big picture with rules, ordinances, dogmas and doctrinal teaching about traditions which get in between us and the Holy Spirit, who was sent to come alongside us to draw us closer to Christ, then the sooner we can get back on mission as manifestations of Christ-in-us, as Christ-like Christians, who listen and hear, who see and perceive, who know and understand.

This world needs understanding before they will ever know love.

This world has taught us all to have a general distrust of absolute truth, absolute faith, absolute obedience – and rightly so. This world seems to produce vile men with evil intent with such ease and regularity that the terrorism of a potentially Fourth World War may eclipse the tragedies of all world wars combined. These evil men, with hateful doctrines and loveless understanding, cannot reproduce by love or peace or joy; they reproduce hate and fear and turmoil that is born from confusion, disorder, havoc and unrest to create more turbulence, instability, chaos – and darkness!

We need understanding more than ever before, but not the understanding that the world gives; we need the understanding that only Christ can offer, through faith, because truth alone will never be enough... we need grace... even greater grace! Yes, Lord, we need grace upon grace in order to see You for who You really are and to experience You with endless freshness of understanding, being renewed moment by moment, as we turn our hearts toward You. If You turn to the left, we will turn left; when You turn right, then we will turn right.

Where You go I will go; what You say, I will say; where You lead, I will follow. Lord, I desire the shadow of your love to be upon me wherever I go in whatever I do. Lord, I desire to bask in Your presence with every breath I take and every step I take. I am no longer bound to the pattern of this world; I desire to be transformed by the renewing of my mind – so that I may understand! I want to know Your thoughts and understand Your ways so that I may be Your hands and feet and arms and legs in a world that is perishing for lack of wisdom, vision and understanding.

Now, do you see why it is so vitally important to understand – and to not let anything get in between you and this divine understanding that may, in any way, obstruct the divine relationship between you and Jesus. Why – and why again? We desperately need to understand. It begins by trusting Who (Jesus) and believing What (Jesus as Truth) to walk in the Way (Jesus only).

Cast ALL your cares upon Him. Trust in Jesus only and love Him with the entirety of your soul. Forsaking all else, abandoning all your cares for this life, seek out Jesus and find Him – and hear His words spoken for you that only your ears can hear – and enter into the divine relationship with fullness of understanding in oneness of newness by abiding in Him.

The Intellect of Man

Throughout most of my adult walk in grace to follow Christ, I have repeatedly heard from church leaders to trust my heart because the mind is rational and cannot be trusted. This is pure hogwash. Therefore, I subscribe to spiritual *'anabaino'* ascent through intellectual exercise of the mind because this is specifically what Jesus taught. "The dual operation of understanding needs to occur in our mind – together with – our heart." [24]

> "Lest they should see with their eyes and hear with their ears, lest they should *understand* with their hearts and turn" (Matt. 13:15)

Some translators teach us that we understand with our heart, and this verse can be used to support the use of *"kardia"* for understanding (as in Eph. 1:18), but allow me to emphasize this scripture using a rigid linear interpretation.

> "Lest they should see with their eyes and hear with their ears, lest they should *understand* [*suniemi- a mental putting together*] with [to put together/in combination with] their hearts – and turn [convert, turn away and turn to]" (Matt. 13:15).

People need to hear the truth and assemble this understanding in their mind (comprehend), as well as build (or plant) understanding in their heart, in tandem **with** each other, as one spiritual operation within the combined function of the spiritual soul of man in order to create true conversion. The door of our mind must be open to understand the things being heard – and the door of our heart must be open to understand the conviction by the Spirit to *'oida' perceive* and thoroughly comprehend the truth of the message.

"They do not know, nor do they understand."

---

[24] These next three paragraphs are excerpts from "Listen: How To Hear God's Voice" by the author.

Jesus wants us to have a personal encounter whereby we experience the truth abiding in Jesus so that we may enter into a divine relationship with Him. This is not the knowing of truth mentally, as one gathers and stores information, but putting together and assembling truth upon truth intellectually in order to '*ginosko*' know the truth experientially that results from having a '*dianoigo*' opening of the mind to '*suniemi*' assemble this truth in order to '*oida*' fully understand, perceive and comprehend divine truth. This is not an intellectual endeavor only; it is a spiritual quest using all faculties of the soul to see and hear in order to know and understand.

Jesus wants us to understand. He came so that we may see His works and hear His truth for one reason: to understand – and live accordingly. Jesus did not do these things to prove to us that He was the Messiah, per se. Jesus knows who He is, and yet, He did not testify unto Himself – until He was confronted by people who thought they knew and understood… but spiritually didn't have a clue. They knew about God informally; however, had they known God '*ginosko*' experientially, then they would have '*oida*' understood completely who Jesus is – and why He came to testify to the truth… as the Truth.

Nearly all of us have heard this scripture quoted to us: "For My thoughts are not your thoughts, nor are your ways My ways," says the Lord" (Isa. 55:8), which is then lovingly shoved down our throat to tell us we can never know or understand the thoughts and ways of the Lord; however, ***this is precisely why Jesus (the Lord) came: to teach us the thoughts and ways of the Lord <u>by the Lord Himself</u>*** so that we may live our lives by imitating His example. This scripture has been used by many teachers to dumb-down believers to adopt the alternate reality's less-than perspective of man *by denigrating and repudiating man* rather than teaching this truth as a challenge from the Lord Jesus for believers to transition into disciples to know the thoughts and ways of the Lord – and live in obedience to them.

No Root Within Us

> "Therefore hear the parable of the sower: [19] When anyone hears the word of the kingdom, and does not understand *it,* then the wicked *one* comes and snatches away what was sown in his heart. This is he who received seed by the wayside. [20] But he who received the seed on stony places, this is he who hears the word and immediately receives it with joy; [21] ***yet he has no root in himself***, but endures only for a while. For when tribulation or persecution arises because of the word, immediately he stumbles. [22] Now he who received seed among the thorns is he who hears the word, and the cares of this world and the deceitfulness of riches choke the word, and he becomes unfruitful. [23] But he who received seed on the good ground is he who hears the word and understands *it,* who indeed bears fruit and produces: some a hundredfold, some sixty, some thirty" (Matt. 13:18-23).

The Parable of the Sower is about seeing our heart as a field for faith to receive the seed of truth *and* grow understanding. There are four types of soil in our heart all the time and we need to understand truth as it comes to us as "understanding" from God. 1. When we hear the truth but don't understand the words, then Satan snatches it quickly before there is any chance for faith to embrace it. 2. When we hear the words with joy but understanding does not occur because our soil cannot understand, having been thwarted by numerous rocks of doubt and unbelief, then understanding cannot take root and the truth withers within us. 3. When we hear the words of truth and embrace the truth, then understanding takes root and begins to mature, but if we allow the cares of this world to corrupt this understanding by looking here or there and by listening to the cares of this worldly pattern that is opposed to (anti) Christ, we will lose our focus on Christ alone and become overgrown by our many cares for this worldly life abiding in human flesh – with no fruit being produced. 4. However, when we receive the truth and then understanding takes root in a heart that has been cultivated and prepared, being thoroughly persuaded and convinced, then divine understanding that comes to us through the Holy Spirit's work within us – whereby understanding takes root in us to produce a harvest 30, 60, and 100 fold.

Jesus said, "The root is not in them" (v.21). What did Jesus mean by this? All seeds have within them the genetic DNA codes to produce a root; however, seed cannot materialize a germination root unless an outward force, like water, acts as a catalyst to stimulate the root-making DNA into action. The outward force in regards to man is the Holy Spirit who abides within us Who is waiting for our soul to initiate the "born anew" process by seeking to become spiritually reborn and regenerated by the Holy Spirit – as a new creation in the (spiritual) kingdom of God.

The word "root" (*rhizo*-G4491; Engl. rhizome) means root, and also implies "metaphorically, of cause, origin, source."[25] The work of the Holy Spirit within us is the cause-agent to begin the spiritual rebirth process, and He is also the origin and source as being One in Triune Oneness with God who created us ("Let *Us* make man" Gen. 1:28). The life-giving breath was breathed into us by the Holy Spirit, and "the Spirit is life" (within us), and thus, the Holy Spirit is the causal reason why we are alive in the first place and He is the reason whereby we are born anew, not with water as before, but according to the Spirit of life in Christ Jesus so that we may do the will of God upon the earth!

When Jesus referred to Himself as "The Root of David" (Rev. 5:5) and "I am the Root and Offspring of David" (Rev. 22:16), He is saying, literally, I am the Origin and Source of David and through him (the offspring/seed of David) Yeshua the Messiah, came. Jesus is both the cause and the effect of not only David, but also the cause and effect of all creation… including you and me!

> "All things were created through Him and for Him" (Col. 1:16).

---

[25] Strong's Concordance.

Well, you may say, is this what Jesus was really teaching? It seems fairly obvious that Jesus was teaching us about receiving the truth, as a seed, and that we need to be focused on nurturing and cultivating seeds of truth into our field of faith to bear much fruit. Well, ok, what is the fruit that Jesus wants us to produce... more seeds of truth? More understanding? Yes, yes – and even more than these... the fruit of righteousness! There is already so much truth in this world that we find it nearly impossible to absorb even small morsels abounding in a veritable ocean of information coming at us all day long from every direction... but the truth that is within this world cannot produce the fruit of righteousness. God desires kingdom fruit: righteousness!

When I read this parable by Jesus, between telling us the Parable of the Sower and then teaching the meaning (truth) with understanding to His disciples, Jesus wants us to understand how the kingdom of God operates. Yes and Amen!

Jesus is literally standing before His disciples and they can see Him – and Jesus is literally teaching them with words and they are hearing Him, but Jesus then tells them – they do not understand. Then Jesus quotes Isaiah to reinforce this concept: it is not enough to see and hear... we must *hear and understand*.

Jesus taught us kingdom truth, and then He taught us parables so that we would seek to find truth that was hidden within the parables, and then He asks *all* His disciples, "Do you understand?"

> "Jesus said to them, "Have you understood these things?" (Matt. 13:51)

The word that Jesus used here is '*suniemi*' (G4920) meaning, "to mentally put together," to assemble the truth as an understanding in your mind. Jesus used this same word (or the Aramaic equivalent) about five times in Matthew 13 alone, and then, to see if we really understand, He changes the word for understand to '*noieo*' (G3539) meaning, "to perceive by exercising the mind and intellect" and finally to '*epiginosko*' (G1921, 1922) meaning, "to completely know" having come from advanced knowledge by participating in the truth "by reason of the intellect."

We can see this transition as open invitations by Jesus to '*ginosko*' know the truth and to '*oida*' thoroughly understand it experientially, as the assembling of truth that you have participated in and experienced – in order to comprehend kingdom reality. It is not enough to know the truth; we must partner with it and incorporate this truth into the very essence of our being – in order to live it out and bear fruit of the kingdom, which is righteousness. This is how we become changed and transformed and renewed by the Holy Spirit through sanctification: we willingly allow the Spirit of truth to change our thoughts so that: we think like Jesus!

> "Let this mind be in you which was also in Christ Jesus" (Phil. 2:5).

Jesus wants us to think like Him so that we can live like Him – and thus… change the world by believing the truth and living according to the heavenly pattern as Christ Jesus instructed. Verily, verily, we need to live our life with the same mind that Christ had. This is not an impossible scenario because Christ abides in us and the Holy Spirit dwells in us, through faith. In one sense, all we need to do is yield ourselves and allow the Spirit of truth to work in us – and in the greater sense… completely yielding and surrendering our will by allowing the Spirit of truth to flow through us. We were sent here to invade earth with the atmosphere of heaven, and to release this atmosphere through us, but if our thoughts have born seeds of doubt – then these prevent us from being who God intended us to be – since the beginning. Unregenerate thoughts become the cork that impedes the flow of heaven through us – and this must stop now!

When we believe the lie – we empower the liar.

When we believe the truth – we are empowered to change the world!

The enemy has only three weapons: doubt, fear and unbelief. If he can cause us to doubt the truth, then he can attack us with fear – and thereby reduce our effectiveness to overcome his kingdom with the light of truth. The enemy will attack the word of God by sowing seeds of doubt in our mind. His plan is simple and it would be working perfectly if not for the Spirit of truth who was sent into the world to instruct us in the way of truth. Consider how the religious leaders of Christ's generation attacked Him because He taught an inconvenient truth. And so it is today, with the hidden saints of this generation who are proclaiming the truth with holy boldness and understanding… which the institutional church will condemn. Why? Because inconvenient truth must either be accepted – or rejected – and in "this world" it is always more expedient that one man should die for the sake of a nation (John 11:50; 18:14).

We need to understand the principles of the kingdom, so let's get started by understanding that there are 16 Greek words in the New Testament to convey understanding (as well as 8 words for doubt), so therefore, it is essential for us to know the inherent meaning of the word "understand" that was communicated by Jesus in order for us to comprehend the message being conveyed by Him.

Understanding Kingdom Principles

The Parable of the Sower is one pivot point in Jesus' earthly teaching ministry. More kingdom truth has been folded within these words of scripture than anywhere else, except perhaps Romans 8. Key words will be highlighted and defined, followed by the living truth contained within the message… and keep in mind the earlier teaching about our field of faith and this message within the context of "understanding."

> "And the disciples came and said to Him, "Why do You speak to them in parables?" [11] He answered and said to them, "Because it has been given to you to *know* (*ginosko*) the mysteries of the kingdom of heaven, but to them it has not been given. [12] For whoever has, to him more will be given, and he will

have abundance; but whoever does not have, even what he has will be taken away from him.
¹³ Therefore I speak to them in parables, because seeing they do not see, and *hearing* (*akouo*) they do not hear, nor do they understand (*suniemi*). ¹⁴ And in them the prophecy of Isaiah is fulfilled, which says:

'*Hearing* (*akoe*) you will *hear* (*akouo*) and shall not *understand* (*suniemi*),
And seeing you will see and not *perceive* (*oida*);
¹⁵ For the hearts of this people have grown *dull* (*pachuno*).
Their ears are *hard* (*bareos*) of *hearing* (*akouo*),
And their eyes they have *closed* (*kammuo*),
Lest they should *see* (*oida*) with their eyes and *hear* (*akouo*) with their ears,
Lest they should *understand* (*suniemi*) with their hearts and *turn* (*epistrepho*),
So that I should *heal* (*iaomai*) them.'

¹⁶ But blessed are your eyes for they see, and your ears for they hear; ¹⁷ for assuredly, I say to you that many prophets and righteous men desired to see (1492-*oida; perceive*) what you see (991), and did not see it, and to hear what you hear, and did not hear it. ¹⁸ "Therefore hear the parable of the sower: ¹⁹ When anyone hears the word of the kingdom, and does not *understand* (*suniemi*) it, then the wicked one comes and snatches away what was sown in his heart. This is he who received seed by the wayside. ²⁰ But he who received the seed on stony places, this is he who hears the word and immediately receives it with joy; ²¹ yet he has no root in himself, but endures only for a while. For when tribulation or persecution arises because of the word, immediately he stumbles. ²² Now he who received seed among the thorns is he who hears the word, and the cares of

this world and the deceitfulness of riches choke the word, and he becomes unfruitful. [23] But he who received seed on the good ground is he who hears the word and *understands* (*suniemi*) it, who indeed bears fruit and produces: some a hundredfold, some sixty, some thirty." (Matt. 13:10-23).

- *Ginosko* (1097) – to know, in process of knowing, sometimes experientially or as a mental construct
- *Oida* (1492) – to understand, thoroughly know and comprehend, perceive, by truth put in practice
- *Suniemi* (4920) – to put together mentally, to understand, assemble truth in the mind
- *Akouo* (191) – to hear with the idea of understanding the thing heard, as compared to *Akoe* (189) the mere sense of hearing as a faculty of the ear's ability to hear sound

Now, let us infuse these words and terms with meaning into the scripture:

"Therefore I speak to them in parables, because seeing they do not see, and *hearing* (*to understand*) they do not hear, nor do they understand (*by assembling truth in their mind*). [14] And in them the prophecy of Isaiah is fulfilled, which says:

'*Hearing* (*in your ears*) you will *hear* (*listen to understand*) and shall not *understand* (*because you will not assemble truth in your mind*),
And seeing you will see and not *perceive* (*comprehend truth put into practice*);
[15] For the hearts of this people have grown *dull* (*pachuno – waxed gross, fatty, thick, stupefied, callous, unmovable pitched tent pegs*).
Their ears are *hard* (*bareos – heavily burdened, weighted down by much toxic teaching*) of *hearing* (*without ever truly understanding*),
And their eyes they have closed (*shut down, no*

> *longer functionally operable),*
> Lest they should *see (perceive from the sense of truth put into practice)* with their eyes and *hear (with attentive listening to hear and understand)* with their ears,
> Lest they should *understand* (mentally *put together and assemble truth in their mind*) with (*to put together/in combination with*) their hearts and *turn (be radically converted to the living and true way),*
> So that I should *heal (spiritually heal, save and restore to wholeness)* them.'

What can we learn and understand from these passages? Jesus wants us to '*ginosko*' know the truth (the mysteries of the kingdom), in order to '*suniemi*' mentally assemble these principles within our mind so that we **understand** and live according to this '*oida*' understanding – as truth believed, truth put into action (not practiced) and truth experienced.

But Jesus does not stop with this limited understanding of kingdom truth; there is much more to comprehend and perceive. Jesus taught the disciples seven more parables – and then He seeks to know if they understand:

> Jesus said to them, "Have you understood all these things?" (Matt. 13:51)

They all answered "yes" and it seems they got it… until the practicum testing of their understanding would reveal 'if' they could put into action the truth they professed to believe. Jesus taught them through word and deed – and many miracles were done in His presence. Jesus sent the twelve disciples out in His authority and they healed the sick and cast out demons. Every time Jesus told the disciples to do something, they were given His authority and power to perform that which was spoken to them because they were operating within His delegated authority – by the power of His word! Saints of God, we must become like Mary,

His mother, who told the Cana wedding servants, "Whatever He tells you, do it" (John 2:5).

Heavenly Test: Truth in ~~Practice~~ <u>Action</u>

The multitudes sought Jesus and by the end of the day were hungry. The disciples suggested to Jesus He should send the people away to get food, but Jesus said to them, "They do not need to go away. You give them something to eat" (Matt.14:16). In the past, when Jesus told them to do it, they were able to do it, so why do you suppose the disciples hesitated? Jesus then tested the disciples to see their response, "Where shall we buy bread, that these may eat?" (John 6:5). They gathered about two hundred denarii, which was insufficient, and then Andrew, Simon Peter's brother piped up and said to Jesus, "There is a lad here with five barley loaves and two fish" (v.9). Aha, at last, someone was thinking outside the box in an inspired kingdom of God sort of way. The revelation mind produced an inspirit thought!

This is a kingdom principle that we all must learn: ***when Jesus tells you to do something, then He also has given you His authority and power to do it.*** His word is more powerful than you can imagine, so if Jesus told you to do anything (*rhema* or in the scriptures), His disciples who hear His voice *will* accomplish it according to His word. It is not about you – it is about Jesus in you and the power of God's kingdom flowing through you.

You feed them! The barley loaves and fish were blessed by Jesus and put into the hands of the disciples, but the multiplication happened *at the hands of the disciples*. And thus, they fed them. Jesus told them what to do, and even though they did not understand what to do, the people were to be fed by the disciples. It doesn't matter how large or unattainable or problematic your circumstances may seem, if you were told to do it, then do it! If your God box is too small, then you will doubt, but if your God box is huge, then anything is possible! Believe the truth!!!

> "Jesus said to him, "If you can believe, all things are possible to him who believes" (Mark 9:23).

Now, consider what happened next with the disciples. Jesus walked on water and Jesus told Peter to come out to Him. And we all know what happened: Peter walked on water. How could he do this as a man that is bound to all the laws of nature just like you and me? Because Jesus told him to "Come" and the power do to it was given according to His word.

But Peter became afraid. He "doubted" when he saw the wind and waves, and once he doubted, he was overcome with fear. Doesn't this sound like the typical MO of our adversary – to plant seeds of doubt in a sea of truth by taking your eyes off of Jesus to consider your phenomenally disastrous circumstances?

Jesus saved Peter and then said, "O you of puny *confidence* (*pistis* – faith), why did you '*distazo*' (G1365- doubt by standing in two ways – wavering – between understanding and unbelief)?" (Matt. 14:31; see also 28:17). What Jesus said to Peter can be said to each and every one of us: why do you doubt? Why do you stand in between two ways? Why, indeed? Believe and understand – or continue with doubt in fear and unbelief.

Jesus said to them, "Hear and (*suniemi*) understand (mentally put it together): it is not what goes into the mouth that defiles a man; but what comes out of the mouth, this defiles a man" (Matt. 15:10-12).

Then Jesus taught them a simple teaching concerning plants not planted by the Father that will be uprooted, and yet, even though this uncomplicated teaching was not on the level of parables, Peter then asked Jesus, "Explain this parable to us" (v.15).

What Jesus said to Peter in this moment of exasperation is the reason why I write so that we may all understand the truth, including myself...

> "Are you still (*asunetos*) *without understanding*? [17]
> Do you not yet (*noieo*) *understand*..." (Matt. 15:16, 17).

Asunetos (G801) was used by Jesus only this once, so it is extremely important to comprehend the meaning implied within this verse; it means, "unintelligent, stupid, foolish, without understanding." And a new word for understand is introduced as well (*noieo*-3539): "to perceive by exercising the intellect," so allow me to insert the implied meanings: [26]

> "Are you still *void of intelligent understanding*? Do you not yet *think and perceive with the intellect by exercising your mind... all that I am teaching you*?"

Think it through for yourself!!! Use your intellect!!! Assemble the truth of Christ in your mind!

The term Jesus used "Do you not yet understand" is radically different than a term we typically use for knowing yet "misunderstanding." Why? When it comes to spiritual truth, either you know the truth and you understand it... or you don't understand it because you don't know it. It's that simple. If you know the truth, then there will be no misunderstanding whatsoever!

When we "agree to disagree" on any interpretation of scripture, it's not because we have a misunderstanding... it's because we do not know the truth.

Equally profound is this new word by Jesus: *noieo* – to perceive by exercising the intellect. In the book "Commission," we learned the soul is composed of two parts: mind and heart. The conscience represents the soul of the person that operates with co-perception in mind and heart oneness. Thus, the soul of man must perceive God's truth by exercising the mind in co-perception oneness "with" the heart. The heart of the disciples, at this point, have yet to perceive with their mind, and thus... do not yet understand. This is most likely because of too much toxic theology; error blinds them from knowing the truth. With this new understanding

---

[26] Terms and definitions were found in Strong's Concordance.

that enables us to perceive the kingdom of God by knowing God's truth, apply this concept to our initial verse:

> "Unless one is born again, he cannot '*oida*' perceive the kingdom of God" (John 3:3).

It this beginning to make more sense now? Perception comes by revelation from the Spirit in renewed minds that are being renewed with truth by the Spirit for born anew people that seek to become aligned with the truth of God! When we '*suniemi*' assemble all aspects of knowing the truth and build truth layer upon layer with the purpose of understanding the truth, we shall perceive and understand, but if we refuse to think and perceive with the intellect of our mind to assemble truth, then we remain unwilling to perceive how the kingdom of God operates… to remain incredibly stupid and unintelligent.

> "For God may speak in one way, or in another, yet man does not perceive it" (Job 33:14).

Life on this planet may seem mysterious and difficult to comprehend, as if we are trying to assemble a giant jigsaw puzzle without knowing what the original image looked like. Well, this is true in many respects and is even more complicated because we've made many terrible assumptions about why man is on earth in the first place… and it's not to get to heaven. We were sent to establish the kingdom of heaven on earth because… we are the host (army) of earth.

If you want to perceive what God is doing, then exercise your intellect – in oneness with your heart.

Do not doubt (*diakrino*-G1252); do not waiver or hesitate by failing to perceive and comprehend deep spiritual truth by not exercising your intellect. In this regard, many pre-existing doctrines and predeterminations may prevent us to perceiving… and understanding! It has happened to me and every one of us… including Peter, the Lord's disciple.

Consider the man, Peter, who had just walked on water and then moments later proclaimed divine truth when Jesus asked the disciples, "Who do you say that I am? Peter answered and said, "The Christ of God'" (Luke 9:20). Then Jesus taught about defilement as what comes out of a man... not what goes into a man (Matt. 15:11) and then the disciples complained to Jesus that the Pharisees were offended by His teaching (v.12). Really? Why are they concerned with the thoughts and opinions of other men? Has anyone in the history of the world or any of those leaders ever walked on water? Yet His disciples seem more concerned by what other people think. You cannot appease God and man, nor can you serve God and mammon.

Then Jesus taught His disciples about leaders that were not planted by the Father who will be uprooted... to just leave these blind leaders alone... and then Peter asks Jesus to "explain this parable." Hello?

Can you sense Jesus' frustration building toward the disciples – and especially Peter? It is as if Jesus, the man, is nearing the boiling point; "Are you paying attention? Do you not understand the spiritual principles and heavenly truth that I am teaching you... or are you more interested in other people's reaction and opinions to My message? Use your intellect and put these concepts together! You twelve were chosen to begin the restoration of all things and now it's time to put two-and-two together to usher My kingdom revolution upon the earth!"

But such is the case when toxic theology has blinded our eyes from seeing the God-moment through the lens of institutionalized religion... and the supernatural becomes unexplainable.

Jesus doesn't need believers who just believe – He wants disciples that understand!

Moments later, Jesus begins to transition His message from teaching principles and truth parables to talking about the kingdom of heaven, including the foretelling of His death and resurrection...

and Peter's reaction is to rebuke Jesus. Peter had just confessed Jesus is "the Christ of God," and Jesus is Lord God, and now Peter is rebuking God. Let me say it again… Peter is rebuking God (Matt. 16:22). Really?

Now, in all honesty, what would you do if one of your best friends did this to you? I pondered the numerous expletives that might come out of my unregenerate mouth, but all I came up with was ARRGGGHHHHHH(*&@*^^$(**%r^%$&($^#% !!!!!!!!!!!!!

> "Jesus said to Peter, "Get behind Me, Satan! You are an offense to Me…" (Matt. 16:23).

If Jesus could say this to Peter, then He can say it to anyone, including you and me. Why was Peter such an offense? Jesus took offense because Peter was more mindful of the things of man (mammon) than the things of God. You can be a pastor or prophet or apostle, but if you are more mindful of what men think or you are "consumed" by worldly cares or public opinion, then Jesus has one word for you: Convert! Either turn around… or get behind Me!

What a great man of God we have made Peter to be, and likewise, many blind leaders are celebrated today. They speak a bold truth and proclaim Jesus as the Christ of God, but deep down, there is not enough puny soil to grow kingdom truth for the multiplication of the final harvest to begin. Where is the deep soil to grow mountains of faith within the church? **Where is the pastoral training of disciples with divine truth and intellectually assembled understanding**? Where is the '*exousia*' delegated authority with power to act? Where are the healings and miracles through faith? Where are the mighty signs and wonders by the working of His *dunamis* power in us and through us? Wake up church, this age is nearly over, and if this is all we've got to offer Jesus, then I can assure you that it doesn't end well!

Changed lives are needed to usher in the kingdom, but this is impossible without divine intellect and understanding through the

Holy Spirit's impartation and instruction. Our minds MUST be sanctified and renewed, to have the mind of Christ, whereby we have the thoughts of Christ – and operate according to His likeness, and thus… imitate His heavenly pattern and operate with kingdom principles according to truth.

We were sent to inhabit earth with the atmospheric joy of heaven bursting within us like ruptured wineskins – with the same spiritual power flowing through us with every breath we take that raised Christ from the tomb. We were sent to have dominion over the darkness, but sadly, it seems the darkness has invaded us just as much as the twelve disciples – we fell asleep and allowed seeds of doubt to be planted in our hearts as well!

How is this possible? How can this be fixed?

It cannot be fixed – we must be changed!

We must be changed and transformed by the renewing of our mind (Rom. 12:2). We need to thoroughly understand the hardened heart dilemma caused by doubt. The disciples did not understand or comprehend because their hearts were hardened – and so are ours! When Jesus got into the boat after walking on the water with Peter, the disciples "were greatly amazed in themselves beyond measure, and marveled. For they had not understood (*suniemi*) about the loaves, *because their heart was hardened*" (Mark 6:51, 52). Jesus and Peter had just walked on water and yet they were still perplexed about the multiplication of bread "by their hands."

We need to understand what is happening here among the disciples because the same thing is happening in the church today.

In my previous book, "Listening," the main reason that we are unable to hear the voice of God is because our heart is hardened. Consider again what Jesus taught us in the Parable of the Sower:

> *"Hearing (in your ears)* you will *hear (to understand)* and shall not *understand (because you will not assemble truth in your mind)*, and seeing

you will see and not *perceive* (*comprehend the truth by putting it into practice*); [15] For the hearts of this people have grown *dull* (*waxed gross, fatty, thick, stupefied, callous, unmovable pitched tent pegs*). Their ears are *hard* (*heavily burdened, weighted down by many teachings*) of *hearing* (*without ever truly understanding*)."

Lest they should *understand* (*mentally put together and assemble truth in their mind*) **with** their hearts and *turn* (*be converted to the living and true way*).

We are going to need a bigger boat of understanding if we are ever going to fulfill our primary mission and first command from God: have dominion!

We need to believe the truth – and starting living like we mean it!

Hardened hearts are the obstacle to getting the Great Commission implemented, so stop blaming the mind and intellect. Jesus told us over and over to assemble the truth in our minds by reason of our intellect – and this begins by removing seeds of doubt that we allowed to be planted in our stony, uncultivated heart by the enemy. We need humility, sincerity, meekness and compassion to soften these hardened hearts, but above all else, we need repentance! And then, without doubt, we must believe the truth and begin to assemble kingdom truths in our mind, to pull down strongholds of doubt, and then invade this present darkness with the light of truth.

I would like to say that the disciples finally got it – but they didn't – and neither have we, because 1.6 billion Christians now living on this planet could change the world within a couple days if we truly believed, trusted, understood, obeyed, did not doubt – and took action!

> "Then Jesus said to them, "Take heed and beware of the leaven of the Pharisees and the Sadducees."

⁷ And they reasoned among themselves, saying, "It is because we have taken no bread." ⁸ But Jesus, being aware of it, said to them, "O you of little *faith (puny confidence)*, why do you *reason (dialogizomai – to reckon or thoroughly deliberate)* among yourselves because you have brought no bread? ⁹ Do you not yet **understand** (*noieo – exercise the mind*), or **remember** (*mnemoneuo – to call to mind, be mindful of, exercise the memory*) the five loaves of the five thousand and how many baskets you took up? ¹⁰ Nor the seven loaves of the four thousand and how many large baskets you took up? ¹¹ How is it you do not **understand** (*noieo – use your intellect*) that I did not speak to you concerning bread?—but to beware of the leaven of the Pharisees and Sadducees."

¹² Then they understood (*suniemi – to mentally put together assembled truth*) that He did not tell them to beware of the leaven of bread, but of the doctrine of the Pharisees and Sadducees" (Matt. 16:7-11).

Hooray! Finally! What did they mentally put together? Five loaves fed five thousand with 12 baskets of leftovers, and yet more loaves fed less people (4,000) with fewer leftovers. It is not about understanding things "more or less" from a natural, physical, earthly perspective; it is all about trusting God to enable you to do the spiritual work that He will empower you to do.

"Do whatever He tells you to do!"

If Jesus tells you to do something, then He is also giving you His authority and His power with His provision to do it.

Selah!

This is the simplicity of the gospel: "Hear His Voice, believe the truth, understand, and obey."

Selah!

Heaven is completely open and the treasuries of heaven are ready for His disciples – with angels, ascending and descending, having been commissioned to assist us in this divine work of grace.

Selah!

Hear His voice and follow Jesus only! Be salt and light; have dominion and change the world!

It is such a simple message – and sometimes I fear that, in my effort to explain the truth as completely and thoroughly as possible so that all will understand... I have made it complicated and too daunting (weighty) to initiate. So, keep it simple, believe the truth that Jesus taught, and live according to faith like you mean it – without any doubt – and it will be done "unto" you. You are the open gateway through which Jesus is passing heavenly grace through in order to change the world. Believe it! Now go ye therefore... make disciples, proclaim Jesus as Lord, do what He tells you – and change this world with the truth!

At this point, I can hear the thought of Jesus, saying... "Now you're cooking with gas!" Jesus wants to give all of His followers and disciples the keys to understand the kingdom of heaven (Matt. 16:19), but there is much danger in giving this much kingdom power and authority into the hands of simple-minded believers that have not assembled kingdom truth. We must understand, now more than ever before, with child-like faith, what it means to really believe, trust, understand and obey – if we are ever going to change the world for Jesus.

How do we do this? And what does it look like?

First, we must be born anew by the Spirit of God before we can understand anything about the spiritual reality all around us (John 3:3-9). Second, we must declare our sovereign allegiance to the Lordship of Jesus Christ to stand together with Him, and we must deny ourselves, take up our cross, and follow Jesus (Matt. 16:24). Third, we must be filled with the Spirit (Luke 4:1) and be converted and, thus, become as little children (Matt. 18:2, for such is the kingdom), being poor in spirit (Matt. 5:3) and walking in meekness. Fourth, we need to ask the Lord to remove our hardened hearts for two reasons: so that we can hear His voice and understand kingdom truth. Fifthly, our answer to the Lord's question must always be yes and amen, in obedience, before we even know the question He will ask. Six, we must be willing to do the impossible... to believe the unimaginable... and to perform the incredible and thus, get rid of all unbelief (Matt. 17:20). And finally, we must be willing to think for ourselves with Spirit-anointed reasoning in order to gain kingdom wisdom with understanding.

> "The Spirit of the Lord shall rest upon Him, The Spirit of wisdom and understanding, The Spirit of counsel and might, The Spirit of knowledge and of the fear of the Lord" (Isa. 11:2).

You have been reading the same scriptures that I have been reading for the past couple years, and in this short period of time, I have written seven books about living according to this new way in Christ, as a servant follower of Jesus who listens to hear His voice – and then does it. I listen to hear Jesus, then I hear, then I (write it down and) do what the Lord tells me because I love Him with all my heart, soul, *dianoia* and strength. There are only three things that enable me to live this way:

1. I have been born anew by the Spirit and the Spirit of Christ dwells in me
2. I know the truth intellectually, with understanding, and I trust Jesus unquestionably
3. I believe this truth without doubt in my heart and yield to the outward flow of Christ as He manifests His life and divine nature through me

> "With God, all things are possible!" (Matt. 19:26).

"Ah, Lord God! Behold, You have made the heavens and the earth by Your outstretched arm. There is nothing too difficult for You" (Jer. 32:17).

"According to your faith, let it be to you" (Matt. 9:29).

"As man acts as the gatekeeper of his soul, so he becomes" (Prov. 23:7 lit. trans.)

"And greater works than these *you* will do" (John 14:12).

"You shall love the Lord with all your heart, and with all your soul, and with all your '*dianoia*' (the thorough and complete understanding in your mind) and with all your strength"

AND

"Love your neighbor as yourself."

AND

"This is **MY** command, that you love one another as I have loved you"

Now go, in the love and strength and authority and power and grace and mercy of Jesus. God is making all things new again – in newness – through truth, change and oneness.

Be the change you always envisioned others do.

Do or do not; there is no try. Do not doubt. Believe the truth… be the living truth – and do it.

"If you want to be perfect, go, sell what you have and give to the poor, and you will have treasure in heaven; and come, follow Me" (Matt. 19:21). [27]

The kingdom of heaven is at hand!

It's all about Jesus – and God gets the glory!!

---

[27] If you want to see global and social change happen instantly, then do this and perceive what happens next.

The Mind of Christ

It is not enough to know the truth – or just believe in Jesus. The truth of the kingdom must be thoroughly understood and comprehended by assembling foundational principles and teachings within the mind – and this belief with understanding, then, becomes the means whereby understanding must be planted and cultivated deep within the heart of man (soul) so that, by putting God's truth ~~into practice~~ in action, *produces the spiritual fruit that God desires*.

What comes out of (through) a man's life is what the Father is interested in.

Jesus spent His entire earthly life teaching us how to walk according to the Spirit, and thus, we are to yield to the Holy Spirit's guidance in order to operate in the likeness of Jesus Christ.

Jesus Christ, who created the heavens and the earth, came as God – to the earth He created, to manifest His Divine presence as a man, who lived in the same manner of all men, but did not sin. Jesus, however, did not operate out of His Divine nature; rather, He lived His life as an example (a pattern) that we can all follow and imitate. Jesus is the God-man, and walked according to the Holy Spirit as our example whereby we can also live according to His pattern by the Spirit's indwelling to accomplish many miraculous deeds and wonders. Just as Jesus was always listening to hear His Father's voice, as a servant yielded to always say and do the will of the Father, likewise, we, as yielded servants, are to hear the voice of Jesus to always say and do what He tells us to do. Jesus manifested Himself as Immanuel, God with us, and through a work of grace, He continues to abide in us, through faith, in unity and oneness with the Holy Spirit, who guides us into all truth – *to have the mind of Christ*.

This is the gospel I preach. Jesus came to teach us and demonstrate how to live according to a certain way, according to the pattern we were originally intended to live from the beginning

– as in the Garden. We are spiritual beings who have forgotten who we are and Whose we are, and we have forgotten what we are supposed to be doing here upon the earth.

There seems to be just one thing that is separating every one of us from walking in the pattern of Christ: hardened hearts. If you want to know the truth and remember what your purpose in life is, then ask the Holy Spirit to guide you in this revelation – and to help soften and remove your stony heart. The Holy Spirit is in you – to guide you and instruct you in the way of Christ, and since He is already within you, even apart from faith… we are all without excuse.

If we soften our hearts to the truth, and have repented, and been born anew by the Spirit, then there is only one thing that remains to be accomplished in order for anyone to live according to the likeness of Jesus upon the earth: believe – and have the mind of Christ. Truly, I tell you, when we think like Jesus, with the Holy Spirit dwelling within us, our actions will become "the greater works" that Jesus told us we would have (John 14:12).

> "So the Lord said, "If you have faith as a mustard seed, you can say to this mulberry tree, 'Be pulled up by the roots and be planted in the sea,' and it would obey you" (Luke 17:6).

There is no difference between you, me or anyone else. The same God created you and He created me, and each of us has been given a measure of faith according to grace to see what we will do with it, because the Lord adds grace upon grace to those who are faithful and desire to live according to the truth of God. The same Spirit who overshadowed Mary to conceive Jesus is the same Spirit who raised Christ from the dead; and this same Spirit who was manifested through Jesus to do mighty works is the same Spirit who dwells in you through faith to perform mighty works "in His name" through you. This same Spirit is given to each of us without measure (John 3:34) and the same works that Jesus accomplished can also be done by those who hear, believe, follow, understand, and therefore… walk in obedience to Christ Jesus.

At risk of redundancy, we need the Holy Spirit! If we have removed our hardened hearts, and we are able to hear His voice and understand what He tells us, then the Lord will accomplish many miraculous things through you – once you have the mind of Christ!

Jesus wants us to think like Him. Jesus knows what will happen to this world (as does the enemy) when we perceive the spiritual reality that surrounds us – and dwells within us. When we are able to think like Jesus, being likeminded and living in one accord in oneness of thought (*noeo* – mind) with Christ, then we truly will have "the mind of Christ" whereby we can do all the exceedingly great and wonderful things that God has prepared beforehand for those who love Him, trust Him unreservedly – and are called according to His eternal purpose.

> "Let this mind be in you which was also in Christ Jesus" (Phil. 2:5).

This scripture is not telling us to have the brain of Jesus, but rather, we are to think in one accord to have the same thought process that leads to understanding regarding how the kingdom of God operates resulting in the release of God's power through faithful obedience to His *rhema* word (spoken utterance).

When we think like Jesus, then we will manifest His word… and this world will become changed by His truth.

When the Lord speaks His word to us, it is because He wants us to accomplish His will upon the earth. Through faith, we have become open gateways whereby God manifests the heavenly reality of His grace within us so that heavens' resources can flow through us in order to bring order to the chaos and to change this world from darkness to light. Whenever God speaks His word and we respond in obedience, then the Lord will always give His obedient servant-listeners and followers (disciples) three things –

the power and the authority and the provision – to do all that He commands (tells) us to do.

This is the simple truth regarding the kingdom of God; we are spiritual beings sent to earth to have a human experience (the mystery of sanctification by the Spirit) and to transform this physical reality shrouded in darkness into the glorious light of God's truth through faith in Christ, as a work of divine grace by the Holy Spirit's empowering who dwells within us.

We need the mind of Christ!

Jesus challenged His disciples to understand the spiritual reality of the kingdom that was flowing through Him. Once they completely and thoroughly understood, this world has never been the same since. Likewise, once we understand the truth and assemble this truth in our intellect (mind), then we will begin to think like Jesus did – and act like His representatives on earth. When we understand the spiritual reality in this manner, it mandates a paradigm shift in the way we think and talk and live; we are converted from living according to an ordinary existence in worldly unbelief to living as an extraordinary demonstration of His manifest presence in our lives – to be the '*epistrophe*' (G1995) **revolution** that He desires for this world (Acts 15:3).

We are world changers. That is who we are predestined to be and we were all born with this same thought: to leave this earth in a better condition than we found it. Does this truth resonate within you? Deep down, it must, or else you did not understand the Father's message.

Think about this: if every one of us came to the same complete understanding that Jesus did, what do you think this world would look like? Exactly right – it would look like heaven! And this is the Father's plan – to use ordinary men to transform the physical and spiritual reality of earth to look like and operate according to the spiritual reality of heaven – "on earth as it is in heaven." This is not a great mystery. We are earthen vessels who were created to be a holy habitation for Jesus, as living tabernacles so that we can live life, being filled with the Holy Spirit, to be another manifestation of Christ upon the earth. If you doubt your ability to change the world, then your understanding (at present) is limited, but if you allow Jesus to operate within you (as a yielded vessel) so that Christ can flow through you, then you are on the threshold of living according to "The Way."

Thinking Like Jesus

Jesus continually taught His disciples how to think and live according to the spiritual pattern that He Himself demonstrated. The scriptures teach us that the Lord's disciples continued to doubt even after they witnessed His resurrection (Matt. 28:17); and we can almost hear the reprimand by Jesus when He suddenly appeared in the upper room...

> "Why do doubts arise in your hearts?" (Luke 24:38).

This word "doubt" is (*dialogizomai*-G1261) meaning – "a discussion; internal discussion or external debate; a dispute" and the word "arise" (*anabaino*-G305) means: "to arise, go up, come up; ascend."[28] In other words... "Why do doubting thoughts arise from within your hearts? Stop disputing the truth – and believe what you see!" Either you believe the truth *and* you alter your understanding to live according to the truth – or you don't believe.

Then Jesus "opened their understanding, that they might comprehend the Scriptures" (Luke 24:45).
- "*understanding*" is (*nous*-G3563) meaning: "the intellect, i.e. the mind; the seat of reflective consciousness"
- "*comprehend*" is (*suniemi*-G4920) meaning: "to put together mentally; understand" [29]

---

[28] Strong's Concordance.
[29] IBID.

Jesus thoroughly understands the spiritual conundrum within man and we have much to learn from Him by studying these scriptures. In order to counter the hardened heart of man where doubts arise, the mind must become opened (by grace) in order for truth to be understood. How incredible is that!!! In order for our field of faith (the heart) to believe the truth, our mind must first be cultivated (softened, then opened) so that we are able to receive and then assemble the truth in our mind and, therefore, we are able to understand the truth whereby an intellectual decision is made by our mind to live accordingly (from out of the heart).

Another scripture within this same vein is:

> "For the hearts of this people have grown dull. Their ears are hard of hearing, and their eyes they have closed, lest they should see with their eyes and hear with their ears, lest they should **understand with their hearts** and turn, so that I should heal them" (Matt. 13:15).

Jesus wants us to *understand* (4920 – *suniemi*, to put together mentally, understand, comprehend) *with* our hearts (*kardia*) and turn; literally, we are to mentally assemble truth in our mind (understand)… and we must do this in tandem (with) our heart (with heart/mind oneness of our soul) in order to operate with the mind of Christ.

Another scripture also…

> "When anyone hears the word of the kingdom, and does not *understand* it (4920 – *suniemi,* to put together mentally, comprehend), then the wicked one comes and snatches away what was sown in his heart. This is he who received seed by the wayside" (Matt. 13:19).

And again,

> "I will put My laws in their *mind* and write them on their hearts; and I will be their God, and they shall be My people" (Heb. 10:8; Jer. 31:33; '*dianoia*' (1271) – completeness of understanding, fully comprehending, meditative, deep thought[30]; Matt. 22:37; Mark 12:30; Luke 10:27).).

And finally… the Lord's commandments for everyone:

> "The first of all the commandments *is:* 'Hear, O Israel, the LORD our God, the LORD is one. [30] And you shall love the LORD your God with all your *heart*, with all your *soul* [*the combined submission of the heart and mind in one accord*], with all your *mind* [*dianoia*-1271 understanding, "*a thinking through, deep thoughts, meditation, reflection*"[31]] and with all your *strength* [*the yielded will and surrender of earthly desires*].' This *is* the first commandment. [31] And the second, like *it, is* this: 'You shall love your neighbor as yourself.' There is no other commandment greater than these." (Mark 12:29-31).

And yet, we are still very much like the Lord's disciples in this regard: without understanding!

> "So Jesus said, "Are you also still without *understanding*? (Matt. 15:16; Mark 7:18; "*understanding* (*asunetos*-G801) meaning: "unintelligent, stupid, senseless, without discernment, without understanding; by implication: wicked, foolish"[32]).

---

[30] A compilation of definition terms from Strong's and Vine's.
[31] IBID
[32] IBID

Either you believe the truth regarding the revelation of Jesus Christ – or you don't. If you want to believe it and you want to understand, then the Spirit is delighted to help you understand, but you must transition yourself (convert) from being a passive onlooker into an active seeker who wants to participate wholeheartedly in the Lord's spiritual revolution that is being birthed within you by the Spirit.

To say you can't believe because you don't understand creates a flimsy excuse to continue in your unbelief and remain "unintelligent." Simply put – such a person does not want to understand because they prefer to live with ignorance in unbelief.

None of us were born with spiritual understanding, which is one of the ways the Lord of glory is weeding us out to see if we want to become disciples who desire to hear, follow and imitate Jesus – or we are goats just pretending to be His sheep. The kingdom of God is already within you, but you must be willing to seek the Lord and live your life according to the guidance of the Spirit and the leading of Christ. Notice – I did not say teaching, because there are multitudes that have heard the teaching of Christ and profess to be a follower of Christ, but they do not do the things He tells them to do. Believers, yes – but disciples, no! This is the greatest tragedy of faith: to profess, but never possess. You can claim to be a Christian with Christ abiding in you, but if you have no interest in the things of Christ or to act more and more like Christ Himself, then you have deceived yourself – and the truth "with understanding" is not within you.

> "But someone will say, "You have faith, and I have works." Show me your faith without your works, and I will show you my faith by my works" (James 2:18).

Jesus created everything. Jesus is Lord of all creation! Jesus created your pinky toe and He gave you intellect. He combined the DNA of two individuals to create a completely new creation as you, and in this moment when two cells became one – His glory was released within you. At that very moment, you became a *living soul* (*nephesh*; Gen 2:7) and you were also given a spirit by God to contain His glory. Through this spirit, the spiritual reality is made known to each of us by the Holy Spirit who comes alongside us to partner with our spirit, as the Paraclete, and to guide us into all truth. It is with confidence that I say, "We are all without excuse" (Rom. 1:20). If we do not know, then this is because we did not place any value in knowing this truth or the implementation of a rigorous search to discover the truth hidden within you. Yes, the truth was hidden within your heart since day one, and on the last day, our own mind (conscious intellect) and heart will either condemn you or defend you when we stand face to face in front of Jesus Christ Himself. Are you counting on Peter to let you in through the Pearly Gates to give you a free pass or have a second chance? **Earth is your second chance**! To think otherwise reveals a lack of any spiritual understanding attributed to having never opened the Bible to read about this truth for yourself. If you are reading this truth (here) for the very first time, then I challenge you to discover this truth for yourself, because it is not just your knowledge of this truth whereby you are held accountable in understanding, but more so – the application of truth itself that only the Spirit Himself can reveal to you as you live in faithful obedience to Jesus. Stop listening exclusively to the teacher and the preacher and the priest: listen to the voice of the Holy Spirit… and live!

"The mind of the Spirit" (Rom. 8:27) and "the mind of Christ" (1 Cor. 2:16)… what do these have in common? Divine intellect with kingdom understanding.

> "But there is a spirit in man, and the *breath* of the Almighty gives him understanding" (Job 32:8; *breath* (*neshamah*-H5397 also translated: *inspiration*).

Who knows the spirit of a man except the spirit within a man? In a similar way, no one knows the things of God except the Spirit of

God; and likewise... the mind of God except the mind of Christ who abides in Oneness with the Spirit.

> "For what man knows the things of a man except the spirit of the man which is in him? Even so no one knows the things of God except the Spirit of God" (1 Cor. 2:11).

> "For "who has known the mind of the Lord that he may instruct Him?" But we have the mind of Christ" (1 Cor. 2:16).

We have the mind of Christ!!! As a disciple of Jesus Christ and holy Apostle, Paul spent the first 14 years of his spiritual journey being guided by the Holy Spirit through direct revelation by Jesus Christ to understand how the kingdom of God operates. His understanding did not come by way of any other teaching or written doctrine (none having been written yet), nor did he receive this revelation from anyone, including super-Apostles; his understanding was divinely inspired (*God-breathed inspiration*) by the Holy Spirit (2 Tim. 3:16). We have his marvelous letters to various people and churches that teaches them how to live according to the way of Christ – and to walk "in" understanding.

Likewise, I was journaling and writing for a year until, on September 27, 2013, I heard the Lord say to me, "You are My writer" and then the Spirit said, "Now write!" For the past two years, since October 12, 2014, I have been writing the "Image Bearer" series and my method is the same every day: listen, hear, meditate, understand – and then write. I do not write what I think, but rather, I write what I hear because "I am His writer" and I no longer live according to my purpose or plan. I am a disciple of Jesus Christ, and I have dedicated my life in service to Him, and as it so happens... He gave me a calling and a responsibility that I thoroughly love. Fresh revelation from Him every day is more precious to me than gold, silver, great riches... and even fresh Virginia peaches in season.

One of the best illustrations of his message "to understand" and "think like Christ" is found in Paul's letter to the church in Philippi. Let's examine the word Paul uses to convey the truth of Christ to understand how we can live *as* the likeness of Christ – by thinking like Him.

'Phroneo' (G5426) – "to think, to exercise the mind; to be minded in a certain way;" "to be like-minded" according to Christ Jesus (Phil. 2:5; Rom. 15:5); "be of one mind" (Phil. 2:2; 2 Cor. 13:11) lit. "minding the one thing"... in one accord; "be of the same mind" (Phil 4:2); to be none otherwise minded (Gal. 5:10)." [33]

When it comes so setting our mind on Christ, it implies we are being mindful to think in a certain way, which in this case, is on Christ – to become like (in the similitude of) Christ Jesus. We are setting the focus of our attention and the fullness of our affection on Christ in order to imitate the way and manner in which He thought and, likewise, lived. We are a nation, that is, a culture of people who have decided, through faith, to live according to certain principles and lifeways as disciples of Jesus Christ. The "one thing" that we have in common (*koinos*)... is to become like Christ Jesus.

The One Thing

As I was meditating on these things, I asked the Lord how we can all get on the same page and "be of one mind," and then I looked in the distance at a trucking company with a fleet of trucks. Then, this understanding came to me: they are all going in different directions with different loads for different purposes, but all are being coordinated by "the one thing" i.e. the dispatcher.

When the Spirit speaks, we are being guided and coordinated by Jesus, through the Spirit (our spiritual Dispatcher), who communicates words from Jesus to guide us and teach us in the way of Christ. When we listen to the Spirit, we are being guided

---

[33] Strong's Concordance.

by the One, to think and act like the Holy One, Jesus Christ, and to operate in oneness "through Him, with Him and in Him," in oneness with one another – according to pattern as exemplified by Christ Jesus. This is how we all must get on the same spiritual page: listen to the Spirit!

The Spirit!!! The Spirit!!! The Spirit!!! We are born anew by the Spirit, and are taught by the Spirit, and are being guided in truth by the Spirit of Christ so that we may become a manifest expression of Jesus upon the earth.... according to the Spirit of life in Christ Jesus.

> "But the Helper, the Holy Spirit, whom the Father will send in My name, He will teach you all things, and bring to your remembrance all things that I said to you" (John 14:26).

> "When He, the Spirit of truth, has come, He will guide you into all truth; for He will not speak on His own authority, but whatever He hears He will speak; and He will tell you things to come" (John 16:13).

If you do not know what to say, then fear not, and listen for the voice of the Spirit...

> "For the Holy Spirit will teach you in that very hour what you ought to say." (Luke 12:12).

If you do not know what to do, then fear not, and listen to the voice of the Spirit...

> "For those who live according to the flesh set their minds on the things of the flesh, but those who live according to the Spirit, the things of the Spirit" (Rom. 8:5).

If you do not know what to think, then fear not, and listen to the voice of the Spirit...

> "For God has not given us a spirit of fear, but of power and of love and of a *sound* mind" (2 Tim. 1:7; (*sophronismos*-G4995) "a disciplined, self-controlled mind"[34]).

> "But you have an anointing from the Holy One, and you know all things" (1 John 2:20).

What more could I possibly say to you in a manner that helps you understand? Well, my words are not what helps you understand, because that is the responsibility of the Inner Witness…

The Inner Witness

One of the most amazing truths we have concerning the spiritual reality that surrounds us is that the spiritual reality is everywhere… and is within us as well.

God is "in you all" (Eph. 4:6) and "the Spirit of God dwells in you" also (1 Cor. 3:16).

> "There is one body and one Spirit, just as you were called in one hope of your calling; [5] one Lord, one faith, one baptism; [6] *one God and Father of all, who is above all, and through all,* ***and in you all***" (Eph. 4:4-6).

God is… everywhere, omnipresent, and all in all; and He is "in you all" i.e. every person. God is already in us, but we oftentimes pretend that He is not really there by creating a separate reality within us that says He isn't. How preposterous!

And the Spirit of the Lord is dwelling within us also…

---

[34] Strong's Concordance.

> "Do you not know that you are the temple of God and that the Spirit of God dwells in you?" (1 Cor. 3:16).

Jesus came to teach us and demonstrate to us how we are supposed to live on this earth as spiritual beings that are having a human experience with the Father and the Spirit dwelling in us. In everything that Jesus did, and by all the words of instruction whereby He taught us, and by His marvelous words, He was teaching divine truths to help us get back to being about our Father's business on earth – according to the Spirit who is at work within us.

One of the most incredible statements by Jesus is in regard to the inner witness. The Holy Spirit, our "spiritual Dispatcher" who dwells within every one of us, has been speaking words of wisdom and truth to us since the time we were born, but somewhere along the path of life we decided to stop listening to "the Voice" of the Inner Witness who testifies to the Truth within us.

> "If I bear witness of Myself, My witness is not true. [32] There is another who bears witness of Me, and I know that the witness which He witnesses of Me is true" (John 5:31, 32).

Many of us have been taught "the Father" is the witness Jesus is speaking about, and this is also true since the Father was dwelling in Jesus throughout His entire life on earth, but we need to see the three-fold witness that is folded within the pages of scripture.

> "This is He who came by water and blood—Jesus Christ; not only by water, but by water and blood. ***And it is the Spirit who bears witness, because the Spirit is truth***. [7] For there are three that bear witness in heaven: the Father, the Word, and the Holy Spirit; and these three are one. [8] And there are three that bear witness on earth: the Spirit, the water, and the blood; and these three agree as one. [9] If we receive the witness of men, the witness of God is

greater; *for this is the witness of God which He has testified of His Son.* **¹⁰ He who believes in the Son of God has the witness in himself**" (1 John 5:6-10).

The Holy Spirit is the Witness of God, whom this world cannot receive…

> "… whose minds the god of this age has blinded, who do not believe, lest the light of the gospel of the glory of Christ, who is the image of God, should shine on them" (2 Cor. 4:4).

The Holy Spirit is "the witness" who was dwelling in Jesus and the Spirit is also "the inner witness" who dwells within each one of us – and was given to each of us by God – so that we may always have access to the Father and the truth through One Spirit (Eph. 2:18) through faith in Jesus Christ (Eph. 4:4).

The Holy Spirit is "The One Thing" who communicates God's messages to everyone so that we may hear, believe and understand the truth of the Messenger, Jesus Christ. The truth is… we have never been alone on this planet! The Holy Spirit, our Paraclete, has been alongside us and within everyone to help us, to guide us, to teach us and to lead us unto the truth in the hope that we may, one day, walk in the Way of Christ and imitate Jesus our Lord.

The Holy Spirit has been speaking to everyone since the beginning, but we cannot know or comprehend the message until we yield our will (and hardened heart) to assemble divine truth in our mind whereby Jesus becomes the Lord of our life. The spiritual reality can only be known in this manner – as the birthing anew by the Spirit of God through the yielded surrender of our will to become obedient servants to Jesus in the kingdom of God – as disciples unto Jesus only!

And it is the Holy Spirit dwelling in us that bears witness with "our spirit" within us that enables us to declare Jesus is Lord…

> "Therefore I make known to you that no one speaking by the Spirit of God calls Jesus accursed, and no one can say that Jesus is Lord except by the Holy Spirit" (1 Cor. 12:3).
>
> "Now hope does not disappoint, because the love of God has been poured out in our hearts by the Holy Spirit who was given to us" (Rom. 5:5)... "who also has sealed us and given us the Spirit in our hearts as a guarantee" (2 Cor. 1:22).
>
> "For as many as are *led by the Spirit of God*, these are sons of God. [15] For you did not receive the spirit of bondage again to fear, but you received the Spirit of adoption by whom we cry out, "Abba, Father" (Rom. 8:14, 15).
>
> "The Spirit Himself **bears witness with our spirit** that we are children of God" (Rom. 8:16).

The Holy Spirit within us is "the inner witness" and "the seal" that authenticates the spiritual reality of God's kingdom *has* taken root in you and is being perfected in you… through sanctification by the Spirit.

> "But the natural man does not receive the things of the Spirit of God, for they are foolishness to him; nor can he know them, because they are spiritually discerned" (2 Cor. 2:14).
>
> "Do you not know that the unrighteous will not inherit the kingdom of God? Do not be deceived. Neither fornicators, nor idolaters, nor adulterers, nor homosexuals, nor sodomites, [10] nor thieves, nor covetous, nor drunkards, nor revilers, nor extortioners will inherit the kingdom of God. [11] And such were some of you. But you were washed, *but you were sanctified*, but you were justified in the

> name of the Lord Jesus and *by the Spirit of our God*" (1 Cor. 6:9-11).

> "But you are not in the flesh but in the Spirit, if indeed the Spirit of God dwells in you. Now if anyone does not have the Spirit of Christ, he is not His" (Rom. 8:9).

The work of Holy Spirit in the kingdom of God is to help everyone hear the truth and understand the message of Jesus Christ by the Messenger's Messenger, the Spirit of Christ Jesus. And this is why Jesus referred to the Spirit as the Doorkeeper for the Door that leads to the Father (John 10:3) because the Spirit of God knows the thoughts and intents of our heart.

> "Now He who searches the hearts knows what the mind of the Spirit is, because He makes intercession for the saints according to the will of God" (Rom. 8:27).

The Holy Spirit is an Intercessor who helps us and guides us according to the will of God. The Holy Spirit is our Sanctifier "through the washing of regeneration and renewing" of our mind by the Spirit (Titus 3:5). The Holy Spirit is our central Dispatcher who distributes messages (prophecies and words of encouragement and exhortation) that unify us and "make us one" in service to "the One," i.e. Jesus Christ. The Holy Spirit is the Project Manager who builds Christ's church and serves as the Administrator of the Church who distributes spiritual endowments (gifts) so we may operate with a diversity of gifts to become the manifest expression of Christ upon the earth as "the body of Christ" in this world – through yielded saints like you and me.

> "… for to one is given the word of wisdom through the Spirit, to another the word of knowledge through the same Spirit" (1 Cor. 12:8).

> "These things we also speak, not in words which

man's wisdom teaches, but which the Holy Spirit teaches, comparing spiritual things with spiritual. (1 Cor. 2:13).

Even so… the Christ in you identifies with the Christ in me – through the Spirit. And yet, the institutional church teaches very little about the Spirit because… it cannot control the Spirit. The Holy Spirit revealed various messages from Jesus to the seven churches in Revelation through John, yet somehow the institutional church puts these words in red letter as being said by Jesus, so… are we not paying attention to the Apostle's teaching and the words of Christ Himself?

> "He who has an ear, let him hear what the Spirit says to the churches" (Rev. 2:7)
> "He who has an ear, let him hear what the Spirit says to the churches" (Rev. 2:11)
> "He who has an ear, let him hear what the Spirit says to the churches" (Rev. 2:17)
> "He who has an ear, let him hear what the Spirit says to the churches" (Rev. 2:29)
> "He who has an ear, let him hear what the Spirit says to the churches" (Rev. 3:6)
> "He who has an ear, let him hear what the Spirit says to the churches" (Rev. 3:13)
> "He who has an ear, let him hear what the Spirit says to the churches" (Rev. 3:22)

> "And we are His witnesses to these things, and so also is the Holy Spirit whom God has given to those who obey Him" (Acts 5:32).

> "But the Holy Spirit also witnesses to us; for after He had said before, [16] "This is the covenant that I will make with them after those days, says the LORD: I will put My laws into their hearts, and in their minds I will write them" (Heb. 10:15, 16).

We need to hear and understand the message revealed to us as coming from the Inner Witness, the Holy Spirit, who enables us and empowers us to do exceedingly great and marvelous deeds for the sake of Jesus Christ "if" only we would listen to the Holy Spirit and learn from Him!

If you want to hear the voice of the Lord your God, then you shall hear it... but if you refuse to hear His voice and continue to make excuses why you cannot, then know this... "you are without excuse" (Rom. 1:20). It is no longer a valid argument open for debate whether primitive cultures or unpreached people groups can be held accountable because they never heard the gospel because...

> "But I say, have they not heard? Yes indeed: "Their *sound* has gone out to all the earth, and their words to the ends of the world." (Rom. 10:18; the word "*sound*" (*phthoggos*-5353) means: "utterance; as in a musical note; to utter a voice."[35])

> "The heavens declare the glory of God; and the firmament shows His handiwork. [2] Day unto day utters speech, and night unto night reveals knowledge. [3] *There is no speech nor language where their voice is not heard.* [4] Their *line* has gone out through all the earth, and their words to the end of the world" (Psa. 19:1-4; the word "*line*" (*qav*-H6957 means: "*a connecting cord*; a musical string or accord"[36]).

Truly, a person must endeavor to be spiritually deaf with great mental rigidity and hardness of heart so as "not to receive" voice messages from heaven!

---

[35] Strong's Concordance.
[36] IBID.

God "*desires all men to be saved and to come to the knowledge of the truth*" (1 Tim. 2:3-5) through faith in Jesus Christ; therefore, He has made sure His sound has gone out into all the earth – by the Voice of His Spirit – Who speaks into our mind "day unto day… and night unto night."

"Be still and know that I am God" and listen to hear the Voice from heaven. Now, therefore…

Do you really want to understand, or do you prefer your prearranged bias and prejudice in support of your own opinions to justify the world you want to live in from your perspective… or do you want to know, understand, comprehend and perceive this world from God's perspective?

If you want to understand, then I invite you to soften your heart, declare Jesus your Lord, ask the Lord to open your mind… and keep reading. The kingdom of heaven is –Here!

> "The grace of the Lord Jesus Christ, and the love of God, and the communion of the Holy Spirit be with you all. Amen." (2 Cor. 13:14).

Change Is The Reason Why

Change is one of the three primary elements of newness (through truth, change and oneness).

But what is change? We know that something is changed when it becomes altered somehow, either by an outward force of greater power or an inward force with greater purpose. Change is a factor of life on earth as well as the universe which represents one of the constants in all creation: everything changes... except God.

Man is changed moment by moment from the instant of conception when two cells become united in oneness until cellular division and multiplication begins to mold this new creation into a unique person that has never existed before. Change happens.

Even from the moment a child is born, dramatic changes occur moment by moment. When a child is very young, they learn to imitate parents and copy their mannerisms, and when they are old enough to communicate, they are often heard saying, "When I grow up, I want to be" or "I'm going to be" or "I am going to be just like____" (fill in the blank). This is part of our human nature to copy, imitate and emulate those around us that inspire us to be bigger than we are.

As adults, we often do the same thing; we seek role models and mentors to show us how to live life that will accomplish our agenda to become – and be – that which we desire to be. What an incredible responsibility is placed on one generation to become the standard for the next generation, and yet, there is another option that we have been given in order to accomplish our purpose on earth: become the likeness of Christ Jesus. When we set our focus on becoming like Jesus, this is not an unachievable goal; in truth, we are able to become like Christ who created us according to His likeness so as to become just like Him... as life-giving spirits.

And yet, the surpassing greatness of achieving this goal to become like Christ is not an insurmountable challenge because all we have to do – is change. Yes, this is easier said than done, so perhaps we need to consider the possibility of becoming like Christ as one part of our spiritual DNA that has been encoded within our soul since the foundation of the world. Once we agree to the change being asked of us, then the Lord of glory accomplishes this monumental task by transforming us by renewing our mind by the Holy Spirit. And again, we think to ourselves, "This is easier said than done." Yet this is only possible once we have accepted the terms of Christ's covenantal agreement with us to be our Lord, as our Master, Savior and Deliverer. This is the purpose of Christ in us – the hope of glory – to change us from the inside out to become what we have all been predestined to become – the manifested likeness of Christ upon the earth.

If you think this is some future-based promise by Jesus that pertains only to when we get to the other side of the resurrection, at the regeneration of all things, then the doctrine of man has sold you a less-than understanding of our reason and purpose for being on the earth.

There is a problem that I have found while studying the scriptures: perspectives influence paradigms. This problem has influenced all biblical scholars and commentaries on the subject of God, man, Jesus, the Holy Spirit, heaven, life, what man's purpose on earth is… and so forth. In essence, we create the paradigm that supports our perspective so that we may understand what we believe in such a way that somehow makes sense to us. In essence, we put on one type of eye-glasses through which we want to see the earthly reality from our perspective and we base our life upon this paradigm (the view we expected to get from the spectacles). So, if you want to change the way you see things – from a different perspective, then you need to put on a different pair of paradigm glasses through which you can see… another perspective.

If, for example, you believe that heaven is to be found in the far reaches of the cosmos, then this perspective will influence your spiritual understanding of life on earth; if, for example, you have been taught the doctrine of sin whereby man is a wretched, miserable, sinful creature void of any goodness or redeeming qualities, then this perspective will influence how you interpret your spiritual understanding of the scriptures and man as having a sinful nature rather than a divine nature; if, for example, you believe that God is vengeful and onerous in His obligatory requirement for us to walk in obedience to attain holiness, then this perspective will influence your understanding of God and Jesus and the Word of God that is devoid of any joy, happiness and glee; if, you believe you are obligated to obey the Laws of Moses which were ordinances given to Israel only, then this perspective will influence your understanding of grace and living according to "the law of the Spirit of life in Christ Jesus;" if you do not believe in the operation of the Holy Spirit's gifts (spiritual endowments) in these days because they were only applicable during the first century Apostolic Age, then that perspective will influence your paradigm as it relates the Holy Spirit's work in you – and through you.

False perspectives lead to false understanding with false expectations within false paradigms.

Here, then, is the follow-up problem: we tend to rigorously defend our perspective when another paradigm challenges our reality. This, in truth, is exactly what Jesus did, but He didn't just teach us about another paradigm – He became for us the exact expression and manifestation of the heavenly paradigm for mankind, as seen from the Father's perspective – and He demonstrated this heavenly reality by words and actions as being "the same as the Father's" for us to imitate. Therefore, we need only to keep our eyes upon Jesus in order to learn from His teaching, imitate His example, and thus… live according to the spiritual reality of the heavenly paradigm on earth "as it is in heaven." This is "the Way" man was originally intended to live – in uninterrupted oneness of Presence and Spirit with the Lord, as Jesus taught us – in word and deed.

Jesus did it – and so can we. "As He is – so are we in the world" (1 John 4:17).

Now, getting back to the subject of change – we need to embrace the paradigm shift that Jesus taught and demonstrated to us in order for us to become aligned with the heavenly reality that surrounds us even now. If we want to become changed and renewed, then we must be changed with the spiritual paradigm of Christ to become more like Jesus – and less like the world around us, whereby the Apostle Paul said it perfectly…

> "But put on the Lord Jesus Christ, and make no provision for the flesh, to fulfill its lusts" (Rom. 13:14).

We need to "*put on*" Christ (*enduo*-G1746-with the sense of sinking into clothing); we not only need to have Christ formed in us through the transformational work of the Holy Spirit to renew (change) our mind (paradigm), we also need to "put on" the outward appearance of Christ upon us as clothing for the new man, and thus… become the manifested image of Jesus Christ upon the earth – as was originally intended for mankind. In essence, in order for this to happen, we need more than a simple make-over with substantive change… we need to be completely transformed into something completely new that did not exist before. And in order for this to happen, the old man must be rendered completely "dead, very dead" (Gal. 2:20) before the newness of Christ in us can begin.

To Change – Becoming New

Let us examine closely several words in the scriptures that denote change: [37]

Allaso (236) – to make different, to make other than it is, to transform, change, as in:
      A) The effect on the body of a believer at Christ's return (1 Cor. 15:51-51)
      B) The final renewal of the material creation (Heb. 1:12)

Egeneto heteron (1096, 2087) – was altered, became different; not the same (nature, form, class, kind); to become, cause to,

---

[37] Terms and definitions taken from Strong's Concordance.

come into being... as other, or different (Luke 9:29)

Metaschematizo (3345) – (5x) to change in fashion, form or appearance; to transfigure, disguise, transform; a transient change that happens (contrasted with *metamorphoo* which is permanent state to which a change takes place) – is said of the believer's body as changed or raised at Christ's return (Phil 3:21); to transform, of Satan and his human ministers, false apostles (2 Cor. 11:13-15)

Metamorphoo (3339) – (4x) to change (permanently) into another form (Engl. metamorphose)
  A) transfigured (said of Jesus, Matt. 17:2; Mark 9:2)
  B) transformed – the obligation of believers to undergo a complete change into another form by the power of God (Rom. 12:2) resulting in changes that are manifested in our outward character and conduct
  C) the expectation that believers will be "changed" into the image of Christ (2 Cor. 3:18)

When Jesus came to earth, He was God Almighty clothed with humanity. He was God the entire time He was upon the earth – being dressed in appearance as a Man. Jesus didn't become the Son of God after the resurrection for having lived a sinless life; He was verily God Almighty before He was ever conceived to a virgin named Mary by the Holy Spirit. Why Jesus chose to come to earth this way is quite mysterious, indeed, but if you wanted to teach mankind how to live like sons and daughters of the Father, then the best way is to become like mankind in every regard including life, death and everything in between – by being born as a man.

Jesus lived His life as an example for us to follow – and imitate – to be changed so that we become transformed into the likeness of Christ Jesus upon the earth... according to His purpose!

Newness – through truth, change and oneness... is what our faith walk is all about.

Change is the one constant man can count on.

Jesus formed us (Gen. 2:7), to be conformed to the image of Christ (Rom. 8:29), by being transformed by the renewing of our mind (Rom. 12:2) for Christ to be fully formed in us (Gal. 4:19) whereby we are transfigured (changed) into the image of Christ (2 Cor. 3:18)…

> **"…who will transform [3345] our lowly body that it may be conformed to His glorious body" (Phil. 3:21).**

This is God's big picture for man to be changed in this life… and eternal life in the resurrection. Our purpose on earth is less about "doing" than "being" (as in) less about "doing" right things, right doctrines, right 'anythings' and more about "being" (as in)… becoming more like Christ.

We were created by Jesus according to His image and likeness – to become an expressed representational image of Him. We are on earth for this reason – according to His eternal purpose in us to become like Him.

Our purpose if life… is to fulfill Christ's reason.

The mystery of man on the earth is sanctification; it is our reason and purpose for being here.

The Transfiguration

When Jesus went up (into) the mountain with three disciples whereby He was transformed before their eyes, with Elijah and Moses being present, we may have been taught this moment was significant as some authentication of Jesus as the Christ of God. Yes, this was important for the disciples to witness on the basic level of faith in Jesus as the Messiah, but it has become exceedingly more important for us to comprehend "why" Jesus did this so that it would be recorded to benefit future generations.

Luke 9:29 records His facial appearance "was altered," yet only Luke uses the term '*egeneto heteron*' (1096, 2087) from the words "(*ginomai heteros*) became different"[38] so as not to give the impression that mere men can be changed into gods, as was frequently taught in the ancient world. Jesus did not transform Himself into something different; only the outward appearance of Jesus was altered, such that the glory of His Divine Nature within Him was revealed when the outward body was transfigured (changed) so as to allow the visible reality of His Divine Self to radiate beyond the limitations of His earthly form. His countenance (appearance) became glorified and radiant – resembling lightning as when it flashes across the sky.

Jesus revealed Himself in this moment – according to who He is – from the inside out.

And the message Jesus keeps trying to teach us is that "who we are" *on the inside* was created according to His likeness so that we might become His representational image upon the earth. Wow! Does this truth change your perspective regarding your understanding of mankind? What about your perspective of you? What about your mission and purpose on earth? Are you just a wretched sinner saved by grace, or are you God's offspring that the Lord redeemed and has activated for duty on account of God's grace and glory within you to do His will? Do you need an intellectual paradigm shift to embrace this understanding?

The transfiguration was also recorded by two other Gospel writers, but they used another term, '*metamorphoo*' (3339) meaning, "to change into another form." The English word we get from this is metamorphosis, which most of us remember as the caterpillar that, after entering into a chrysalis, emerges some time later as a beautiful butterfly. The nature of the animal has not changed, but the outward appearance and form has become altered and changed. And it is within this concept that man needs to see himself… as a spiritual being within a physical form that is being renewed within

---

[38] Strong's Concordance, study on *metamorphoo*-3339.

the mind in order to be transformed (changed, altered) by the truth of Christ in this life – and thus, will be transfigured by glory in the life hereafter.

> "And do not be conformed to this world, but be *transformed* [*metamorphoo - transfigured*] by the renewing of your mind, that you may prove what *is* that good and acceptable and perfect will of God" (Rom. 12:2).

Jesus wants us to become transformed (*metamorphoo*) by the renewing of our mind to become radiant and brilliant… resembling lightning as when it flashes across the sky!

The inherent meaning of Christ's transfiguration remains constant in all three accounts whereby the scriptures are consistent even when different terms are utilized; and it is of monumental importance to see two additional times the Apostle Paul used this term with pinpoint accuracy.

Rom. 12:2 describes the transformation '*metamorphoo*' of the inner man by the renewing of man's mind by the Holy Spirit – and the implications are significant. When the mind of the inner man is renewed in order to live according to the Spirit (the heavenly paradigm of Christ in us), the inward man is literally "being transformed – *metamorphoo*" to become consistent with this "new man" according to Him who created him in order to become who he was created to be… the image and likeness of Jesus our Creator. In this regard, the inner man is being revealed according to Him who created us according to His likeness – in glory.

While this truth is marvelous on the basis of faith unto salvation, it is significantly more important to understand this truth as it relates to our "transfiguration" in the resurrection on the day of Christ. When we are raised in resurrection, who we are (that is – the inner man – our soul) will be raised in newness and clothed with an incorruptible body that is superimposed upon us. The inner man, our soul, will remain the same, but the new body we receive will be a glorified body just like the one the disciples witnessed at the transfiguration of Jesus. The changed appearance is revealed to us from within us – as glory.

Jesus said… "In the resurrection, [we will be] like angels that are in heaven" (Matt. 22:30). Jesus said we will be like angels according to their nature (form).

> "And of the angels He says: "Who makes His angels spirits and His ministers a flame of fire" (Heb. 1:7).

Close your eyes and imagine this for a moment: angels are a flame of fire, heavenly beings radiant from the glory of God within them and upon them. Can we see ourselves like angels in the resurrection, with glorified bodies, becoming like Jesus at His transfiguration, or do we still desire earthly bodies with all the carnal trappings?

Since we are given a new body that is superimposed upon us as coming down from out of heaven, then how can this appearance come to us from within? What an excellent question! The answer is "both-and." The resurrection body that we receive comes to us from out of heaven, yet is within us now (that is, our spirit). God's glory will illuminate this new body once again, as it was originally in Eden. Adam and Eve lived like this in the Garden, but when they entered into sin, a different outer garment was superimposed on them and the glory within them became veiled; they saw themselves as they are – separated from God's oneness – and naked in appearance. (This truth will be very important when we learn more about the spirit within us.)

When Jesus comes again – apart from sin – "we shall see Him as He is" in glory, and we shall be seen as we truly are "like Him" (1 John 3:12)… yet without these earthly garments (Heb. 9:28).

> "Beloved, now we are children of God; and it has not yet been revealed what we shall be, but we know that when He is revealed, we shall be *like*

Him, for we shall see Him as He is" (1 John 3:2).

Jesus is in glory form right now – and we shall become *like* Jesus when He comes in glory. This should not come as a complete surprise to any of us since Jesus created us in His image according to His likeness. The word *"like"* is *'homios'* (G3664) and means "similar in appearance or character; like, resembling, the same as" – "of ability, condition, **nature**." [39] And used again by Paul…

> "Therefore, *since we are the offspring of God*, we ought not to think that the Divine Nature is *like* gold or silver or stone, something shaped by art and man's devising" (Acts 17:29).

We were created with "spiritual DNA" to operate in the ability and similitude of Jesus according to a remnant of the Spirit within us (Mal. 2:15); He seeded the earth with His glory placed within man, and "crowned him with glory and honor" (Psa. 8:5). During this current age on earth, men were created and positioned a little lower than angels, but in the age to come – the sons of men become sons of God and will judge angels.

> "Do you not know that we shall judge angels? How much more, things that pertain to this life?" (1 Cor. 6:3).

Jesus has invited us to partner with Him and to be partakers of the divine nature to accomplish all that He has *prepared beforehand* for us to walk in (2 Pet. 1:4);

> "that He might make known the riches of His glory on the vessels of mercy, which He had prepared beforehand *for glory*" (Rom. 9:23).

> "For we are His workmanship [masterpiece], created in Christ Jesus for good works, which God prepared beforehand that we should walk in them"

---

[39] Strong's.

(Eph. 2:10).

Do we not often preach from the pulpit about the great reward we will receive in service to God? Why is this so difficult for us to comprehend, then, that Jesus would make us like *elohims*, in the similitude of *Elohim*, God Himself (Psa. 82:6; John 10:34), so that we may rule and reign with Him in eternity? Not only does Jesus want us to get to the other side... He also wants us to have and possess things when we get there and govern creation and kingdoms with Him.

> "Now he who plants and he who waters are one,
> and each one will receive his own reward according
> to his own labor" (1 Cor. 3:8).

> "If we endure, we shall also reign with Him. If we
> deny Him, He also will deny us" (2 Tim. 2:12).

The great reward we receive is an inheritance commensurate (given in equal measure) according to our faithfulness to Christ. Now, this next point is highly significant: we cannot earn our inheritance, as we perceive "earnings" in this life which result from working to produce something. The Lord is our Provider in this life whereby the provisions we receive and acquire in this life are the result of the Lord providing it for us... through our efforts to produce. Our inheritance is not the result of accumulating or earning heavenly treasure on earth, but rather... through deeds of righteousness, our *recompense* is forwarded into our faith account to be used by us in the hereafter, whereby our faithful stewardship and deeds of righteousness in obedience to Christ becomes our eternal *reward* that is "sent ahead" for our after-life benefit. For even the earthly inheritance we receive from another person is not something that we have earned... it is given to us based upon the graciousness of another person out of their abundance and generosity. We cannot earn an inheritance, nor are we "entitled" to receive an unmerited inheritance because such a gift is according to the graciousness of the benefactor, which operates apart from works-based performance with compensation – or entitlements –

according to John 1:13.

What we did for the sake of Christ (good works) will be rewarded in the hereafter; however, any good that we do apart from Christ that does not give glory to God will be regard as self-righteous vainglory chaff and thrown into the fire… yet we (the redeemed) may be saved as one barely escaping through the flames.

> "When you pass through the waters, **_I will be with you_**; and through the rivers, they shall not overflow you. When you walk through the fire, you shall not be burned, nor shall the flame scorch you" (Isa. 43:2).

> "If anyone's work is burned, he will suffer loss; but he himself [his soul] will be saved, yet so as through fire" (1 Cor. 3:15; words [added] by the author).

Yet those who disregard the Lord will face His indignation with fire…

> "So the Light of Israel will be for a fire, and his Holy One for a flame; it will burn and devour His thorns and his briers in one day" (Isa. 10:17).

> "A fire devours before them, and behind them a flame burns; the land is like the Garden of Eden before them, and behind them a desolate wilderness; surely nothing shall escape them" (Joel 2:3).

Please keep in mind: since Jesus is your Lord and Master, then you are truly saved even if your limited understanding debilitates you from walking according to the Spirit of life in Christ Jesus; however, if your understanding does not produce seeds of righteousness that gives all glory to God in faithful obedience to Jesus Christ, than your self-righteous good works performed by human effort will be burned by fire, yet you yourself [your soul] will be saved… but without an inheritance. We don't go up to get it; it comes down to us when we get to the other side.

When you get to the other side, will you have an inheritance or will everything be burned away?

The world consists of two basic people types: saved through faith in Jesus and unregenerate. And the faithful consist of two basic types: those with an inheritance and those without.

The Light of Glory

What did Jesus mean by 'light' as in, "you are the light of the world"? Is this a metaphor for something more than mere illumination, and if so, then what? In my opinion, light is a metaphor for God's truth *and* God's glory revealed (manifested) within man.

> "What is man that You are mindful of him, and the son of man that You visit him? [5] For You have made him a little lower than the angels, and *You have crowned him with glory and honor*" (Psa. 8:4, 5).

"God made man upright" (Eccl. 7:29), and God crowned us with glory and honor; however, all glory belongs to God our Maker. God placed a deposit of His glory in *everything* He made, including all creation, but man gets to decide "to whom" he gives this glory that we received from God. The rebellion that happened in heaven, whereby angels lost their proper habitation and were cast out, is also happening to all of us on earth and God is testing our allegiance to see whether we will love Him, serve Him and give Him glory – or not. If we remain rebellious on earth, then we will also lose our proper habitation (earth) and be cast out.

Now, consider this glory that was given to all men from God and "to whom" the Psalmist David gave "his glory"…

> "To the end that ***my glory*** may sing praise to You and not be silent. O Lord my God, I will give thanks to You forever" (Psa. 30:12; said by David).

> "For the Lord God is a sun and shield; *The Lord will give grace and glory*; no good thing will He withhold from those who walk ***uprightly***" (Psa. 84:11).

> "O God, my heart is steadfast; I will sing and give

> praise, ***even with my glory***" (Psa. 108:1).

> "Give to the Lord the glory due His name; bring an *offering*, and come into His courts" (Psa. 96:8; *bring an offering of His glory*).

God has given a measure of His glory to all men, including nations and leaders of nations...

> "You, O king, are a king of kings. For the God of heaven has given you a kingdom, power, strength, *and glory*" (Dan. 2:37; spoken by Daniel to King Nebuchadnezzar of Babylon).

> "It is the glory of God to conceal a matter, but the glory of kings is to search out a matter" (Prov. 25:2).

Consider Job who, in the bitterness of his afflictions, lamented the removal of his glory by God:

> "He has stripped me of my glory, and taken the crown from my head" (Job 19:9).

We cannot seek our own glory and expect it to be like God's glory:

> "It is not good to eat much honey; so to seek one's own glory is not glory" (Prov. 25:27; which is vainglory, see Phil. 2:3).

And there is a reason why God gave His glory to man, which we will discuss in a moment, but if we refuse to give God the glory due Him...

> "*If you will not hear, and if you will not take it to heart*, to give glory to My name," says the Lord of hosts, "I will send a curse upon you, and I will curse your blessings. Yes, I have cursed them already,

because you do not take it to heart" (Mal. 2:2).

Everything concerning man upon the earth is about giving glory to God. Either we give our glory to God, or we deliver it to Satan to build his kingdom...

> "And the devil said to Him [Jesus], "All this authority I will give You, *and their glory*; for this has been delivered to me, and I give it to whomever I wish" (Luke 4:6).

In the Garden, on account of sin, mankind delivered to Satan the glory given to them by God, but Jesus reclaimed this glory through His sinless victorious life whereby Jesus said...

> "All authority has been given to Me in heaven and on earth" (Matt. 28:18).

When we give glory to Jesus Christ, the Lord, we have access to the Father and become one with the Father...

> "And the glory which You gave Me I have given them, that they may be one just as We are one" (John 17:22).

These verses are highly significant: Jesus received all authority in heaven and earth, and now we also see Jesus giving glory to His disciples. This glory being given to the disciples can be interpreted two ways: either Jesus is giving them the glory that He recovered from Satan – or Jesus is giving His disciples His glory. In one regard, getting our glory back from Satan liberates us from our captivity and bondage to him, which is incredibly good news; however, if Jesus is giving us His glory, then this is even greater news indeed... which involves a greater grace!

Even though Satan told Jesus "he gives glory to whoever he wishes," yet this is not his glory to give, so it seems he will tempt us to embrace a lie to exchange our glory in order to receive more glory; however, only Jesus is able to do this... and thereby we give our glory to Satan in error – which he continues to steal from us with more lies and false promises. For this reason among many, Jesus came to set us free from the lie and the multitude of many false promises and doctrines regarding who man is – and who our Father in heaven is so that we may walk in the way – as sons and daughters of God our Father.

In this regard, as it pertains to "who" we give our glory to, either we become like Jesus or we become like Satan, and we determine this according to whom we give the glory within us. When we give the glory to ourselves, this is exactly what Satan did while in heaven; he received God's glory and kept it for himself (iniquity was found in him)... and then he left[40] the presence of God to build his own kingdom (which, by the way, is upon the earth). Satan tempted Eve and Adam to do the same thing – and they acted independently of God by believing upon his enticing words and they trespassed into sin (i.e. separation from God's presence). Man's separation is only temporary and is reconciled through repentance from sin by entering "into faith" in Jesus Christ, but Satan's separation is permanent, whereby a special place in Hell has been reserved for him – and a similar place has been reserved for those who will not give to God the glory due Him. So, what does God's word say about man's former condition as darkness before repentance and declaring Jesus as your Lord and Savior?

> "For you were once darkness, but now you are light in the Lord. Walk as children of light ⁹ (for the fruit of the Spirit *is* in all goodness, righteousness, and

---

[40] There are two accounts of Satan's expulsion from heaven: the most popular version says he was "cast out" and thrown to earth (Rev. 12:9) which Jesus witnessed (Luke 10:18); the other account says he "took" with him one-third of heaven with him. I believe both versions explain what happened in heaven... he left the presence of God on account of iniquity being found in him (robbing God of His glory to use for his own purpose, which he accomplished by stealing one-third of heaven's angels) and then he was cast out of heaven. The drama in the Garden is a type and shadow of what happened in heaven between God and Lucifer – and continues to happen between God and the sons of men upon the earth.

truth), ¹⁰ finding out what is acceptable to the Lord. ¹¹ And have no fellowship with the unfruitful works of darkness, but rather expose them. ¹² For it is shameful even to speak of those things which are done by them in secret. ¹³ But all things that are exposed are made manifest by the light, for whatever makes manifest is light" (Eph. 5:8-13).

Through faith in Christ and by becoming His disciple, the glory of man has been restored unto him, but only through faithful obedience as disciples to Jesus as our Lord. In this regard, the Lord Jesus, our Sovereign, calls us friends when we remain in total obedient allegiance to Him.

Now, therefore…

> "For it is the God who commanded light to shine out of darkness, who has shone in our hearts **to give the light of the knowledge of the glory of God** in the face of Jesus Christ" (2 Cor. 4:6)…
>
> "that the God of our Lord Jesus Christ, **the Father of glory**, may give to you the spirit of wisdom and revelation in the knowledge of Him" (Eph. 1:17).

Jesus told us that we are the light of the world. God sent us into the world *with His light* (the light of His glory) in order to dispel the darkness and disregard the prince of darkness, but the first two inhabitants of earth succumbed to Satan's temptation and our original mandate to have dominion over the earth (Satan's dominion of darkness) became a rescue and recovery mission for Jesus. Read carefully what Jesus says about light and darkness being within us…

> "The lamp of the body is the eye. If therefore your eye is good, your whole body will be full of light. ²³ But if your eye is bad, your whole body will be full of darkness. If therefore the light that is in you is darkness, how great is

that darkness!" (Matt. 6:22, 23).

> "But if your eye… the knowledge of your understanding, focuses your attention and affection on serving anyone or anything other than God, and thereby gives God's glory to any 'other,' then your whole body has become a foothold for Satan's darkness. If, therefore, **the light of the knowledge of the glory of God** that is within you that is supposed to dispel the darkness has been given over to serving darkness, then how great is the darkness of evil within you" (Matt. 6:23 paraphrased by the author).

Who is your spiritual father? Well, what comes out of you either gives glory to "God alone" or to "any other." Manifest the love of one father or the other – because what comes out of you indicates the father you '*oida*' *know*, love and obey. Those who profess Jesus is Lord but continue to walk according to the sinful ways and pattern of "this world" have been deceived and tricked by the father of lies to believe a less-than gospel in order to surrender and deliver their glory to Satan, the Deceiver…

> "… whose minds the god of this age has blinded, who do not believe, **lest the light of the gospel of the glory of Christ**, who is the image of God, should shine on them" (2 Cor. 4:4).

We may find it difficult to consider why God would give the light of His glory to men to do with whatever we want… who even commands us to have dominion on earth with this glory *and* His authority as well, yet this is exactly what He has done… which He did for two reasons: 1) to test our allegiance to Him, and 2) with the hope that we may produce an increase of this glory and return all of this glory unto Him who gave it to us. God is not lessened one bit in doing this; God reaps where He does not sow… yet because He seeded us with His glory – He expects us to produce something worth reaping.

And here is the unifying thought of seed, light and glory: we are light-bearers and glory bearers for the kingdom of God... and the Lord (Jesus) seeded us upon His field (the earth) as bearers of His truth and glory in order to produce more glory and then give all glory to God.

If all you produce are thistles and thorns that gives glory to your self-made kingdom with the glory you received from God, or if all you do is bury your talent in the soil that does not benefit anyone or advance the kingdom of God upon the earth, then it seems clear, now, what happens to such thorny persons: their glory will be taken from them and their soul will be thrown into the fire of God's judgment in outer darkness.

Yet the reason we may not understand this, and believe it, is because the doctrine of sin by sin merchants teaches us that man *was not* created good, is exceedingly sinful and has a sinful nature; and thus, the doctrine of grace has been thwarted by the doctrine of sin, and the promises of God make little if any sense to us. And yet, on the other side of the church pendulum swings the faith and works merchants who teach us it is all about an emotional appeal to believe and feel good about ourselves and receive God's grace on our own greasy-grace terms when, in reality, it has already been given to us whereby we must give an accounting of what we did with it – on God's terms!

Are you using God's glory to build your kingdom? Does 'your' life glorify God?

All glory belongs to God! *Use it* according to righteousness that glorifies God – *or lose it*!

Two More Scriptures

And yet, there are two scriptures in Isaiah that say, ""My glory I will not give to another" (Isa. 42:8; 48:11).

- "I *am* the Lord, that *is* My name; and My glory I will not give to another, nor My praise to carved images" (Isa. 42:8)
- "For My own sake, for My own sake, I will do *it;* for how should *My name* be profaned? And I will not give My glory to another" (Isa. 48:11).

Jesus is "the Lord" and with very clear words given to Isaiah, says… "My glory I will not give to another" because Jesus will not give His glory to anyone or any "other" that sets themselves as a god or as lord with the glory that belongs to Him – and in so doing… profane His name. Does this make more sense now? Yet, Jesus gave His glory to His disciples (John 17:22) and will also continue to give His glory to those that believe in their testimony that Jesus is Lord, the Son of God, and King over all creation – because Jesus wants to give His disciples a share in His glory who will magnify His name!

> "And now, O Father, glorify Me together *with* Yourself, **with the glory which I had with You before the world was**" (John 17:5).

> "I do not pray for these alone, but also for those who will believe in Me through their word; [21] that they all may be one, as You, Father, are in Me, and I in You; *that they also may be one in Us*, that the world may believe that You sent Me. [22] **And the glory which You gave Me I have given them**, that they may be one just as We are one: [23] I in them, and You in Me" (John 17:20-23)

When the Lord God makes a declaration or an oath by raising His hand, has He ever changed His mind? Never! God does not change – and God does not change His mind. When the Lord makes an oath, then you can count on it; however, there is at least one example when the Lord promised to bless Israel, but changed His mind because… "I acted for My name's sake, that it should not be profaned before the Gentiles" (Ezek. 20:5-15). This may be just my opinion, but perhaps the only reason we have not seen the glory that Jesus promised, which Jesus had "before the world was" which He gave to His disciples, is because we may have profaned His name among the Gentiles, just as Israel has done.

But you ask… how have we profaned the name of the Lord? So I ask you, what is His name? What is the name above all names? Why do we still talk about "God this" and "God that" within generalized God-speak (which the world even does) when God Incarnate came and revealed Himself clearly to us as "the Lord" in personal terms that we might intimately know and identify Him as "the Lord who is near to us" in every regard? We touched Him and we beheld His glory, and yet, how often do we even say the name "Jesus" in *His* church anymore? We gather together for sacred assemblies in the name of God the Father, but God cannot be our Father unless we have boldly declared our obedience to Jesus as Lord. Anathema!

> "For you are all sons of God through faith in Christ Jesus" (Gal. 3:26).

> "For through Him we both have access by one Spirit to the Father" (Eph. 2:18).

Are there two types of glory? Yes, it seems so. Jesus Christ has His own glory, which He obtained His from the Father, and He is also regarded as the "Lord of glory" (James 2:1). His glory *He will not give* to just any other; however, *He will give His glory* to those who dedicate their life in service to Him as His disciples – as "the Lord's beloved"… "because God from the beginning chose you for salvation through sanctification by the Spirit and belief in the truth."

> "But we are bound to give thanks to God always for you, brethren beloved by the Lord, because God from the beginning chose you for salvation through sanctification by the Spirit and belief in the truth, [14] to which He called you by our gospel, ***for the obtaining of the glory of our Lord Jesus Christ***" (2 Thess. 2:13, 14).

Jesus gave a measure of His glory to Moses when His manifest presence appeared before him on the mountain, but this glory was temporary and fading because the Lord's presence did not remain with him, and as a result, Moses wore a veil to conceal this fading glory. When we remain in the Lord's presence, the veil is removed and a measure of His glory will remain with us until we see Him as He is – and we become like Him in glory.

> "But if the ministry of death, written and engraved on stones, was glorious, so that the children of Israel could not look steadily at the face of Moses because of the glory of his countenance, which glory was passing away, [8] how will the ministry of the Spirit not be more glorious? (2 Cor. 3:7, 8).

Are you a true believer and worshipper, in spirit and in truth – or merely a make-believer?

Does the church even teach about sanctification? The mystery of man *IS* "sanctification by the Spirit," yet we prefer to preach about the easy road and how God gives 'melba-toast-believers' every good and perfect gift because God loves us immensely on account of our puny confidence in Christ. We go to church for fifty minutes and consider this our fulfilled obligation in keeping the Sabbath in service to Jesus, who (by the way) is also "Lord of the Sabbath" (Luke 6:5). How dare we tempt the Lord's indignation!!! "Where is My reverence, says the Lord?"

The Lord's oaths and promises are true and dependable, but *Jesus is not going to fulfill His promises according to faith if we have been unfaithful in keeping His commands.* He withheld His blessing from Israel, so what is to stop Jesus from withholding His blessing for the church? His promises to us mean absolutely nothing unless, through sanctification, we are chastened [41] for our

---

[41] Chasten, defined by the dictionary as: "To correct by punishment or reproof; take to task; discipline; to inflict suffering upon for purposes of moral improvement." In contrast, 'chastise' means, "to make pure; to warn, advise,

unbelief regarding Him and, thus, also become hated by the world just as Christ was hated (Heb. 12:5-11; John 17:14; Rev. 3:19).

> "But if you are without chastening, of which all have become partakers, then you are illegitimate and not sons" (Heb. 12:8).

If sanctification and chastening is not what you have been taught to believe, then perhaps you should spend more time listening to the words of Jesus by the hearing of His voice. Let the Spirit of truth guide you rather than the doctrines of man and, by hearing and doing, become a partaker of the divine nature (2 Pet. 1:4).

> "Enter by the narrow gate; for wide is the gate and broad is the way that leads to destruction, and there are many who go in by it" (Matt. 7:13).

The Glory of Jesus Christ

Just as Jesus has His glory, there are many types of glory as well (1 Cor. 15:40-42). There is one glory seeded within man that we must all give an accounting of before God, and there is one glory we receive in the resurrection, and there is Christ's glory that He shares among His disciples according to the Spirit of grace so that we may partner with Him (go shares with), being enlivened and enlightened by the *"Spirit of glory"* to continue the work of Christ upon the earth, as partakers of the divine nature He placed within us – according to His image and His likeness through Whom we were *all* created – whereby we act as His ambassadors to establish the kingdom of heaven upon the earth –thereby filling it full of His glory. This is the big picture of faith in Christ, not just to believe, but to dedicate the entirety of our lives to become His disciple – with wisdom and understanding – and have a share in His glory! This, my friends, is your reasonable service (worship) in Christ Jesus (Rom. 12:2).

---

instruct, admonish; punish, criticize (someone) harshly for doing something wrong."

Jesus is not interested in immature believers or passive admirers – He desires disciples!

> "If you are reproached for the name of Christ, blessed are you, for the ***Spirit of glory*** and of God rests upon you. On their part He is blasphemed, but on your part He is glorified" (1 Pet. 4:14).

Jesus is the Lord of glory and has commissioned the Spirit of glory to work within us by renewing our mind so that we may walk according to the Way of Christ. Jesus will not give His greater glory as a working of the Spirit to another or any "other" if their sole purpose is to use Christ's glory to build their own kingdom. We were created in Christ Jesus for good works, through sanctification… and greater works, by the Spirit of glory… and yet, if you profess Christ abides within you, then let me ask you this: do you still look like the rest of the world? Does the world love you? Do you still walk in the same evil practices like the rest of this sinful world? This, my brethren, should not be so!

God has given to all men (seeded within them) some of His glory in the hope that (according to God's purposes in Christ Jesus) we may bear the fruit of righteousness and good works; however, when we believe in Jesus Christ and become His disciple, we receive His greater glory in addition to the glory seeded within us (our soul). Jesus did not do this for us to continue living according to the worldly pattern or the old covenant with onerous statutes and judgments (Ezek. 20:25) that He rendered obsolete by His new covenant (Heb. 8:13); He did it because His name *shall* be magnified and glorified in all the earth – through the church (Eph. 3:10)!

> "All nations whom You have made shall come and worship before You, O Lord, and shall glorify Your name" (Psa. 86:9).

> "Who shall not fear You, O Lord, and glorify Your name? For You alone are holy. For all nations shall come and worship before You, for Your judgments

have been manifested" (Rev. 15:4).

But even if we can't operate in Christ's glory because we do not walk in obedience to Christ, then know this: God has numbered our days when He will take back the seeded glory that belongs to Him – and everything else without (apart from) His glory will be burned.

Everyone was created as a unique expression of God's glory on the earth as He lives within each of us; however, if we do not give Him all the glory for the life we are living (because it is His '*zoe*' life that was given to us), then we must give an account for our disobedience… and such a soul will complete the remainder of their existence in hellish torment.

Now, consider this… if a greater glory exists for those who follow Christ, as His own disciples witnessed and experienced, according to the Spirit of grace and of glory, is there a greater judgment that awaits those who walk away from Christ? Well…

> "Anyone who has rejected Moses' law dies without mercy on the testimony of two or three witnesses. [29] Of how much worse punishment, do you suppose, will he be thought worthy who has trampled the Son of God underfoot, counted the blood of the covenant by which he was sanctified a common thing, and insulted the Spirit of grace? (Heb. 10:28, 29).

> "Nevertheless the solid foundation of God stands, having this seal: "The Lord knows those who are His," and, "Let everyone who names the name of Christ *depart from iniquity*." (2 Tim. 2:19).

Are the scriptures, here, talking about backsliding or about full abandonment of faith in Jesus? There are many who talk about God's grace and mercy as if we cannot ever fall from grace once we have made a profession of faith… but… was this *a full profession* that included your allegiance to Him to become His disciple – or just a partial profession to escape the fire of hell? They will often quote "no one can snatch them out of His hand" (John 10:28, 29); however, we are free to walk out of His hand any time we desire the lusts of the flesh and to live according to the ways of this world. Let me ask this: are you living according to the doctrine of mediocrity – or do you desire to be a disciple of Jesus?

Stop standing in between two ways; if Jesus is your Lord, then serve Him and declare His name!

If this message sounds true and resonates within you, then ask Jesus what He wants you to do! Don't listen to me and stop listening to others tell you what Jesus wants you to do; if Jesus is your Lord, then hear His voice, become His disciple and do what He tells you. Let the Holy Spirit guide you into all truth because, after all… this is why Jesus sent Him… to come alongside us and help us get back to the way of following Jesus Christ, the Lord.

Temples and Tabernacles

Consider, now, that we are tabernacles for the Lord – and temples of the Holy Spirit…

> "Or do you not know that your body is the temple of the Holy Spirit who is in you, whom you have from God, and you are not your own?" (1 Cor. 6:19).

> "Heaven is My throne, and earth is My footstool. What house [tabernacle] will you build for Me? says the Lord, or what is the place of My rest?" (Acts 7:49).

Do we so easily forget that we are earthen temples – created by Jesus as tabernacles to host the presence of God, and if His glory is manifested by His presence, then – according to "Christ in us – our hope of glory"... His greater glory abides within us as we host His Presence and Spirit within us?

> "The glory of this latter temple shall be greater than the former,' says the Lord of hosts. 'And in this place I will give peace,' says the Lord of hosts" (Haggai 2:9).

Are not all Jewish temples a shadow of the One True Temple, Jesus Christ (John 2:19)? And now, since God is in us and His Spirit is dwelling within us, may we understand the scripture... "and I will fill *this* temple with glory,' says the LORD of hosts" (Haggai 2:7).[42] And yet, the church spends more time talking about rebuilding the Jewish temple according to an old, worn out pattern that was rendered obsolete than teaching the faithful to become disciples of Jesus, as temples of the Holy Spirit, and as tabernacles for Jesus Christ, the One True Living God, the Lord... who created the earth "By Himself" and its' fullness for His glory! When Jesus returns in glory, did Jesus promise the disciples any reward based upon Jewish promises? NO!

> "So Jesus said to them, "Assuredly I say to you, that in the regeneration, *when the Son of Man sits on the throne of His glory*, you who have followed Me will also sit on twelve thrones, judging the twelve tribes of Israel" (Matt. 19:28).

How incredible is that! We have been saved by Jesus with better promises and sealed for redemption by "the Holy Spirit of promise" as a guarantee so that we may enter into the glory of the Lord, Jesus Christ, when He comes again – in glory (Heb. 8:6; 2 Cor. 1:22; Eph. 1:13; 4:30).

---

[42] The greater outpouring that many prophets are speaking about today, in regard to the Third Great Awakening, is this greater glory that will be released within Christ's disciples by the Spirit of Glory. The expression always precedes the manifestation... if you have ears to understand, then let them hear. Read all of Haggai, chapter 2, and consider this: the Jewish temple (since 70 A.D.) will never be rebuilt... so what it the Lord Jesus referring to?

Jesus is the Lord of Glory – to the glory of God, the Father.

Jesus is the Lord, our Creator, our Deliverer, our Redeemer, the Lord of the Sabbath, the Lord of Glory, the Christ of God, the manifested image of the invisible Father (Heb. 1:3), Lord of heaven and earth, and now... thoroughly understand and comprehend this: the entire universe is under His command!

Indeed...

- "The earth is the Lord's, and all its fullness, the world *and those who dwell therein*" (Psa. 24:1).
- "The earth is full of the goodness of the Lord" (Psa. 33:5)
- "The heavens are Yours, the earth also is Yours; the world and all its fullness, You have founded them" (Psa. 89:11)
- "Lord, how manifold are Your works! In wisdom You have made them all. The earth is full of Your possessions" (Psa. 104:24)
- "The earth, O Lord, is full of Your mercy" (Psa. 119:64)
- "And one cried to another and said: "Holy, holy, holy is the Lord of hosts; ***the whole earth is full of His glory***" (Isa. 6:3)
- For "the earth is the Lord's, and all its fullness" (1 Cor. 10:26)

Everything about man upon the earth is all about giving God all the glory... including the glory that He placed within us, and most especially... the pearl of great price, that is, Jesus Christ!

Jesus wants to partner with us and become partakers of the divine nature within us (with His Spirit) so that the glory of the Lord fills the earth. This is our high calling in Christ Jesus whereby the works we do become the "greater works" that release God's glory throughout the earth – in the face of His enemies.

> "Again, the kingdom of heaven is like treasure hidden in a field, which a man found and hid; and for joy over it he goes and sells all that he has and

> buys that field. ⁴⁵ "Again, the kingdom of heaven is like a merchant seeking beautiful pearls, ⁴⁶ who, when he had found one pearl of great price, went and sold all that he had and bought it" (Matt. 13:44, 45).

Jesus is teaching us about the mystery of God's kingdom which He describes in terms we may understand, but few ever comprehend the meaning of the message. *Anything that has been hidden from us is intended for us to seek and find*, and if the treasure that has been hidden within our field (that is, the glory of God hidden within the soul of man) is found by us, then we should esteem this treasure as greater than all other treasure on earth, such that all worldly glory appears utterly worthless in comparison.

> "For what profit is it to a man if he gains the whole world, and loses his own soul? Or what will a man give in exchange for his soul" (Matt. 16:26).

And rather than searching to acquire the multitude of many teachings by various teachers, much like a merchant seeking beautiful pearls, rather, we should best spend our time with Jesus, who is the Pearl of enormous value such that all other worldly pearls appear… worldly indeed! We are to "guard carefully" (*tereo*-G5083) this *pearl of great price* (Christ's glory within us) and not give it to another, nor let it be trampled upon by anyone.

> "Do not give what is holy to the dogs; nor cast your pearls before swine, lest they trample them under their feet, and turn and tear you in pieces" (Matt. 7:6).

This world has disregarded God as the source of all glory and will tear you to pieces to prevent the light of God's glory from shining through you, and even more so… those who have Christ's greater glory within them. "You are the light of the world. A city that is set on a hill cannot be hidden" (Matt. 5:14). Once we find the hidden treasure of God's glory within us, we will become known according to 'whose father' we are, but once we are positioned in Christ as His disciples, our inner man will be "transfigured, transformed, changed, altered" *from within* as a result of this radiant glory being revealed (displayed) by God for all to see. "You are My witnesses" when the light of Christ's glory within us shines radiantly like lightning before men. When this happens, either people will believe Jesus is the truth and surrender everything they possess to have the same peace, grace and glory of God's light which you possess – or they will tear you to pieces because – darkness hates light!

> "If the world hates you, you know that it hated Me before it hated you" (John 15:18).

> "And you will be hated by all for My name's sake. But he who endures to the end will be saved" (Matt. 10:22)

Do you still desire just parts of Jesus as patches put upon your old wineskin – or do you want the total package according to the Spirit of life in Christ Jesus? Count the cost... but count everything this world has to offer 'as loss' except for the exceeding greatness of following Jesus as His disciple... by offering yourself as a living sacrifice that is holy and acceptable to God (Rom. 12:1). For this purpose Jesus called you – so that Christ's Spirit may have His way within you (James 4:6) and a greater *grace* (*charisma*- G5486, spiritual endowment) may be given to you.

> "You are the salt of the earth; but if the salt loses its flavor, how shall it be seasoned? It is then good for nothing but to be thrown out and trampled underfoot by men." (Matt. 5:13).

Once we've lost the saltiness of Christ's glory within us, it cannot be re-seasoned, so don't lose the saltiness of His glory within you by returning (to turn anew again) to follow the ways of this world, as was done by the Galatians (Gal. 1:6; 4:9). Insipid salt that has become insidiously corrupted by evil intent is "good for nothing"! Do you still consider yourself a wretched sinner saved by grace –

or has the grace and truth of the gospel of Jesus Christ finally become real in your heart – and will be manifested through you – to the praise of God's glory in Christ Jesus!

> "And whoever does not bear his cross and come after Me cannot be My disciple. [28] For which of you, intending to build a tower, does not sit down first and count the cost, whether he has enough to finish it— [29] lest, after he has laid the foundation, and is not able to finish, all who see it begin to mock him" (Luke 14:27-29).

Count the cost – and consider, also, the afflictions when unbelieving and unregenerate men of this world come against you on account of Christ's grace and truth being revealed through you…

> "For our light affliction, which is but for a moment, is working for us a far more exceeding and eternal weight of glory" (2 Cor. 4:17)… "that in the ages to come He might show the exceeding riches of His grace in His kindness toward us in Christ Jesus" (Eph. 2:7).

> "For I consider that the sufferings of this present time are not worthy to be compared with the glory which shall be revealed in us" (Rom. 8:18)… "but rejoice to the extent that you partake of Christ's sufferings, that when His glory is revealed, you may also be glad with exceeding joy" (1 Pet. 4:13)… "and also a partaker of the glory that will be revealed" (1 Pet. 5:1).

The seed and the light have been interpreted by many teachers and preachers to mean "truth" – but what is truth? What is knowledge without understanding? And where can wisdom be found? Yet, when we consider the reason why Jesus kept teaching us about the mystery of the kingdom of heaven where the fullness of God's glory resides, then perhaps we need to reexamine these applications – including the word 'heaven' to imply "the state of being wherever the fullness of God's glory and presence resides." And therefore, Jesus, then, is heaven personified… and by faith, Christ abides in you!

And if God's Presence and Spirit abides in you, then God's manifest glory also dwells within you.

> "I do not pray for these alone, but also for those who will believe in Me through their word; [21] that they all may be one, as You, Father, are in Me, and I in You; *that they also may be one in Us*, that the world may believe that You sent Me. [22] ***And the glory which You gave Me I have given them***, that they may be one just as We are one: [23] I in them, and You in Me; that they may be made perfect in one, and that the world may know that You have sent Me, and have loved them as You have loved Me. [24] Father, I desire that they also whom You gave Me may be with Me where I am, that they may behold My glory which You have given Me; for You loved Me before the foundation of the world. [25] O righteous Father! The world has not known You, but I have known You; and these have known that You sent Me. [26] And I have declared to them Your name, and will declare *it,* that the love with which You loved Me may be in them, and I in them" (John 17:20-26).

United in oneness – by Grace – in Christ's glory.

> "But we all, with unveiled face, beholding as in a mirror the glory of the Lord, are being *transformed* [*transfigured*] into the same image from glory to glory, just as by the Spirit of the Lord" (2 Cor. 3:18; *metamorphoo*-G3339).

This is our high calling in Christ Jesus: for Christ to be fully formed in us so that we may be transformed, from glory to glory – into the image of Christ. We are exchanging the outer glory for the inner glory, and exchanging the inner glory of man for the glory of Christ. Therefore, the inner man is being renewed according to the image of Christ our Creator by becoming transfigured into the likeness of Christ in us and, thus therefore… we become an expression of His '*charakter*' on earth… to the praise of His glory.

Amen.

    It's all about Jesus – and God gets the glory!!

Seeds of Truth and Glory

We are all children and offspring of God; however, we can only call God "our Father" through faith in Jesus Christ. (Gal.3:26; Eph. 2:18)

The Lord has sown us as seed upon the earth *and* He has sown the seed of truth and glory in our heart; therefore, it is incumbent upon us to cultivate this seed to produce a harvest as our inheritance that not only benefits us, but also promulgates and expands the kingdom of God through us. We are stewards and caretakers of these seeds (talents, oil, etc) given to us by the Lord; what we have been given, we are responsible for… yet we are to do more than just protect it from theft or hide them in the soil… we are instructed to produce an increase upon that which we were given (The Parable of the Talents; Matt. 25). Our Lord is a hard manager who reaps where He did not sow… and we are to imitate His example. If, however, we do not do anything with the heavenly resources we have been given…

> "For whoever has, to him more will be given, and he will have abundance; but whoever does not have, even what he has will be taken away from him" (Matt. 13:12; see also Matt. 25:1-30).

This scripture doesn't apply to just understanding… it applies to everything within the kingdom of God. If we do nothing with the spiritual talents, gifts and resources that we've been given, we forfeit more than just the increase that could have been credited into our account… we forfeit our entire account (our soul) into eternal torment in outer darkness.

> "For to everyone who has, more will be given, and he will have abundance; but from him who does not have, even what he has will be taken away. [30] And cast the unprofitable servant into the outer darkness. There will be weeping and gnashing of teeth" (Matt. 25:29, 30).

Most Christians have been taught to believe an unscriptural doctrine that cannot even be regarded as truth: once saved always saved. As we can see by the words of Jesus Himself (above), unprofitable servants will be cast into outer darkness. Jesus is referring to "servants" that have made a profession to be a servant, but did not live their life like a servant; they lived for themselves according to their ego, self-determination or whatever. God does not give His glory to us to use for our personal pleasure and financial betterment – He gave us His glory so that we might produce more glory for the praise of His glory.

> "In Him we have redemption through His blood, the forgiveness of sins, according to the riches of His grace [8] which He made to abound toward us in all wisdom and prudence, [9] having made known to us the mystery of His will, according to His good pleasure which He purposed in Himself, [10] that in the dispensation of the fullness of the times He might gather together in one all things in Christ, both which are in heaven and which are on earth— in Him. [11] In Him also we have obtained an inheritance, being predestined according to the purpose of Him who works all things according to the counsel of His will, [12] that we who first trusted in Christ **should be to the praise of His glory**" (Eph. 1:7-12).

This incredible scripture is perhaps one of the great "fullness of the gospel" scriptures in all Christendom, which is sandwiched between two more "praise of His glory" (Eph. 1:6, 14). The Apostle Paul understood the big picture and the eternal importance of being a servant and bondservant of Christ. Jesus commissioned him to be a light of truth to the Gentiles and nothing could separate him from his covenantal agreement with Jesus Christ to fulfill this commission. He became more than just an Apostle, he became Christ's manifest body and ambassador of the gospel into the world; he completely understood that Jesus was abiding in him and operating through him – to the praise of His glory. The only way anyone can become this sold out for Jesus is to have a radical grace awakening by experiencing the truth firsthand – and this goes for every one of us! Paul understood!

We all need a radical grace awakening. We need to understand truth – and walk in it.

"If you do well" is another way the Lord is saying to us… "Do the right thing." We have all heard His Voice and He has called every one of us to perform a task to advance the kingdom of God upon the earth, so now… "Do the right thing" – but – "if you do not do well…"

> "If you do well, will you not be accepted? And if you do not do well, sin lies at the door. And its desire is for you, but you should rule over it." (Gen. 4:7).

The Lord commissioned every one of us as seeds of light, truth and glory that were sown into the earth to produce more glory – to the praise of His glory. We are His image bearers and we are already acceptable in His sight because we were created "in His image according to His likeness," and we must be faithful to do all that He commands and "be His light unto the world." Our name is already written in the Book of Life, but it is "we" who erase our names on account of disobedience (Rev. 3:5). We must all give an account of what we did – and didn't do (Matt. 25:19). We must hear His voice and obediently follow Jesus – and we *shall* be saved; yet He has given us an eternal choice: either to hear His voice and walk in the way of righteousness, or we can reject His counsel to pursue many schemes and live according to self-determination.

> "And if it bears fruit, well. But if not, after that you can cut it down.'" (Luke 9:13).

Why did Jesus use so many agricultural metaphors? Truly – because we are seeds, and He used the language of plants and plantings to convey deep spiritual principles regarding life on earth from a kingdom of God perspective. We are seeds that have been sown to produce fruit, but it is *up to us* (our responsibility) to cultivate our soil to remove rocks of doubt and not become entangled by the cares of this life or be overtaken by the weeds of this world!

Glory Revealed in Metaphors

Most of my Christian life, I saw light, seeds, and coins as metaphors for God's truth, but now it seems clear that light, seeds and coins can also refer to God's glory which has been entrusted to us so that we may produce an increase… but an increase of what? for whom? more wealth, fame, power and self-seeking glory for the purpose of building our own kingdom? What are we supposed to do with the light of truth He gave to us? Give the light to others!!!

> "For it is the God who commanded light to shine out of darkness, who has shone in our hearts ***to give the light of the knowledge of the glory of God*** in the face of Jesus Christ. [7] But we have this treasure in earthen vessels, that the excellence of the power may be of God and not of us" (2 Cor. 4:6, 7).

"The earth is filled with the glory of the Lord" or stated another way… the Lord fills the earth *with* His glory. Either way, we are vessels that contain the seed of His glory, being created and then commanded by God to be fruitful and multiply, not just according to our physical seed, but also according to the spiritual seed (singular) that was placed within us – according to our ability.

We are to fill the earth with the presence (glory) of the Lord.

And what, shall we suppose, is the pearl of great price? I have always interpreted this to mean Jesus Christ who is the most important truth we might ever possess in this life, so consider this alternative: the newly acquired field where this pearl is hidden (planted in soil) is the new-birth field of our heart given to us by

God that we are now using to cultivate seeds of glory to glorify the Lord of heaven on this earth. In the new birth, we are given a new heart and a new spirit (Ezek. 36:26), and the treasure we acquired as a result of being born anew and transformed by the Spirit whereby our renewed mind puts all our efforts into cultivating this new field is to produce an increase of glory for the Lord Jesus. Are we talking about making money to acquire wealth for our own pleasure... or are we using metaphors to describe expanding the kingdom of God with the resources He has given us?

Alright, then, now let's get this dominion mandate started – and produce a bumper-crop!

The field of faith that Jesus mentions is our soul in two dimensions: now – and hereafter. The soul, with heart and mind oneness, is the elemental substance of "who" we are as we sojourn on the earth for one season of eternity... with which we shall also serve the Lord in the new earth that follows the regeneration.

> "For where your treasure is, there your heart will be also" (Matt. 6:21; Luke 12:34).

Why do we think that there will not be an element of who we are in the hereafter? We talk about recognizing loved ones, as if this is going to be a social gathering of sorts, yet we will become like angels that are in heaven – and even they have a purpose in God's kingdom as well. Why do we trouble our hearts with the multitude of many things that don't seemingly matter in the least, yet regarding those things that pertain to heavenly matters... we remain purposely ignorant. Why don't we consider the big picture regarding "who" we are that will be raised up and live again in newness without end of days? Are we so blind that we cannot sense eternity waits for no one?

You do not have a soul; you are a soul – and your soul is eternal... "That he should continue to live eternally" (Psa. 49:9). The operative word is "continue."

We were sown by the Lord upon the earth as seed of truth to produce an abundant harvest of goodness, and this is our God-given task and responsibility (Eccl. 3:10), but Satan has also cast seed of doubt to perform deeds of unrighteousness (Matt. 13:39). Since the devil's seed of doubt that leads all into disobedience and rebellion has been sown into our heart, it is our responsibility to acknowledge it and remove this evil from our midst. Thus, we have a dual responsibility: to produce goodness and depart from evil. Let me expound on another scripture within this vein…

> "Therefore hear the parable of the sower: [19] When anyone hears the word of the kingdom, and does not understand it, then the wicked one comes and snatches away what was sown in his heart. This is he who received seed by the wayside" (Matt. 13:18, 19).

The "wayside" has often been interpreted to mean the shoulder of the road, and in many regards this is true; however, do you cast seed on top of a road and expect any seed to germinate? The word "wayside" is a combination of two words (*hodos*-3598; road, a route; metaphorically, a course of conduct *or* way of thinking) + (*para*-3844; alongside of, beside, near or contrary to).[43] Keep in mind that this parable is about how we receive truth (in the mind) in order for a root of understanding to take effect in our heart. The wayside represents, in one aspect, seed that is sown along one (correct) side of the road that willfully adopts the proper course and seeks this way of thinking so as to gain understanding, as opposed to the other (incorrect) side of the road that remains inattentive and obstinate thereby permitting the enemy to steal truth without allowing understanding to occur. This person may accept the truth in one manner, either factual '*ginosko*' or intellectual '*epiginosko*,' however, they will reject this truth because it is "*para*" i.e. "contrary" to the way they want, which is contrary to the "*suniemi* way" that allows understanding to occur in the heart through an open mind, thus giving Satan an advantage by creating doubt or fear that results in '*distazo*' (wavering

---

[43] Strong's Concordance.

between understanding and unbelief). To give us a better sense of *'para'* as it relates to "wayside," consider the word *'nous'* (mind) with two opposing prefix's: *paranoia* (to think contrary things that are in opposition to truth) versus *dianoia* (to think things through resulting in understanding).

The seed sown along the wayside was not misplaced seed poorly cast by the Lord; the truth has gone out (seed sown) so that everyone has heard whereby we are all without excuse, but these individuals have decided (in their mind) *not* to be open minded thereby rejecting the truth. Understanding hasn't got a chance!

"In Regenesis, I taught about the four types of soil in our hearts whereby we are able to receive truth; we all have wayside, rocky, thorny overgrowth and fertile soil in our hearts, but now I want to talk about the seed as words of truth that produces four types of understanding – partnered together with understanding in our mind:

1. the seed *apart from* understanding
2. the seed *of limited* understanding
3. the seed *growing in* understanding (amidst adversity)
4. the seed *with* fruitful understanding

"The seed that was sown by the wayside" is the casual response to the initial hearing of the gospel message with *'akoe'* – "by the sense of hearing you will hear," but because they do not, choose not, cannot, or refuse not to understand the message, the deceiver quickly snatches the seed of truth from the listener's heart. People in this respect, even though they may have made a verbal profession of faith, flicked their wrist, been baptized and even attend church every Sunday… they only have save-not faith. It is not what we say or do that determines our salvation – ***but what we hear and understand that results in obedience to the Lord***!!!"[44]

---

[44] Excerpts from "Listen" section titled "Ears Of Our Mind."

The "wayside" is, therefore… an alternative way "alongside of" the True Way of righteousness that results in life eternal. Within this context, I refer to religion as the "wayside" manner in which we hear truth apart from abiding in a personal relationship with Jesus Christ that compels us to become disciples. It looks good and teaches good doctrine, but it does not result in life eternal.

The "way" of the Lord also has two sides along it: the prescriptive and predetermined way that leads to salvation – and the permissive and restrictive way that leads to destruction. This, also, is deep understanding to guide us in the way.

The outward man of flesh wages war against the inner man of the soul with spirit. The outward man resists the things of the Spirit directed life until such time they chose to seek the truth, being awakened by reasoning within the mind to walk alongside understanding – and thus, the new birth (with '*nous*' G3563) happens. Otherwise, none of this new creation stuff makes any sense nor is there any purpose under heaven why man must endure and persevere against many obstacles. Knowing "why" helps us understand what we are and why we do what we do.

Very early in my listening to hear the Voice of Truth, the Spirit began teaching me the error of man's "sinful nature doctrine" to explain why we do the things we do not want to do (Rom. 7). Jesus created us "in His image according to His likeness" and placed within us His nature and divine attributes so that we may become partners and partakers of the divine nature. Jesus did not sow imperfect or corrupt evil seed in us, nor did He put a nature within us that would contradict, conflict with, or work against His eternal purpose for man upon the earth. God does not oppose or work against Himself!!! There is another book on the horizon that discusses the errors of the sinful nature doctrine and the mystery of iniquity, but until that day happens, I will leave you with this teaser:

> "The kingdom of heaven is like a man who sowed good seed in his field; [25] ***but while men slept****, his enemy came and sowed tares among the wheat and*

> *went his way.* ²⁶ But when the grain had sprouted and produced a crop, then the tares also appeared. ²⁷ So the servants of the owner came and said to him, 'Sir, did you not sow good seed in your field? How then does it have tares?' ²⁸ He said to them, 'An enemy has done this.'" (Matt. 13:24-28; hint: the servants (v.27) are angels).

Saints of God Most High, we need to stay awake (keep our eyes on Jesus), remain alert (be attentive) and be agonizingly vigilant to oppose the many deceitful schemes of the enemy. Once we thoroughly understand how God created us and intended us to live – and become fruitful "in" understanding – we must continuously walk in fresh revelation truth from the Lord *daily*; embrace wisdom and experience His newness by grace every day. Let revelation happen!

> "Where there is no revelation, the people cast off restraint" (Prov. 29:18).

One of the saddest stories I've ever read in the scriptures is about a young boy who hears his name called by the Lord in the middle of the night and goes to his spiritual advisor thinking that he called him, but he denies it. The Lord called Samuel's name again and once again he goes to Eli to see what he wanted. Then Eli realized what was happening and counseled the boy to say: "Speak Lord, for Your servant hears" (1 Sam. 3:9). Eli's words had wisdom with understanding, and Samuel's ears were listening attentively, yet (the sad part) Samuel was living in a community where revelation had not occurred in a very long time.

> "Now the boy Samuel ministered to the Lord before Eli. And the word of the Lord was rare in those days; *there was no widespread revelation*" (1 Sam. 3:1).

The small, still Voice of the Spirit is still active and continuously speaks to attentive listeners that want to hear, but now, it seems, the heart condition of the church is repeating the same offenses as Israel, yet far worse in one regard: the church disregards the Voice of the Spirit because the Lord only speaks to us through His written word. The early-church period experienced revelation so that we might have holy script, but revelation for the institutional church today, which has never ceased, is largely ignored and aggressively silenced. Revelation truth is oftentimes inconvenient when it occurs… because it happens when we least expect it.

It is impossible to replicate the miraculous works of the early church as they walked with the Spirit without the scriptures – versus the current church model that walks with scriptures in hand yet apart from the Spirit. Anathema!

The problem isn't what we believe; the problem is "how" we implement "what" we know.

Who Am I Lord

Is who I am now… the best I can offer to God?

Even so, who I am is irrelevant because – He who dwells within me is all that ever matters!

Consider all the spiritual metaphors for men as fruit and trees; even though men act more like vegetables, we are in fact, created like fruit with internal seeds. We cannot judge a book by its cover, but we can get a fairly good idea of the seed within us by examining the fruit we produce. Does our life look like those around us who maintain a status quo appearance, or are we motivated by our '*dianoia*' love for Jesus to produce exceedingly excellent and praiseworthy fruit that increases the kingdom of God and righteousness upon the earth?

The seed that was planted by God and the new crop that is being cultivated within us will bear fruit of one type (nature) for goodness and righteousness, but the seed sown by the enemy, the devil, will produce yet another crop according to its kind (nature) for evil. How many seeds within you are being raised up into everlasting newness as harvestable fruit in righteousness? The seed of righteousness and God's attributes of grace that have sown in us will be cultivated in our field of faith (by us) to become our inheritance in the resurrection to come; therefore, our eternal reward is predicated upon our faithful endurance to produce a spiritual harvest of righteousness within our soul... for the glory that awaits us.

> "You will guide me with Your counsel, and afterward receive me to glory" (Psa. 73:24)

You, my dear friends in Christ, are cultivating your own reward – and you are Christ's reward.

We get out of life what we cultivate – and the fruit produced by our soul in obedience to Christ goes into our account.

> "And when the Chief Shepherd appears, you will receive the crown of glory that does not fade away" (1 Pet. 5:4).

A man reaps what he sows in this life – and into the next. What is your focus for living on earth that will survive the test of eternity? What will your inheritance look like? Will it be that of a pauper, or as someone barely escaping the flames, or will it be that of a priest or a king with a kingdom, or sadly... none of the above?

> "Set your ***mind*** on things above, not on things on the earth" (Col. 3:2; affection-KJV; *phroneo*-G5426-to exercise the mind; be minded in a certain way).

May this become our lifelong prayer: "Take my life away. I want to exchange my life for Your life, so Jesus, please... take my life away so that I may live according to Your life within me."

> "For I consider that the sufferings of this present time are not worthy to be compared with the glory

which shall be revealed in us" (Rom. 8:18).

"For our light affliction, which is but for a moment, is working for us a far more exceeding *and* eternal weight of glory" (2 Cor. 4:17).

"Therefore I endure all things for the sake of the elect, that they also may obtain **the salvation** which is in Christ Jesus **with eternal glory**" (2 Tim. 2:10).

Set your mind on things eternal!

Transition

Transition can be defined as the process of change between what was… to what will be; to make a change from one state, place, or condition – to another.

For man, transition is the period of time and activity upon the earth to become that which he was meant to be. The focus is not on what was or that which is, but rather… focusing on those things that are becoming that which they were meant to be. It is future based and compels us to keep moving forward – and become.

Newness through truth, change and oneness is the nature of the spiritual reality that surrounds us whereby we are changed and renewed, by truth and grace, according to the Spirit, to become what God intended us to be – oneness "in" Him.

Change is the only constant in this earthly reality – and transition is the most difficult!

Everything changes.

The static physical reality that we experience on earth is, for lack of a better word, temporary. Everything that we are about on this earth is in transition from what was to what will be. The physical elements that we perceive as permanent are actually a just a shadow of those invisible spiritual elements that were put into place long ago… and will be restored once again within the new earth reality. The hardest part of any transition is simply… getting through it. It is the time when the past becomes less relevant than pressing into that which is meant to be. This is the time of "is" and it never lasts long… because change makes certain that it changes.

We have always known since the beginning that there is more going on around us than we can prove, as if a hidden plan with hidden players is being obscured from observation and present day comprehension. Even the analytical aspects of math and science prove that there is infinitely more that awaits our discovery which in due time can be analyzed, deduced and realized; however, the answers we arrive at are mere expressions within a larger framework that continues to unfold and express itself in a myriad of unexpected and mysterious ways.

Such is life. Change is inevitable.

We are scientists and mathematicians – and we are sojourners in search of truth in order to help us perceive this spiritual reality and form the basis for understanding many things, including many mysteries that currently escape our comprehension. We only know in part and see in part (1 Cor. 13:9, 12) and the truth has always been with us, but it is *we* who must seek the truth in order to perceive the spiritual reality that surrounds us… which is verily only a little farther than what we can tangibly experience during this season of "is."

"There is nothing new under the sun," yet man likes to think in terms of newness all the time, as if something new is going to be discovered that will inexpressibly alter our reality to help us live within an orderly existence apart from a worldly system bound by hatred, pain, chaos and suffering. We long for this paradise on earth, and the yet-to-be-discovered panacea within utopia that offers everyone the chance to live in love and peace, but it cannot happen within the current parameters that are constrained by the elements of darkness and patterns of "this world" that remain upon the earth. What these invisible elements are, we know little of, but we know that there are principalities and powers, demons, and wickedness that wages war against us, and Satan himself who walks to and fro over the earth to see whom he may devour – to prevent us from transitioning into the new earth reality. This aspect of change – is destructive.

Today, I am currently experiencing transition and, as often happens, I will experience headaches and some disorientation by it, such that I seem compelled to write about the subject of transition that humanity continues to move through and experience, and likewise, to express why it is ok to experience some confusion during transition. In the big scheme, life on earth is, in itself, a transitional period from what was (paradise lost) to what will be (Eden once again). When we look at the many epochs of time and various kingdoms upon the earth, these have been merely transitional periods built one upon the other that are taking us on a journey through the ages until we get to the final period – the age to come – and then life eternal in Paradise. Man continues to express his opinions about what this age will be like according to an earthly bliss, but attaining it continues to be elusive. In the 1950's, we envisioned a future where machines would make life easier with more free time for recreation, entertainment and the arts, but the opposite happened; life with machines became fast, more complex and we traded simplicity for anxieties that torment the soul. Other changes brought about by education and the computer age in the age of enlightenment predicted a more intelligent way of living life better, but the opposite happened; we are working more and enjoying life less.

If we want what is best for our generation and that of our children, then why does humanity continue to grind itself into meaningless dust that is blown away by every whim and fancy?

Newness is not a gadget – it is a spiritual process whereby we are changed and transformed to become that which we were originally created to be: sons and daughters of God Most High.

What will it take to get off the proverbial modernity hamster-wheel? Well, all I can say is that we are in yet another transitional period that will result in significant changes on earth. We cannot fix earth; we can only change who we are becoming within a worldly system that seeks to destroy us – and swallow us in death. But there is a plan to help us escape called: faith in Jesus.

Transition periods are often painful, stressful and messy. There is no way to predict what will happen or how long this period will last because the future is unpredictable; there are simply too many unknown variables within dynamic fluidity whereby the elements of change, free will, earthly dominion and divine providence are all working as complimentary and contradictory forces at the same time to create dynamic tension in a future clouded by mystery. The push and pull of life itself is evidenced much like the ebb and flow of ocean tides with wave upon wave crashing upon the shore; every wave is different and every sand deposit is unique, but the only constant is: this process will keep repeating itself. And this is good to meditate on: everything changes continually and yet… everything stays the same.

> "One generation passes away, and another generation comes; but the earth abides forever" (Eccl. 1:4).

What makes transition so difficult for man is that we are oftentimes caught within the ebb and flow of the transition process without knowing what is happening or why; it creates periods of uncertainty that oftentimes produces confusion with anxiety and fear with trepidation. We can no sooner accelerate the process to get out of it than we can slow it down to make a course correction; it may seem that we are stuck treading water in a stagnant pool, yet nearby the stream continues to flow swiftly toward its final destination where it will meet the tides and waves once again. There is a purpose for everything under the sun! And nothing is new!

> "That which has been is what will be, that which is done is what will be done, and there is nothing new under the sun" (Eccl. 1:9).

> "Is there anything of which it may be said, "See, this is new"? It has already been in ancient times before us" (Eccl. 1:10).

> "That which is has already been, and what is to be has already been; and God requires an account of what is past" (Eccl. 3:15).

> "Whatever one is, he has been named already, for it is known that he is man; and he cannot contend with

Him who is mightier than he" (Eccl. 6:10).

Solomon, the author of Ecclesiastes goes on to write about the futility of man upon the earth; his final analysis is… everything is foolishness and all is vanity. "For what has man for all his labor, and for the striving of his heart with which he has toiled under the sun?" (Eccl. 2:22). What, after all, has man truly accomplished in 6,000 years that has produced a permanent goodness that resulted in world peace? What has he got to show for it? Is it not even undone by the next generation without comprehending the sacrifice of many who gave their life for the good of all… only to have it squandered by those who fail to remember a time when goodness and truth were themselves under attack by evil itself?

> Again, and I say again… "One generation passes away, and another generation comes; but the earth abides forever" (Eccl. 1:4).

This philosophic banter is not meant to imply hopelessness shall overtake reason; for everyone who trusts in the Lord will be saved. The ultimate sense of security and greatest reason for hope in this life that humanity shall ever experience is only found in faith and obedience to the Lord of heaven and earth, Jesus Christ.

This dynamic tension between a seemingly ever changing present reality that continues to evolve into a future dimension that is marketed and over-hyped as being better than the past has generated much skepticism by many former and present day philosophers, poets and songwriters making light of this futility about life in general, whereby… "Let us eat and drink, for tomorrow we die" (Isa. 22:13). "Don't worry, be happy." And also, "Get yours while the getting is good."

What, then, is the purpose of life if everything changes and yet stays the same; if anything gets better only to become worse again, what manner of madness is life on earth that results in such fearful futility? Why arise each morning to fulfill a manifest destiny to only again repeat tomorrow the same things performed yesterday?

If there is no meaning to this earthly merry-go-round, then why does the Lord keep us in suspense within an unpredictable future? Where is our hope? This is what Solomon was seeking to discover.

If this message is nothing more than a harbinger of bad news, then what is to stop anyone from focusing on having fun? Nothing at all – and in fact, the Lord wants us to have fun and enjoy our days upon the earth. While this may seem like an unfamiliar truth that is hidden within the scriptures, the Lord does want us to have fun… *as* we delight ourselves in the Lord. The Lord must be our focus – and nothing else, and the Lord Jesus wants us to keep our eyes upon Him and simply… faithfully endure. Life can be fun and is not to be considered drudgery even if none of us are getting out of earth alive; earthly humanity is the transitional phase between those former things and life eternal. What we will become is not known, but we will be changed from glory to glory – to be that which we were originally created to be: the host of earth and children of God. We are spiritual beings that are having a human experience for one season of eternity. Once we are done with this humanity phase, and we faithfully endure all things in Christ until the end, we will transition into a new glory phase "in" oneness with the Lord… upon the new earth.

> "To them God willed to make known what are the riches of the glory of this mystery among the Gentiles: which is Christ in you, the hope of glory" (Col. 1:27).

So, what is our hope if we essentially die without changing anything? What is the meaning of life? Why even strive for excellence or live according to the most excellent way if all the good we do is meaningless vanity and a chasing after wind? Nothing on this planet makes any sense without hoping in something that is far greater than death itself! And indeed, there is just one thing… and therefore, nothing on earth is greater than the resurrection that is found in Christ.

> "If, in the manner of men, I have fought with beasts at Ephesus, what advantage is it to me? If the dead do not rise, *Let us eat and drink, for tomorrow we die!*" (1 Cor. 15:32; *Isa. 22:13*).

Even the Apostle Paul used cynical arguments to prove his point about the resurrection. Indeed, if everything is utter futility and meaningless vanity, what advantage is there even in being good if there is no resurrection? Solomon, the second wisest man to ever live (second to Jesus) kept asking the rhetorical questions beginning with 'what' and 'why,' but it seems the author put all the pieces together to explain life on earth except for one: all is meaningless and a chasing after wind apart from having a personal relationship with God in Christ Jesus and living according to the Spirit of God in you. If you aren't living with Jesus as the center of your life – then everything *is* vanity and a chasing after wind.

The Apostle Paul also came to the same conclusion; "O wretched man that I am! Who will deliver me from this body of death?" (Rom. 7:24). And he answers this cynical quandary in the only manner possible: "I thank God—through Jesus Christ our Lord!" (v.25).

Jesus is Lord! Jesus is the key to this earthly quagmire to safely escape the coming fire that will burn away everything that does not give glory to God. Please take note: I did not say faith in Jesus is the key; believing in Jesus – and having a love and trust personal relationship with Jesus are two entirely different things. One espouses a factual belief that operates apart from faith while the other manifests a lifestyle of godly righteousness according to faith; the former simply believes while the latter puts into ~~practice~~ action the elements of faith in Jesus Christ having been thoroughly persuaded and convinced to live according to the most excellent way… the way of Christ.

If, however, we know that we will each be asked to give an account and be individually judged for our past, then we must endeavor to live by grace and walk in God's goodness as Christ taught us. We need to put our trust in the only One who can deliver us – Jesus Christ, Lord Almighty.

> "Blessed is the man who trusts in the Lord, and whose hope is the Lord" (Jer. 17:7).

Transitional Places

Have you ever been stuck in one place for such a long time that all you ever wanted to do was leave? It didn't matter where you went as long as it was somewhere else.

Perhaps that does not resonate with you. Have you ever been in one place for such a long time that the thought of having to move or change location caused fear and anxiety?

These scenarios represent the push and pull of our human existence upon the earth. We were created by the Lord to be sojourners and agents of His change upon the earth, but if we have become complacent and comfortable with this worldly system such that we prefer status quo more than doing the unthinkable to accomplish the impossible, then perhaps our sedentary life-as-usual cannot see the larger picture that is hidden beyond the veil which is called: life eternal.

There is more to this life. There is another life after this life.

Transition is not often an enjoyable process to go through because it involves change within an element of uncertainty; if, however, we knew how the Lord was changing us and what the Lord was changing us into and what we were going to be doing after we were changed, we might embrace this change with willingness and anticipation. Sadly, this information is hidden behind the veil. All we can do at this point is trust in Christ – and this hope will not disappoint us.

What awaits us on the other side? There are many opinions and I have some as well.

When I read the scriptures to consider the ordination of man upon the earth, the Lord tells us many times that He knew us before we were born and He knitted us in our mother's womb (Prov. 8:22-31; Psa. 22:10; 139:13). This period of time when we existed with God, before this life on earth began, I refer to as the life of the soul apart from the flesh. We were a spiritual being with God ... a soul abiding in His presence, and we were "daily His delight" (Prov. 8:30). God's plan always intended for us to be the host of earth because this planet is our proper domain and habitation; earth is our eternal home – in this life – and the life hereafter.

"The word "*habitation*" (*oiketerion*-G3613; *residence*) refers to: A) the former home of angels that did not keep their "first estate, proper domain" residence in heaven on account of unlawful deeds (Jude 6), and B) it refers to our new "habitation" residence/tent/body (as '*ex*' coming "from out of" heaven; 2 Cor. 5:2) which we will inherit in the resurrection as we abide upon our "first estate and proper domain" – earth.[45]

If this message contradicts what your tradition taught you regarding where you will go after your body dies, namely – heaven, then you should read the book "Here: The Kingdom of Heaven is." There is not one reference in the 692 scriptures about heaven that says "man goes to heaven." Not even one – yet we obsess on it! Jesus didn't promise it, the Apostles didn't preach it and our Creeds don't teach it. We, the redeemed, were promised life eternal by Jesus in the kingdom of heaven – which includes the new earth as the eternal habitation for "the host of earth."

Since our eternity is going to be spent upon the earth in the hereafter, in the Paradise of God called Eden, then what do you think you might be doing upon the new earth? Your new earth resurrection '*oiketerion*' clothing will be put upon you just as your first earthly garment was put on you in the womb; however, this one will never see corruption nor will you experience pain. This new earth body will be glorious, much like the resurrection body

---

[45] Excerpt from "Here: The Kingdom of Heaven is."

that Jesus had when He was raised from the dead (Matt. 25:21; 1 Cor. 15:43; 1 John 3:2) and the body that angels have in heaven (Matt. 22:30). It will be like the body which Adam and Eve had before they fell from grace, such that, being without glory on account of sin, they were able to see their nakedness; however, there will be no sin or doubt in the hereafter that will ever separate us from the love of God and the glory of His presence. That former time will not be just a faded memory of a previous life on earth... it will not even be a life anyone will remember.

> "For behold, I create new heavens and a new earth;
> and the former shall not be remembered or come to
> mind" (Isa. 65:17).

Is anything to difficult for the Lord to accomplish? Jesus stretched out the heavens and the earth by Himself and He has created an everlasting way for man to inhabit the earth according to His eternal plan. He alone has done it. He clothed us in the womb and formed our inner parts; He gave us a mind with intellect in order for us to make our ways straight before Him; He fashioned a heart within us that might not practice guile or deceit; and He gave us a spirit to partner with His Spirit to direct our paths so that we may walk according to the will of God in steadfast faithfulness and love toward Him. He made the Way – and it's up to us to walk in it.

So, what will we be doing in the new earth? We will be master craftsmen, builders, and servants of the Most High God, Jesus Christ. We were created for His glory – and we will manifest His glory in the new earth after He triumphs over His enemies to become His footstool.

In this life we will have pain and suffering, but in life eternal, we will be delivered from even death itself where "God will wipe away every tear from their eyes; there shall be no more death, nor sorrow, nor crying. There shall be no more pain, for the former things have passed away" (Rev. 21:4). The former trials and tribulations that we experienced during this transition phase in earthen vessels shall not be remembered nor come to mind (Isa. 65:17). This, I believe, is on account of His great mercy! The joy that awaits us will far surpass the pain we endured in this life of the flesh, as the faint fleeting memory of a time when the enemies of God were positioned against the sons of men for earthly dominion with venomous cruel hatred toward us... all on account of Christ our Lord and Redeemer.

Man was sent to earth to have dominion over the earth; this is God's eternal plan for man and the earth. There are no accidents or mistakes in this plan even though it seems our failure is monumental; all we must do is keep our eyes focused on Christ – and faithfully endure.

- Don't give up. Don't give in.
- Be steadfast and resolute. Endure trials and tribulations.
- Endure to the end of this age... because another age is coming soon.
- Eternity is eminent. It belongs to those whose hearts are steadfast in the love of God.

What shall we be doing on earth for all eternity? It seems we will be doing much the same as we are doing now: building, farming, creating, stewarding the earth and declaring the glory of the Lord... except, in this new earth reality, there will no longer be any doubt or sin that separates us from the love of God because all will know the Lord because the glory of the Lord will be with us and as oneness "in" us... and all will worship Him in one accord. From the least to the greatest, all will acknowledge the Lord and give Him all the glory for He alone is great and mighty and worthy to be praised.

Can you imagine such a place?

> "Behold, You desire truth in the inward parts, and in the hidden part You will make me to know wisdom" (Psa. 51:6).

The outward man will pass away, but the inner man that is

redeemed will never experience the second death when truth and wisdom are worn like sashes and breastplates of righteousness. Indeed, the forever eternal place will never experience transition – ever again. And neither will you! If you can comprehend such a reality, then perhaps now is the time to start living according to the manner in which you were created… as the host of earth. The Lord gave us the command to have dominion over the earth and His enemies. For those who remain faithful and true to His commandments, He will reward each one according to their deeds.

Our battle is not against flesh and blood; our battle is against spiritual forces of darkness and wickedness and against principalities and powers that have established themselves in heavenly places on earth's domain to contest the sovereignty of Jesus Christ, the Lord of heaven and earth. We were sent by the Lord to reestablish His sovereignty by declaring His lordship *over us* as His disciples – and *through us* by the pulling down of spiritual strongholds that have raised themselves up against (anti) the knowledge of Christ.

> "For we do not wrestle against flesh and blood, but against principalities, against powers, against the rulers of the darkness of this age, against spiritual hosts of wickedness in the heavenly places" (Eph. 6:12).

Faithful ones, the host of heaven (angels) wage war against spiritual hosts of wickedness in heavenly places, and Jesus wages war against Satan, the Prince of Darkness, and the host of earth (sons of men in transition of becoming sons of God) are waging war against principalities and powers in heavenly places on earth. We are at war and we have been sent to declare and decree this battle cry: "The kingdom of heaven is at hand. Repent!" Those words will never be uttered in the new earth, so choose this day Whom you will serve – and declare your allegiance to Jesus Christ the Lord.

This present life is worth fighting for because your life hereafter depends on it.

Dominion happens – and God has given everyone free will to make an eternal choice.

What will you inherit in the age to come? Are your deeds and faithfulness being stored up as treasure in heaven to await the resurrection and regeneration of all things – or are you forfeiting even your inheritance and legal birthright as saints of Almighty God in order to enjoy the pleasures this world has to offer which are paltry compared to the glory that awaits? What does it take for us to come to our senses and awaken from this grand illusion sold to us by the forces of wickedness whose only interest is to deprive us of what was rightfully ours to begin with by defrauding us with lies, deceit, trickery, and deception through doubt and unbelief? They cannot inherit what was promised to us, so their intent is to deprive us of the glorious inheritance of the saints because they hate us with cruel venomous hate.

Saints of God – what manner of men aught we to be? Victims – or servants of the Lord.

If Jesus is your Lord, then serve Him… and obey His commands. Have dominion in the name of Jesus, for the praise of His glory, now and forever. Amen.

And this is the purpose of His Church, the Bride of Christ… "to the intent that now the manifold wisdom of God might be made known by the church to the principalities and powers in the heavenly places" (Eph. 3:10). May we, the church, begin to make known the manifold wisdom of God to the host of men upon the earth while the light is still light.

Endure. Declare. Advance. Proclaim. Faithfully endure.

Transition Tales

Let's take a look at two spiritual giants in the bible to learn several aspects about transition.

The Lord called Abram (Abraham) to go to the land that He would show him. The journey began with Abram's father, Terah, taking Abram, Sarai, and his grandson Lot (son of Abram's brother, Haran) along with many servants, multitudes of livestock and great wealth to go with him on a journey. Terah leaves the land of Ur of the Chaldeans to go to the land of Canaan, but halfway there settles down in a place he named after his deceased son, Haran, where he himself dies. The exact location of Ur is debated, but the most probable location places Ur and Haran about 730 miles apart. This journey, which began with a great many people and livestock, would likely have taken many years.

After Terah died, Abram continued the journey to the land the Lord would show him. *Abram did not know where he was going*, but by faith, he left his country (the land of his father's house) and traveled with Sarai and a multitude of people and livestock. At least 318 men, not including women and children, are attributed to Abram when he went to rescue Lot (Gen. 14:14), so this journey was like moving a large town along with tents, flocks, herds, food and other belongings. Traveling a distance of 700-800 miles or more would have taken many years with considerable planning while encountering many obstacles in unchartered territory, yet Abram did it because he believed and trusted God.

Abram left his father's territory, left his family of origin, traveled through unfamiliar territory for many years with all their belongings, and then arrived at "a place" the Lord promised to show him many years later. Abram was in transition the entire time… from what was – to the beginning of something new and unknown. All he had were words and promises from the Lord to go, and for some… that is all it takes, and history regards Abraham as "a man of faith."

Imagine traveling day after day through unfamiliar territory, through inclement weather, through changing seasons that would have made food acquisition difficult, through terrain often difficult to move swiftly, dealing with typical events like broken equipment, injured servants, infant births, lost animals, searching for grassland to forage, soils too muddy to travel upon during rainy seasons, inhospitable residents who question why you are passing through their land to stop for periods of refreshing, and lastly… the soft-spoken discussions around campfires that question what the leader is doing because he doesn't know exactly where he is going. All they know is that "the Lord will show him" when he gets there.

Transition isn't easy – and oftentimes is not popular.

Now, let's consider Moses who, much like Abraham, was asked by the Lord to lead a very large group of people with many possessions out from one country to go to the land that was promised to them – the land of the Canaanites, Hittites, Amorites, Perizzites, Hivites and the Jebusites. For four hundred years, the Israelites were slaves in Egypt and earnestly prayed for deliverance, but once the people were set free from bondage and delivered by many miraculous events, they sought to grumble against their leader, Moses. Not only did these people put Moses to trial with much testing, they also tested the Lord.

These people had not known freedom in four hundred years and now they were expressing themselves with great liberty of thought and action leading to open rebellion against Moses and the Lord, so when the people made a golden calf to worship, the Lord determined this generation would never enter the promised land. Imagine for a moment what the next forty years would have been like for Moses and Joshua as they wandered around the desert and the mountain of God until all those rebels died. Perhaps millions perished along the journey with great affliction and constant grumbling; now imagine that you are that leader who is being blamed for all their self-inflicted woes. Is it no wonder that Moses became very angry with these people?

The Lord was transitioning this rebellious group of people to become His chosen nation… which took forty years, and then some. History has since recorded many similar generations who have vacillated in their obedience to the Lord; numerous kings and rulers did evil in the sight of the Lord, priests were more interested in legalistic righteousness than teaching people to have a personal relationship with the Lord, prophets boldly spoke the words of the Lord whereby all of them were killed for it. It seems the transition process for Israel remains ongoing to this day because they failed to acknowledge their one true King when He manifested Himself to them. If you are not becoming what you were originally intended to become, then the Lord continues to be gracious, merciful and longsuffering up to a point, and then… it's time to graft a new branch onto the vine.

Thirty years ago, after I was saved by grace and baptized in the Spirit, I found myself in the midst of transition; I was raised Roman Catholic but I became increasingly disconnected from church traditions and teachings that contradicted the message Jesus preached, especially having to do with salvation and infant baptism. Months before my first child was born, I made the decision to break away from hundreds of years of family tradition (on both sides) to raise my children in a Christ-centered Protestant manner. This created a schism between me and my family which became palpable at family events, and I have (and continue to) endure many trials as a result of this decision. My life became, literally, a transition element between a former family tradition rooted in Catholicism and a future family tradition for my children to walk in the way of truth and to love Jesus (without all the religious trappings and baggage).

There are many lessons to be learned from this. We are all in transition to become what the Lord planned long ago. Even the church finds itself in transition between the church age and the kingdom age because she no longer desires to listen to the Voice of her first love, the Lord Jesus – or the Holy Spirit for that matter. The Lord desires us to abide with Him in Presence and Spirit, to hear His voice, to walk according to the Spirit and to do all that He commands; however, the church has drifted off course and now finds herself within transition once again.

Transition Safety

Whether you are on a sojourn between places or you dwell in one residence, transition will be experienced by everyone, but not everyone will have a safe and smooth transition. By safe, I mean a place without hostility, strife or immediate danger where a person can meditate (day and night preferably) on what the Lord is revealing to them and to listen intently without inordinate distraction. As I sojourner from place to place, my primary concern was finding a safe place to sleep at night. Perhaps my fear seems obsessive to some, and yet there are a great many who have experienced trauma of one sort or another when they were most vulnerable – when they thought they were safe enough to go to sleep. The place where a person rests and recovers at night is not something to be taken for granted. This one element was a common core value as I lived among homeless people in Florida and elsewhere; in Canada, this core value was deemed the highest in order to transition people from homelessness to productivity in society, such that safe housing was "the number one" priority above education, jobs, substance abuse prevention or other forms of rehabilitation. Safety is important to everyone. By offering it to strangers, you may be entertaining angels unwittingly (Gen. 19:1; Heb. 13:2).

Trans To Trans

While in transition, we are being transformed by glory and grace to become gateways of glory and grace. Transition is often resisted because it implies being changed into something else in order to become someone else, but this is a misnomer: you are what you are. Before God can change the "who" part of us, He has to convince about the "what" part of us. And in this regard, the Lord is deeply concerned about the what.

> "*What* is man that you are mindful of him?" (Psa. 8:4).

Our culture is obsessed with personal identity. There are thousands of self-help books, programs, organizations, TV shows and positive-thinking pundits that are consulted every day to help us know who we are, but the "who" part of us cannot be known apart from knowing "what" we are, and if we think our what is one thing but our what is completely other, then our who will be trapped in the middle of an identity crisis between what and whatever. Let me explain…

If you are a child of God Who knows you by name, and knows the number of hairs on your head, but you have been taught that God is angry or ambivalent, then you will struggle to believe the truth about how much God loves you. If you have been raised within an atheistic house and taught God does not exist, then your "who" will always be in conflict with "whatever." And there are some that have created an entirely new "what" in order to be "who" they wanted to be, only to result in confusion and disorientation.

We are all in transition of varying degrees in order to be transformed from what we were so that we may live according to the manner in which we were created – as sons of God.

- "For as many as are led by the Spirit of God, these are sons of God" (Rom. 8:14)
- "For you are all sons of God through faith in Christ Jesus" (Eph. 3:26)
- "For the earnest expectation of the creation eagerly waits for the revealing of the sons of God" in the new earth (Rom. 8:19)

Now Therefore

> "I beseech you therefore, brethren, by the mercies of God, that you present your bodies a living sacrifice, holy, acceptable to God, which is your reasonable service. ² And do not be conformed to this world, but be *transformed* by the renewing of your mind, that you may prove what is that good and acceptable and perfect will of God" (Rom. 12:1, 2).

Sons and daughters of God Most High – we need to own this scripture!

Many of us, in the early days of conversion, were given a scripture by the Spirit that left an impact crater upon our soul, which the Holy Spirit has used to guide us over and over again – and encourage us to keep moving forward. These scriptures became a "spiritual lens" through which our lives would be directed and transformed in order that we may become a living testimony of His word made manifest, being living and active as a double-edge sword in us and through us that not only transforms us – but changes and influences others as well. The scripture above literally jumped off the page and became implanted in my mind at my conversion, and as you can tell by the substance of this book, the Lord has been pouring much wisdom and understanding into my transformed mind with His living word.

The word "transformed" is *'metamorphoo'* (G3324) also translated "transfiguration" and denotes a continuous process of being changed and renewed – to reveal the glory within.

As I mentioned earlier, transition can be an awkward and painful period; not long ago I went through a transition period and became overcome by deep grief and sorrow. There are many psyche and other factors that contribute to these emotions, but it is important to know that Jesus was also a "Man of sorrows" and "acquainted with grief" (Isa. 53:3). Jesus knew the truth about the cruelty and brutality of this worldly reality versus the peace abiding in the kingdom of heaven that surrounds us, and He consistently tried to teach His disciples about this truth so that they might be liberated from many doctrines and toxic theology from hard-hearted teachers that very often frustrate the soul. Jesus knew the answer to their problem (and it wasn't an anti-depressant)… because Jesus is the Answer, but it was hard even for His disciples to follow Him. He simply said, "Believe in Me" and sometimes, when we are way over our head in transition and transformation… that is all we really need to do. Believe!

Transition always has a purpose: to help us become what we ought to be. Transition is not about us getting to where we need to be because "is" is not place-based; it is future based. The single most difficult part of transition is this: we don't know what "what" is! We are told by the Spirit of the Lord to get going and keep at it, but oftentimes we have no clue what we are supposed to be doing or (like Abraham) know where we are going. One thing I have learned while on my sojourn is this: it doesn't really matter where you go… if you are guided by the Spirit, you will always be where you are supposed to be. So, then, 'where' is somewhat irrelevant, yet '*get going*' is mission critical. The Lord knows who you are and He is abiding within you, so you will never be alone on this journey. Surrendering control of the situation was perhaps the hardest thing for me to perceive, and to be perfectly candid… I still don't have a clue. Yes, the Lord called me as His writer and I have been writing seven books concurrently which He told me to put on the internet for free, and I transitioned from living in tents for six months and just recently transitioned out of living in my car for three months to live out of a minivan (a tiny RV), and when I awake tomorrow, I still have no earthly clue where I will be or what will happen; however, I *do know* that My Lord is with me every step of the way and my passion to write what the Lord tells me to write has only grown stronger and stronger with each struggle, trial and tribulation I encounter. So perhaps it is for this reason that I experience these things so that I may write about it and encourage someone else … to get going, don't stop, keep at it and above all… trust in Jesus the Lord! "What" always makes sense according to "is."

None of us are getting off this planet alive, so the best or greatest good that I might possibly do is to serve the Lord with the fullness of my attention and affection, and perhaps encourage others to do the same. The Lord of glory has called each of us to walk according to His calling upon our life, which is actually His life being revealed in you and through you, but it is up to us to respond to the Lord's invitation and say… "Here I am, Send me" (Isa. 6:8).

Noah answered the call (Gen. 6:22); Abraham answered the call (Gen. 12:4); Samuel answered the call (1 Sam. 3:9); David answered the call (1 Sam. 17:32). ***ALL*** the giants of faith *answered* the call of faith. But… will you?

And one more thing… it seems the Lord plays to our weakness and not our strength, so when you think all the odds are against you and you lack the strength to go on, it is then that the Lord picks you up, brushes you off and sends you back into the very matrix that either wants to minimize you or take you out of the race completely. The Apostle Paul had this happen to him many times and he fervently petitioned the Lord three times to take away the thorn in his side. Just when you think you've become valuable to the plan of God, the unexpected happens and then your veracity or integrity or whatever will be called into question whereby your strength becomes nullified and the only thing that remains… is your love and trust and utter dependence upon the Lord of grace and mercy to carry you through it.

My dear brothers and sisters in Christ, let me tell you one of the most valuable lessons that I've learned: it isn't about you! **It… is… not… about… you!!!** If you are unable to give God the glory in your weakness, then it's only a matter of time… and patience is a virtue. God gets the glory! in everything!

In all we do, we are to honor Him. Consider this: the Lord of Glory came to earth and suffered far worse things than we can imagine, so now, do you regard yourself as better than Jesus? Jesus knew Who He was at the age of twelve and still persevered until the age of about thirty in order to begin His long-awaited three-year sojourn into Jerusalem to be butchered by truth-less men who disregarded Truth Incarnate. So, you think you've got it bad? Ha! Maybe one day my private journal will be released to share the painful misery of rejection and the ridicule of others, being alone yet writing in obedience without house or home, never knowing if my mission to write what I heard from the Lord will be completed before my last breath is given to me – or if anyone will ever read it! Even now, deep sorrow fills my heart and mind for my family and loved-ones who only know in part and see in part, who are willing to snack on crumbs along the wayside of institutionalized religion when an entire banquet table has been set before all His faithful ones who answer the call, live in truth with understanding, and give their entire life to love and serve Jesus, forsaking the cares of this life, to glorify the Lord of glory with their life.

Life... what an interesting concept................

The Third Person

Many years ago, I was leading an organization from near bankruptcy to operational stability. There were many unique factors and players that needed to be coordinated in this turn-around effort, yet every now and then I could sense some resistance to the change process. After several unexpected events began to pop up and sidetrack significant progress being made, it became obvious to me that there was an invisible element that had a hand in this... which I called "the third person." This became a valuable lesson for me to learn and to teach to others in management positions as well... to "look for the third person."

Oftentimes, we do not understand why our best laid plans sometimes go awry or even how poorly planned and unmanaged ideas become serendipitously successful beyond reason. It's as if an invisible force is guiding the process of change upon the earth to produce the outcomes needed for continuity. America's founding fathers called it "Divine Providence" to explain the favor and blessing they encountered when all odds were against them in their defiant act of independence from the mightiest nation on the planet with far superior military, navy and financial resources. Every nation has experienced this during their history as well because the Lord is a nation builder, such as when an invading Armada was suppressed by an unexpected storm or a dictator was suddenly deposed during the night. Divine Providence!

If God is for us, who can be against us! This is not a question, but a prophetic exclamation!!!

The third person that I am referring to in these scenarios is the hand of God being administered by the Holy Spirit of God, Who continues to hover over the earth (and dwell in us through faith in Christ) to accomplish the will of God throughout the earth. This is not science fiction or urban legend; the Holy Spirit works the will of God and intercedes for us in miraculously unseen ways. When we lack wisdom, He provides truth; when we lack strength, He provides 'dunamis' power; when we lack stamina to carry on, He encourages us to keep going forward in faith. The Holy Spirit is the invisible hand and guiding force to manifest grace upon grace on us, in us and through us. We are not alone and have never been alone; the Holy Spirit is always with us even if we are not walking by faith or living according to the Spirit. The Holy Spirit will never abandon us or forsake us because Jesus promised Him to us for these reasons: believe, understand, and continue in the course of faith.

There is, however, another viewpoint to the Invisible Hand we can trust; there is an invisible force of evil upon the earth that works to maintain darkness and chaos throughout the earth that seeks to prevent the restoration of God's kingdom upon the earth. The invisible reality of these spiritual forces is being manifest in the hearts of (evil-minded or Spirit-guided) men to build one kingdom or the other… for earthly dominion. The tearing down and the building up of nations and kingdoms has been going on since the dawn of history, so this cannot be construed as an overactive imagination or zealous religious ideology; the dynamic tension to push up and pull down strongholds has witnessed the rise and fall of many empires (Babylonian, Assyrian, Persian, Greek, and Roman from the ancient world alone, plus countless empires since). Alliances have been formed and dissolved, treaties have been forged and broken, and promises to preserve and protect have often been ignored in an effort to seek some military, economic, religious or political advantage.

All in all, the will of God that allows mankind to have dominion upon the earth is governed by the same Hand that effects God's plans and purposes – through the agency of man's heart. The Lord controls the reins of man's mind with thoughts that influence the motivation of the heart, and yet, the elements of change have always been left up to man. Why does the Lord allow this? Because God has given mankind the command to have dominion upon the earth... and it was for this purpose that we were created. For better or worse, He gave us authority to do it; promoting goodness or wickedness – or establishing righteous or evil has always been the moral responsibility of man upon the earth according to the will of God... and we have only ourselves to blame when we allow evil to flourish upon the earth. Verily, we are living in the world of our own making, such that the reality of heaven or hell is made manifest on earth – through the hearts of men.

The gateway of heaven or hell upon the earth – is made manifest through the soul of man.[46]

If we desire to see changes that result in righteousness upon the earth, then we must allow our souls to be transformed by the renewing of our mind by the Holy Spirit (Rom. 12:1, 2). The heart can only manifest what the mind has planted (Matt. 13), and understanding the spiritual forces at work upon the earth is predicated by knowing the truth *and* living according to it, which can only be accomplished by being born anew according to the Spirit of God (John 3:3-8). Either mankind allows the Spirit of God to rule and reign in our hearts through faith in Christ Jesus to perceive this truth, or by default... the forces of evil shall continue to wage war against the mind of man to pervert the truth with lies, kill other men, and obliterate all goodness and godliness upon the earth.

In the end, the kingdom of God is victorious ... even if mankind does little to honor God with the life-breath and the glory they were given. The Lord is going to re-establish righteousness in the earth in the regeneration of all things with or without us; the question for us is this: do you want to partner with it – or work against it? And if you want to be a partner with Jesus, do you desire the better resurrection? (Heb. 11:35).

> Jesus said... "For he who is not against us is on our side" (Mark 9:40).

---

[46] Read "Gateways" to fully understand this principle.

The Mystery of Man

Perhaps the best way for me to explain man's reason for being upon the earth is what I call: the mystery of sanctification. We are being sanctified for a very good 'eternal' reason

> "For both He who sanctifies and those who are being sanctified are all of one" (Heb. 2:11).

Yet before I discuss sanctification, I want to discuss an "unofficial" description for the word – Christ.[47] We attribute this word to Jesus in every regard, and when it appears independently of His name as an epithet, it conveys Jesus by expressing Him as "the Anointed One." Jesus Christ is: Jesus, the Christ, the Messiah, the Anointed One, the Son of God, Lord God, God Almighty, and *El Elyon* – God Most High that represent at least 111 names for Jesus in the scriptures. There is no question in our mind regarding His Divinity, but I want to express an understanding that was given to me that will help us see man's spiritual reality within a heavenly context.

The word "Christ" conveys "manifestation of God." Jesus "the manifestation of God" appeared for God and as God in every regard as the '*charakter*' – "the *express image* of His person" (i.e. Divine Nature; Heb. 1:3). When I insert the terminology "*the manifestation of God*" in substitution of the word "Christ," the scriptures provide a greater means of understanding two things: 1) Jesus is "the Manifestation of God" and the Shekinah 'manifest Presence of God's' glory; and 2) man is a spiritual being "in" relationship *with* God through Christ.[48]

For example:

---

[47] Christ (Christos-G5547) from (G5548) means anointed, i.e. the Messiah; Strong's Concordance.
[48] With one exception, which the gospel writers also do, the word for Jesus in the possessive case is rendered Christ's because it seems awkward to add an apostrophe after the name Jesus'.

- "When 'the manifestation of God' who is our life appears, then you also will appear with Him in glory" (Col. 3:4)
- "The woman said to Him, "I know that Messiah is coming" (who is called 'the Manifestation of God'). "When He comes, He will tell us all things" (John 4:25)
- "He first found his own brother Simon, and said to him, "We have found the Messiah" (which is translated, 'the Manifestation of God')" (John 1:41)
- "He [Jesus] said to them, "But who do you say that I am?" Peter answered and said to Him, "You are 'the Manifestation of God'" (Mark 8:29)
- "Then if anyone says to you, 'Look, here is 'the Manifestation of God'!' or 'There!' do not believe it" (Matt. 24:23; said by Jesus).
- "And demons also came out of many, crying out and saying, "You are 'the Manifestation of God,' the Son of God!" And He, rebuking them, did not allow them to speak, for they knew that He was 'the Manifestation of God'" (Luke 4:41)
- "If You are 'the Manifestation of God,' tell us." But He [Jesus] said to them, "If I tell you, you will by no means believe" (Luke 22:67)
- "Ought not 'the Manifestation of God' to have suffered these things and to enter into His glory?" (Luke 24:26)

Consider the implications of these scriptures as well:

- "*The manifestation of God*' in me – the hope of glory" (Eph
- "But when you thus sin against the brethren, and wound their weak conscience, you sin against [the manifestation of God in them]" (1 Cor. 8:12)
- "Having a good conscience, that when they defame you as evildoers, those who revile your good conduct in 'the manifestation of God (in you)' may be ashamed" (1 Pet. 3:16)

Please understand this explanation without unnecessary dramatic alarm; I am not being sacrilegious or irreverent to Christ or the scriptures... I am trying to communicate very deep understanding. Through faith in Jesus, "Christ" is in you, and since 'the manifestation of God' is in you, then you are His tabernacle as well as His image bearer who was "created in His image according to His likeness" for this express purpose: to become another manifest expression of God (i.e. Christian) in the world. This is what we have been reading and understanding throughout hundreds of pages in the Image Bearer series – and it all comes down to this: manifest God – in you and through you – in the similitude of Jesus Christ, your Lord and God.

Why do we find this so difficult to comprehend? Why is it so difficult to perceive this truth – and receive this truth into our lives... that God wants to manifest Himself in us? God is ALREADY in us and God wants to release His glory and power through us, yet it is we who deny this truth abiding within us and, thus, deny the most beautiful aspect of man's existence on earth, as well as man's experience on earth. *This is what the new earth reality will be like – as Paradise inhabited only by those inhabited by God*.

> "Now He who establishes us with you in Christ (*Christos*-G5547) and has anointed (*chrio*-G5548) us *is* God, [22] who also has sealed us and given us the Spirit in our hearts as a guarantee" (2 Cor. 1:21, 22).

The Anointed One anointed us!!! Our earthen tabernacle was anointed and is being sanctified by "He" who sanctifies us to become a holy habitation for the Lord our God, who *establishes* us (*bebaioo*-G950; built up from within) "in Christ" and sealed us by His Spirit. Jesus was not merely teaching us how to live better... He was teaching how to live like Him, according to His likeness, with the thorough knowledge that God is in us.

> "I am in the Father and the Father in Me" (John 14:11).
> "I and My Father are One" (John 10:30)

With Christ in you, then you, likewise, are in the Father and the Father is in you!!! YOU and your FATHER are ONE!

Where does your spirit end and where does God's Spirit begin? Beloved – you are one!

> "I do not pray for these alone, but also for those who will believe in Me through their word; [21] ***that they all may be one, as You, Father, are in Me, and I in You***; ***that they also may be one in Us***, that the world may believe that You sent Me. [22] And the glory which You gave Me I have given them, that they may be one just as We are one: [23] I in them, and You in Me; that they may be made perfect in one, and that the world may know that You have sent Me, and have loved them as You have loved Me" (John 17:20-23).

"I in them and You in Me" (v. 23). Jesus left absolutely no room for equivocation! Through faith, Jesus is in you and the Father is in Jesus. Thus, therefore... the Father is in you on account of faith in Jesus 'the Manifestation of God' and furthermore... you are now the 'manifestation of God' upon the earth as His representative, His ambassador, His *elohim* and His beloved!

Saints of the Most High God... when we believe this truth, we will be set free from the self-imposed bondage of religion and the self-inflicted blindness of sin that so easily ensnares us and separates us from the love of God who dwells within us richly. "The fullness of the Godhead" dwells within you bodily when you have fully yielded your earthen vessel into the Lordship of Jesus Christ, the Holy One of God... and thus, you have now become another manifestation of God upon the earth "through Christ Jesus our Lord."

Why, then, sanctification? God may express Himself through ordinary common vessels, but He will not manifest His presence in unsanctified vessels – or release His glory through them.

> "Therefore if anyone cleanses himself from the latter, he will be a vessel for honor, sanctified and useful for the Master, prepared for every good work" (2 Tim. 2:21).

Sanctification prepares us to be useful to our Lord and Master, Jesus 'the manifestation of God,' having been "created in Christ Jesus unto good works" (Eph. 2:10). Jesus was absolutely pure and holy, and Jesus is Jehovah Tsidkenu – "God our righteousness" yet Jesus sanctified Himself, not because He had any reason to be sanctified, except one: to become a tangible example and demonstration as 'a man' whereby all men must be sanctified before being anointed and authorized by God to manifest the works of God. Not only did the Father sanctify Christ's vessel, but Jesus also sanctified Himself.

> "Do you say of Him whom the Father sanctified and sent into the world, 'You are blaspheming,' because I said, 'I am the Son of God'? (John 10:36)

> "And for their sakes I sanctify Myself, that they also may be sanctified by the truth" (John 17:19).

This prophetic fulfillment by Jesus, which was spoken by the prophet Ezekiel, is another confirmation of His identity as the Lord: "Thus I will magnify Myself *and sanctify Myself*, and I will be known in the eyes of many nations. Then they shall know that I *am* the Lord.'" (Ezek. 38:23). Jesus *IS* the Lord… and there is no room for equivocation here either! Sanctification is what all earthen vessels must go through in preparation for the manifestation of God's work through us. We are called, sanctified and then preserved in Christ for greater works.

> "Jude, a bondservant of Jesus Christ, and brother of James, To those who are called, sanctified by God the Father, and preserved in Jesus Christ" (Jude 1:1).

And sanctification helps us comprehend the new earth reality that we will share with others:

> "So now, brethren, I commend you to God and to the word of His grace, which is able to build you up and give you *an inheritance among all those who are sanctified*" (Acts 20:32).

> "I will deliver you from the Jewish people, as well as from the Gentiles, to whom I now send you, [18] to open their eyes, in order to turn them from darkness to light, and from the power of Satan to God, that they may receive forgiveness of sins and *an inheritance among those who are sanctified* by faith in Me.'" (Acts 26:17-19).

What is our inheritance? Is it not the new earth? And who will be with us? Is it not those who are also sanctified and preserved in Christ Jesus among us? And what is our great reward? Is it not our fruit of righteousness that we will exchange for greater glory in the resurrection?

> "For both He who sanctifies and those who are being sanctified are all of one, for which reason He [Jesus] is not ashamed to call them brethren" (Heb. 2:11).

The mystery of man upon the earth is sanctification! And for this reason Jesus offered Himself as a living sacrifice, holy and acceptable to God… for our sanctification.

> "For by one offering He has perfected forever those who are being sanctified" (Heb. 10:14).

Why would God come to earth and become a man to then be butchered by men? Why would God strive and agonize through so many inordinate scuffles with man in order to sanctify man? And why give him a divine nature? Why, why, why? ***Because (the big picture understanding) God wants us to become like Him so that***

we may govern the new earth in the same manner that He would – according to our Divine Example – Jesus Christ!!! Jesus came in meekness as our Divine example… and "Blessed are the meek, for they shall inherit the earth" (Matt: 5:5).

What, then, is sanctification? In one word: 'hagios.'

"Man was created to be more, to desire more, to thirst for more, to seek goodness and perfection. The faithful in Christ are counted as saints worthy of God's election by grace and our souls crave holiness because we were created to be holy as God is holy. We are being sanctified by the Holy Spirit as we are washed with the word of God's truth. Our sanctification is not just for our benefit; we belong to God. We have been called into newness of life and are being sanctified for the purposes of God – and we are being sanctified for His glory. It is not for our benefit only but for His inheritance that we believe and are being saved. We have been called according to His purpose (Rom. 8:28).

"What do the words holy, sanctified and saints have in common? They all have the same Greek root word: '*hagios*' (G40). By utilizing all three words in various combinations, we will understand why God loves us and has called us into a personal relationship with Him. Saints (G40) are holy (G38) and sanctified (G37). Sanctification makes saints holy. Holiness constitutes a sanctified saint. We are consecrated vessels who have been called out (*ecclesia*) and set apart for service according to His purpose. We are Christ's workmanship, holy and acceptable, which is our reasonable service (Eph. 2:10; Rom. 12:1, 2). We were created for holy service to worship as saints of the most High God. We are consecrated vessels, and instruments of worship, as holy articles for true worship, in spirit and in truth. You are a sacred vessel to God, a sanctuary (*hagion*-G39) who was created upright and very good for divine service. You are more precious than gold and silver, more costly than jewels and more valuable than diamonds and pearls. You are the precious things of God –and He loves you so much. You are a tabernacle for the Divine. The Father's name in hallowed (*hagiazo*-37). Why do you resist His tug on your heart? How can you resist His love?" [49]

Perfection, in this regard, is not based upon holiness codes set by man "as doing" but rather "becoming and being" according to what Jesus tells us – by living according to His example. Jesus ate with sinners, touched lepers, conversed with tax collectors, allowed prostitutes to perfume Him, and yet – He walked on water. He did wrong according to everything that was "customary" in Judaism in order to be "what" He was intended to be: Yeshua, our Messiah.

Sanctification is all about "holiness to the Lord" as our response to the Divine Presence of God within us; we do not act pious – holiness is our "divine nature" response to 'the manifestation of God' within us.

How the institutional church misunderstood the purpose of salvation as "the only step" rather than just the first step in a never ending process of sanctification in preparation for the new earth leaves me utterly baffled, speechless and immensely grieved.

> "For you are not mindful of the things of God, but the things of men" (Mark 8:33).

> "Set your *mind* on things above, not on things on the earth" (Col. 3:2).

Manifesting God in us and through us – is man's reason for being on the earth, but before God can manifest Himself in us – He needs to weed out all elements of doubt through sanctification wherein the trees of righteousness may flourish once again upon the new earth.

What On Earth Are We Doing Here

What an excellent question, indeed. Allow me to express the presence of man upon the earth from a "mindful of the things of

---

[49] Excerpt from "Regenesis" chapter titled "The Spirit of Man" by the author.

man" perspective. For no earthly reason does man seem to be here – and if mankind were removed from the planet, the earth would keep going and going without interruption. In some regards, man has made it better, but in most cases the earth has been inextricably altered and disfigured to suit the needs of man; and yet even in this, when man vacates a place, nature has an incredible capacity to reclaim and renew itself in such a manner so as to erase any and all evidence of man's presence. And yet even in this, outer space objects have erased nature many times over and left impact craters the size of oceans as nature itself creates both mountain and ocean abyss by tectonic forces that, by comparison, dwarf the puny impacts of man.

What is man that nature is mindful of him? Absolutely nothing, really. However… "What is man that God is mindful of him" (Psa. 8:4; 144:3). Much in every regard!

Attempting to understand any reason for man upon the earth without the indwelling presence of God's Spirit is – well – meaningless vanity. So, why are we here – and what is God's purpose for man? There are numerous schools of science, theology and philosophy that have endeavored to explain this mystery for thousands of years. Science and philosophy look at man's existence from an anthropocentric view and theology has oftentimes has done the same thing – by trying to explain the divine reality and spiritual reality from a man-centered perspective, but I will go back to one point that I keep making over and over again – the Spirit! The Spirit! The Spirit! Apart from the Spirit of God, we can know nothing without the mind of the Spirit, or God's intent… because "No one knows the *mind* of God except the Spirit of God," thereby we understand significantly less than that. All three theories make very good comprehensive and holistic explanations for the world in which man lives with radically differing conclusions… that is… until the "why" question comes up. Yes, there are subatomic particles, but why? Yes, we discovered DNA and Higgs Boson (the God particle), but why? Yes, there are consistencies of thought among all cultures, but why? Yes, the human mind can store three million years worth of data, but why? Yes, the cosmos were knowingly explained many years ago and then Hubble found millions more galaxies that are moving away and contracting at the same time, but why? We have been looking into eternity in two directions (microscopic and telescopic) to find something, but why? What are we looking for and what are we hoping to explain? Precisely – the what question begins the process, followed by why, to explain "is." And yet, even after we've gone around the mountain several thousand times, man is no closer to explaining who he is – apart from seeking truth with the assistance of the Spirit of God dwelling within him.

> "For what man knows the things of a man except the spirit of the man which is in him? Even so no one knows the things of God except the Spirit of God. [12] Now we have received, not the spirit of the world, but the Spirit who is from God, *that we might know the things that have been freely given to us by God.*[13] These things we also speak, not in words which man's wisdom teaches but which the Holy Spirit teaches, comparing spiritual things with spiritual" (1 Cor. 2:11-13).

And yet I am amazed by the volume of words that seem non-essentially necessary to teach truth to convey understanding in order to perceive the spiritual reality that surrounds us – and dwells within us as well – but don't ask me why! Ask Jesus. Let the Spirit guide you into all truth because I am just a gardener who writes what he hears.

Two Schools of Thought

There are two spiritual schools of thought that explain man's existence upon the earth: the doctrine of sin and the gospel of grace. These two opposing yet oftentimes complementary schools of thought represent two ways in which spirit-minded men have sought to understand man's ordination upon the earth… but they reach different conclusions. And perhaps the best way for me to explain man's purpose on earth, as it relates to man's sanctification, is to compare and contrast A) the doctrine of sin, versus B) the gospel of grace – by their attributes:

Doctrine of Sin	Gospel of Grace
Sinful nature	Divine nature revealed
Sinful world	New earth
Corrupt	Created a little lower than angels
Contemptible	Crowned with glory and honor
Sinful and evil	Upright and very good
Religion	Relationship
Works	Greater works through grace
Faith with works	Supernatural miracles
Know the truth	Understanding the truth
Sin	Trust and obedience
Sinners	elohims, priests, and kings
Laws	Hear His voice and follow
Sacrifices	Mercy and compassion
Obligation	Love
Commandments	Spirit of grace to imitate Jesus
Safety net	The reality of Christ in us
Hope deferred	Promise assured
Worship "what we know"	Worship in spirit and in truth
Give a tithe	Surrender all
Glad	Exceedingly joyful
Ginosko	Oida
Type and Shadow	Substance
Essence	Manifestation
Alternate reality	Jesus is our Lord and eternal King
Know in part	Dianoia understanding
Less than	Greater than
Fading glory	Greater glory
Immortal	Eternal
Immanuel – God with us	God in us
Heaven	New Earth

This list could go on and on, but the greatest difference is within the realm of the eternal; the new earth reality understands the origin of man from an eternal perspective such that God placed eternity in our hearts for a reason (Psa. 49:9; Eccl. 3:11). We are spiritual beings experiencing one season of eternity on earth as humans (in the flesh), but our origin did not begin at conception because our Source is God Himself who made and created everything by the thought of His intellect (Gen. 2:2-4) before anything was created and formed by the power of His word – through Jesus Christ.

A new age is coming soon to the earth, as well as a great tribulation – and then the Regeneration will occur whereby the temporary pause in eternity for one season upon the earth will end – and eternity will resume again – with newness and oneness in one Lord and one God, Jesus Christ.

What are you willing to exchange in order to embrace the eternal reality you have been promised?

Thoroughly think through this question and assemble the truth with understanding in the oneness of your heart and mind (soul). You were created for an eternal purpose! Are you willing to lay down your life and your kingdom of self-attained glory in order to follow Jesus… at all cost?

Consider this…

If the only people who inherit eternal life are those who exemplify the attributes of Jesus, then I perceive only a very small number because only very few are willing to agonize through the narrow gate to become like (imitate) Jesus.

> "And you shall love the LORD your God with all your heart, with all your soul, with all your mind, and with all your strength.' This *is* the first commandment. [31] And the second, like it, is this: 'You shall love your neighbor as yourself.' There is no other commandment greater than these" (Mark 12:30, 31).

These are the divine attributes that Jesus exemplified, and the meek that live according to His example on earth here and now – will inherit the new earth with life eternal

> *"For many are called, but few are chosen." (Matt. 22:14).*

Thorough Thinking Through (dianoia)

Of all the messages that I hope to successfully communicate to the faithful in Christ who want to walk in a greater-than awareness of Christ in their life, this is my hope: that we '*suniemi*' assemble the truth in our mind to seek a greater understanding and our reason for "being" on earth by yielding to the Holy Spirit's transformational work in you (your inner man) through the renewing of your mind (*dianoia* thought process). Every book I write is about our sojourn to remember who we are, which begins by understanding "what" we are in relation to Jesus our Creator who created us as image bearers – in His image according to His likeness.

We were created as gateways and "throughways" so that God's grace, glory and heavenly things may pass through us – and fill the earth with the glory of the Lord.

Now, let's discuss a deeper level of understanding called '*dianoia*.' This is not the type of truth that comes simply by exercising the intellect (*noieo*) or by assembling truth with the intellect (*suniemi*) – '*dianoia*' is the means whereby the Holy Spirit is able to transform us by renewing our mind (*nous*) into a spiritually-focused mind that is able to thoroughly think things through "with" the mind of the Spirit in order to think operationally with understanding. This next point is very important: we are not using our mind to create new imaginative truth, which is the way of the world; we are yielding our will to the operational work of the Spirit to create "throughways" of thought within our mind that results in divine revelation that enables us to understand the spiritual paradigm of God's kingdom that is consistent with the truth of God.

Let us revisit several terms to put this into context.

'*Nous*' (3563) is defined as "the intellect, i.e. the mind, the seat of reflective consciousness, comprising the faculties of perception and understanding, and those of feeling, judging and determining"

[50] (Luke 24:45; Rom. 1:28; 14:5; 1 Cor. 14:14, 15 (twice), 19; Eph. 4:17; Phil. 4:7; Col. 2:18; 1 Tim. 6:5; 2 Tim. 3:8; Titus 1:15; Rev. 3:18; 19:7).

'*Dianoia*' (1271; *dia*-1223; channel, through + *nous*-3563; mind) means "to channel, through the faculty of the mind; deep thought, meditation, thorough thinking through." [51]

If '*nous*' represents "this new nature belongs to every believer by reason of the new birth (Rom. 7:23, 25),"[52] then '*dianoia*' represents our new nature intellect spiritually empowered by the Holy Spirit with '*megas*' greater understanding that operates according to prophetic vision, wisdom, divine understanding and revelation for one principal purpose: to establish the kingdom of God upon the earth.

When we compare and contrast "the wayside" as an area alongside the "normal thought process" that is contrary-in-mind (*para-noia*) to the truth, we can clearly see '*dianoia*' as the throughway through which wisdom, understanding and revelation truth is being manifested by those who have: cultivated their field (softened their heart), removed all seeds of doubt, and are being '*metamorphoo*' transformed by the Spirit of God to think according to a certain way… so as to have the mind of Christ! '*Dianoia*' enables us to perceive the darkness around us in order to pierce the darkness with God's truth to live as God intended – as imitators of Christ Jesus.

In what appears to be a significant intellectual reversal in a world view sense, the spiritual reality of "Christ in us" which is often portrayed as stupid, crazy and delusional (para-noia) is thus… intellectually enlightened and superior when we '*dianoia*' think with "the mind of Christ" which, as a bonus, also includes eternal life benefits.

---

[50] Vines, word study on MIND.
[51] Strong's Concordance.
[52] Ibid.

> "We know that we are of God, and the whole world lies under the sway of the wicked one" 1 John 5:19).

'*Dianoia*' does not merely sit back passively and marvel in awe and amazement when divine revelation comes; this enhanced level of understanding motivates saints to go deeper in their personal relationship with Jesus which compels them to live in righteousness and holiness as disciples of Jesus to become another manifestation of Christ upon the earth. '*Dianoia*' saints are compelled to walk by grace, in divine revelation, with prophetic utterances, to operate the spiritual gifts they have been given – to manifest Christ in the earth. These saints don't do it for personal gain, power, wealth, influence, prestige, accolades or the praise of men as when others marvel at the size of a ministry – these saints have sacrificed everything for the sake of serving Jesus, as one of His obedient servants who listen for His voice *and* do all that He commands. They have surrendered *all* for the sake of Christ Jesus. This, my friends, is diametrically different than the model within the current church. When Jesus told us to build His church, He meant: "make disciples" and then turn them loose to revolutionize the world with truth! A time is coming when saints with radical love and affection for Jesus are going to be revealed that are currently being hidden… and each of these unique expressions of Christ's faithful ones will become "manifestations of God" in them to release greater glory *through* them.

He who dwells within you – is all that ever matters!

The Dianoia Way

> "Jesus answered him, "The first of all the commandments *is:* 'Hear, O Israel, the LORD our God, the LORD is one. [30] And you shall love the LORD your God with all your heart, with all your soul, with all your (*dianoia*) mind, and with all your strength.' This *is* the first commandment. [31] And the second, like it, is this: 'You shall love your

> neighbor as yourself.' There is no other commandment greater than these" (Mark 12:29-31; see also Matt. 22:37 and Luke 10:27).

It is very interesting to read all the footnotes, citations and references in various Bibles to help us understand the impact of this scripture, yet none seem to perceive the impact of this one word to help us understand and comprehend what Jesus is teaching us.

Perhaps the best way for me to convey deeper understanding is to insert my exposition of the verse: the fullness of loving the Lord your God (Jesus) with the fullness of your soft-hearted heart, in tandem with heart and mind oneness of the soul, that has been thoroughly persuaded by the truth to walk in divine understanding with revelation, whereby you exert all human effort to live according to this deep understanding – is the first commandment.

Foremost in importance is loving the Lord your God, Jesus Christ. Secondly, love your neighbor as yourself. Jesus, who is God, who is the Preeminence, gets the preeminence (Col. 1:18) and all other sons of men are to be regarded with love and respect. This is the way of the kingdom of God according to the truth of God, but the alternate reality offers an alternative way to follow:

> "There is a way that seems right to a man, but its end is the way of death" (Prov. 14:12).

However, there is a *dianoia* way that is not conformed to the pattern of this world, which leads to eternal life. This is the Way of Christ!

There are two ways of going about life on earth: the way of death or the way of life. The only way anyone will ever be able to discern the difference between the two is to listen to the Voice of Truth – and be guided in the way of the Spirit to gain understanding. Seeking to search out and find truth to gain understanding with a desire to live according to the pattern of God's kingdom while upon the earth – is the first step in the way the Spirit transforms goats – into sheep who desire to live obediently to Jesus and imitate His example.

Either we 'give in' to God – or we continue to 'give over' our mind to live according to disobedience as an enemy of God's kingdom.

'*Dianoia*' occurs thirteen times in the scriptures that describe two camps of thought upon the earth: with Christ – or – '*para* (contrary to) *anti* (opposed to)' Christ. Consider these wayside examples of *dianoia*…

> "And you *He made alive,* who were dead in trespasses and sins, [2] in which you once walked according to the course of this world, according to the prince of the power of the air, the spirit who now works in the sons of disobedience, [3] among whom also we all once conducted ourselves in the lusts of our flesh, fulfilling the desires of the flesh and of the '***dianoia***' mind, and were by nature children of wrath, just as the others" (Eph. 2:1-3).

> "And you, who once were alienated and enemies in your '***dianoia***' mind by wicked works, yet now He has reconciled [22] in the body of His flesh through death, to present you holy, and blameless, and above reproach in His sight— [23] if indeed you continue in the faith, grounded and steadfast, and are not moved away from the hope of the gospel which you heard, which was preached to every creature under heaven, of which I, Paul, became a minister" (Col. 1:21-23).

> "He has shown strength with His arm; He has scattered the proud in the '***dianoia***' imagination of their hearts" (Luke 1:51; cross-over Hebrew is prob. '*sheriyruwth*' (H8307) in the sense of twisted imagination, as a hostile enemy; opponent)

> "This I say, therefore, and testify in the Lord, that you should no longer walk as the rest of the Gentiles walk, in the futility of their mind (*nous*-3563), [18] having their '***dianoia***' understanding darkened, being alienated from the life of God, because of the ignorance that is in them, because of the blindness of their heart" (Eph. 4:17, 18).

As we can see by these scriptures, the *dianoia* mind can become thoroughly persuaded and convinced to operate according to ignorance in darkness *as an enemy opposed to God.* Such people will strenuously defend their right to live however they want, and perhaps even talk about God's love for them – yet never even understand that their deeds are tantamount to lawlessness in blatant rebellion against God… because of the blindness of their heart on account of sin.

When we give in (yield our life) to God and allow His Spirit to guide us into all truth with understanding, we will begin to live according to the pattern and operating system (of the Spirit) in God's kingdom with a '*dianoia*' mind that has been thoroughly persuaded and convinced by God's truth to live like a true citizen in God's kingdom.

- "I will put My laws in their '*dianoia*' mind and write them on their hearts; and I will be their God, and they shall be My people" (Heb. 8:10)
- "This *is* the covenant that I will make with them after those days, says the LORD: I will put My laws into their hearts, and in their '*dianoia*' minds I will write them" (Heb. 10:16)
- "Therefore gird up the loins of your '*dianoia*' mind, be sober, and rest your hope fully upon the grace that is to be brought to you at the revelation of Jesus Christ" (1 Pet. 1:13)
- "Beloved, I now write to you this second epistle (in both of which I stir up your pure '*dianoia*' minds by way of reminder), [2] that you may *be mindful of* (3403-*remember,*

remind, call to mind) the words which were spoken before by the holy prophets, and of the commandment of us, the apostles of the Lord and Savior" (2 Pet. 3:1)

The net result of living according to the truth produces '*dianoia*' understanding within our mind to walk in the Way of Christ…

- "That the God of our Lord Jesus Christ, the Father of glory, may give to you the spirit of wisdom and revelation in the knowledge of Him, [18] the eyes of your '*dianoia*' understanding being enlightened; that you may know what is the hope of His calling, what are the riches of the glory of His inheritance in the saints (Eph. 1:17, 18)
- "And we know that the Son of God has come and has given us an '*dianoia*' understanding, that we may know Him who is true; and *we are in Him* who is true, in His Son Jesus Christ. This is the true God and eternal life" (1 John 5:20)

Beloved, we are in transition, we are being renewed through '*dianoia*' and are being sanctified according to newness through truth, change and ones so that we may become – sons and daughters of God in the new earth.

The mystery of sanctification and the revelation of Christ in you through a *dianoia* mind will help us understand, comprehend and perceive the true reason why man is upon the earth…

Imitate Jesus according to His example.

This is your reason for being on earth – and the meaning of life

Be a 'manifestation of God' upon the earth.

It's all about Jesus – in you and through you – and God gets the glory!!

Understand Oneness

Much of what we are taught within church today is to have faith in God so that we may attain greater things, namely heaven, which was never promised to us; however, we already have everything "in Christ" that we will ever have, including exceedingly great and precious promises, and yet, we continuously strive to attain that which we already possess. So I ask the main question behind all real and illusive quandaries… why? Why has the church misunderstood the Lord's instructions to us? Why, indeed? Because we are still operating in performance orientation to "do things" in order that we may "have and attain things," which incidentally – is the pattern language and *the way* of this world.

Jesus kept teaching very simple lessons, so it is no wonder that we remain in awe of the deep wisdom He revealed to us whereby we failed to understand this truth: the spiritual reality of heaven is all around us – and the kingdom of God is within you as well.

> "The kingdom of God is within you." (Luke 17:21).

> "by which have been given to us exceedingly great and precious promises, that through these you may be partakers of the divine nature, having escaped the corruption that is in the world through lust" (2 Pet. 1:4).

Since Jesus is in you through faith, and the Holy Spirit is dwelling within you as well, then the Father is also abiding in you. Truly I tell you, the fullness of the Godhead is dwelling within you bodily and yet we pretend this is not true, so we attend meetings in order to experience a new manifestation of God's presence – when the fullness is already within is – on account of faith in Christ and the new birth!

Just as Jesus said, "I and My Father are One" (John 10:30), likewise, you are also able to say the same thing… "I and My Father are One." You and the Father are abiding in oneness within the singularity of one person – exactly like Jesus and according to

His example. We treat many of these statements by Jesus as being mysterious revelations about His unique Divinity while appearing as a Man upon the earth, but His entire life was spent showing us how we are supposed to live, as spiritual beings, and also what is intended to happen to us at every stage along our spiritual journey as sojourners who were sent from heaven by the Father to do the will of God on earth.

When Jesus taught His disciples He was going to die, He began speaking deep mystery to us.

> "And now, O Father, glorify Me together with Yourself, with the glory which I had with You before the world was" (John 17:5).

The Lord Jesus has His Glory – and you have your glory as well. God's Glory always relates to His Presence and Spirit! Jesus was teaching us over and over that we are spiritual beings and that God's glory dwells within you because His presence also abides within you. Since God is in you, then His glory (the hidden treasure) is also within you, as is the Pearl of Great Price (the Lord of Glory) – which is why Jesus said, "The kingdom of God is within you" (Luke 17:21). And even more so, Jesus has given us the keys of the kingdom as well (Matt. 16:19)!

What part of this don't we understand? Just because it's too incredible doesn't mean it isn't true.

God's glory is His presence – and God's presence is His glory. "God is everywhere," and "The whole earth is full of His glory" and "God is in you all" (Psa. 24:1; Isa. 6:3; Eph. 4:6). We do not need to be a mathematician to add all three of these verses to come to one unifying answer in singular truth: God's glory is already within us. And because the Father dwells in us richly and has adopted us as children to be heirs of the kingdom *through faith in Christ Jesus*, then why do we lightly consider the reason for this glory which He placed within us – or its very existence? Do we not consider that we are supposed to do something glorious with it? Yes, indeed! We are to grow it, multiply it 30, 60, 100 fold, magnify the Lord with it, and most of all – we are to manifest it to the entire world so that all may see the truth that dwells within us. This is "the light" that we are to shine into the whole world – and this is the truth that was sown into us – to manifest God's glory in us and through us, and in doing so, we give glory to God – and by doing so, we become a vessel for Shekinah Glory: God's Manifest Presence!

> "Everyone who is called by My name, Whom I
> have created for My glory; I have formed him, yes,
> I have made him." (Isa. 43:1).

Everything we do on earth is to give glory to God with the seed of truth/light/glory that was placed within these earthen vessels. This is the purpose of man and our reason for being, as well as the meaning of life: we were created for His glory! And whenever we excel exceedingly more than we might ever hope or imagine, then we must give all praise and honor and thanksgiving unto Jesus and glorify God because – it is not us doing it – it becomes us allowing God to do it in us and through us as yielded earthen vessels according to the working of His Spirit within us. We were given glory to produce more glory so that we should give all glory unto God our Father – through Christ Jesus our Lord.

> "… that the God of our Lord Jesus Christ, the
> Father of glory, may give to you the spirit of
> wisdom and revelation in the knowledge of Him,
> [18] *the eyes of your understanding* being enlightened;
> that you may know what is the hope of His calling,
> what are the riches of the glory of His inheritance in
> the saints…" (Eph. 1:17, 18).

Do we prefer to further limit our understanding in order to remain '*asunetos*' unintelligent and thereby tempt the Lord's indignation – or are we going to accept Christ's command to become expressly like Him in all regards as His disciple? He calls us brothers and friends of God, and yet we minimize this truth in order to remain as we are – within status quo enclaves of religion.

Listen my friends, this is not new supernatural revelation as some would suppose – this truth has been made known to us for 2,000 years and this is the true nature of the spiritual reality that surrounds us <u>*and dwells within us*</u> even now; however, we have been taught the opposite such that we can never have and attain true holiness and perfection in the similitude of Christ because 'we are wretched sinners.' Well, I am here to boldly say that "yes and amen" you can... yet with two exceptions: you are not Divine (you have a divine nature but cannot be God) and you are not sinless (you are being set free from the power of sin and are being empowered to avoid sinful temptations so as to walk according to your spirit-nature being partnered with the Holy Spirit).

> "Not that I have already attained, or am already perfected; but I press on, that I may lay hold of that for which Christ Jesus has also laid hold of me" (Phil. 3:12).

Let me tell you a mystery: the more you walk according to this revelation according to glory that dwells within you whereby everything you do, from least to the greatest, is an occasion to exalt the Lord and give Him all glory, an amazing thing happens... everything being done to you, in you, with you and through you is being done for God's glory and for His sake – and because you recognize this and you are giving all praise, honor, glory and recognition to Jesus, the Father will release more glory through you because you are a faithful and obedient disciple of Jesus.

This is something we *can* attain – when we willingly choose to completely empty our vessel.

> "To them God willed to make known what are the riches of the glory of this mystery among the Gentiles: which is Christ in you, the hope of glory" (Col. 1:27).

Many years ago, while I was receiving revelation every day and communicating non-stop with the Holy Spirit, I asked the Lord,

"Where does my spirit stop – and where does Your Spirit begin?" Our conversation had become so seamless that I was beginning to question whether it was me doing all the talking and also me with a lot of divinely pretentious thoughts, so I asked Him that question… and then the Spirit spoke very clearly to me: "We are one!" The distinction between the two of us, which I thought had become blurred, was actually becoming seamless. I was operating in oneness with the Lord of all creation… according to the Spirit!

> "But he who is joined to the Lord is one spirit with Him" (1 Cor. 6:17).

> "There is one body and one Spirit, just as you were called in one hope of your calling; [5] one Lord, one faith, one baptism; [6] one God and Father of all, who is above all, and through all, *and in you all*" (Eph. 4:4-6).

During the final moments of Jesus Christ's earthly life (i.e. visit #26), Jesus spoke even deeper truth to His disciples because He knew He was nearing the time of His death. This is what people tend to do when they get close to the end of their life: they drop wisdom bombshells on us to help us focus on the real purpose and meaning of life – and to thoroughly comprehend.

> "I have glorified You on the earth. I have finished the work which You have given Me to do. [5] And now, O Father, glorify Me together with Yourself, with the glory which I had with You before the world was" (John 17:4, 5)…

> "I do not pray for these alone, but also for those who will believe in Me through their word; [21] that they all may be one, as You, Father, *are* in Me, and I in You; *that they also may be one in Us*, that the world may believe that You sent Me. [22] *And the glory which You gave Me I have given them, that they may be one just as We are one*: [23] I in them, and You in Me; that they may be made perfect in

one, and that the world may know that You have
sent Me, and have loved them as You have loved
Me" (John 17:20-23).

Jesus had yet to be glorified in His resurrection, and yet Jesus is teaching us He already has His glory residing within Him upon the earth, which He previously revealed to us by His transfiguration. Jesus is teaching us that we have our glory and His disciples are also being given a share of *His* glory – as partners and partakers of His glory – to do two things: 1. to make us one, and 2. to finish the work of Christ upon the earth (to have dominion over Satan) through the church. We are not waiting for the resurrection to receive our glory – we are already operating in the glory given to us whereby we will receive an even greater glory according to our faithful obedience to Jesus – in the Resurrection of Life (John 5:29).

And when we have completed the work which God has given us to do on earth, in the similitude of Jesus, the Father will glorify us with the glory which we had before "the world" was… and we will, once again, become like angels that are in heaven (Matt. 22:30; Mark 12:25).

Wow!!! Glory be to God!!! Jesus is one with the Father, and through faith with Christ in me, I am one with the Father – and the Father and I are one! And likewise – so are you!!! You can likewise say, "I and the Father are one." Say it, believe it, own it and live like you mean it.

God is in us. God is with us. God is for us. You are not alone! Now it's time … to BELIEVE!!!

Newness – through truth, change and oneness is what our true spiritual life on earth is all about. Lord – make us one! And let's get this dominion mandate started!

However, many of our motivational Sunday services are designed according to an old worn-out, obsolete tradition that keeps us in bondage to a sacrificial system – that is opposed to grace. We are told to go to church, listen attentively, give generously and perhaps come to the altar for prayer so that we can get closer to God and hear His voice; the very things that we attend by hoping to attain more of God's Presence in our lives – are actually keeping us addicted and dependent upon the pastoral and priestly "juice of godly encouragement" so that perhaps, just maybe, we will experience God and receive a Sunday blessing from God. Anathema!

This is not what God intended. We were created by God to host His Presence and Spirit, and to fill the earth with His glory!

> "God, who made the world and everything in it, since He is Lord of heaven and earth, does not dwell in temples made with hands" (Acts 17:24).
>
> "Thus says the Lord: "Heaven is My throne, and earth is My footstool. Where is the house *that you* will build Me? And where is the place of My rest?" (Isa. 66:1)
>
> "'The glory of this latter temple shall be greater than the former,' says the Lord of hosts. 'And in this place I will give peace,' says the Lord of hosts" (Haggai 2:9).

Connect the dots! **God does not dwell in houses made by human hands – He dwells in houses that have human hands**! Your body (house) is God's building. We were created to be tabernacles *of* His glory – and *for* His glory!!! We are many members of one body: the church. **Rest, in this regard… is the permanent place where God's presence abides – with/in you**! And the glory of your latter temple in the resurrection will be greater than the former earthen vessel that is currently reading these words. Christ in you… is all that ever mattered from day one.

> "Or do you not know that your body is the temple of the Holy Spirit who is in you, whom you have from God, and you are not your own?" (1 Cor. 6:19),

God is in "the house" when you walk through the door and bring Him with you. You are a tabernacle for Jesus and also a temple of the Holy Spirit, and the Father is abiding within you as well. So then, why do we go to church to be closer to God? Because we have been taught by the doctrines of man to think this way – which is contrary to what Jesus taught us. We are being taught religious things that are actually keeping us restricted from walking in oneness with the Lord and manifesting His glory in us and through us. We have been indoctrinated and inculcated to accept the business practices of operating a church to gather members to support the financial work of the church – instead of making disciples that desire to hear the Voice of Truth and follow Jesus as His disciples – and ***build His church*** with greater works! How many programs does your church support? How wonderful! Now let me ask this – is there even one program that teaches discipleship? This is the primary responsibility of pastors and priests, to make disciples that follow Jesus (not disciples according to Paul, Apollos, John, James, the Pope or according to other men's teachings or doctrines), and yet we elevate godly leaders to near worship status to become a disciple of Wesley, Calvin, as well as other super-preachers of mega-churches today. Even the church has been guilty of creating an alternate reality! Are there any programs in your church about greater works? How about supernatural grace gifts, prophecy or revelation? Are we going to continue to contend in this manner, as less than believers that pretend *not* to be filled with the Holy Spirit, or do we desire to be saints of the Most High God, Jesus Christ, that operate in the prophetic with revelation to build *His* church whereby we manifest His glory with understanding to produce greater works!

The Lord's disciples lived this way – and likewise, so should we. Many of their teachings represent a pulling away from tradition-laden Judaism even while they continued to live according to many of those customs; however, when we read about the Apostle Paul's radical message of grace and grace alone, with revelation and the manifestation of miraculous healings, signs and wonders accomplished through him, is it any wonder the Lord added to their numbers daily through his gospel. The church today often uses fear and guilt – but the Lord of glory prefers to employ grace and glory in us and through us.

Grace, grace, awesome wonderful grace; ***grace upon grace unto works and greater works in order to release glory and greater glory***. This is the ministry of the church in obedience to Jesus Christ… and the gates of Hades shall not prevail upon this earth!

> "To me [Paul], who am less than the least of all the saints, this grace was given, that I should preach among the Gentiles the unsearchable riches of Christ, ⁹ and to make all see what *is* the fellowship of the mystery, which from the beginning of the ages has been hidden in God who created all things through Jesus Christ; ¹⁰ to the intent *that now the manifold wisdom of God might be made known by the church to the principalities and powers in the heavenly places,* ¹¹ according to the eternal purpose which He accomplished in Christ Jesus our Lord, ¹² in whom we have boldness and access with confidence through faith in Him" (Eph. 3:8-12).

Saints of God Most High, this is what the ministry of the church must be about – again.

It seems the Lord is using these words to create a shock-effect within the church. The Lord is seeking newness in us – through truth, change and oneness – and we have been reading about truth and change within the context of wisdom and understanding, but we are never going to enter into the oneness that the Lord desires until we turn the fullness of our mind's attention and heart's affection to focus on Jesus and to do all that He commands – by hearing His voice.

Am I telling anyone to stop attending church? Absolutely not! We need to stay in *koinonia* fellowship with other believers, but the "man show" has gotten out of control. More time is spent every Sunday reading announcements, collecting money and telling anecdotal stories about what happened to you this week… than worshipping the Lord of glory, Jesus Christ. And some churches have the audacity to call this a worship service when all they do is sing three little hymns "at" God instead of offering reverence and praise that exalts His glorious name.

By faith, with Christ in you – your earthen vessel is now "the body of Christ" as He abides within you to do the will of God "through" you. We were called out and set apart, and sanctified and consecrated – so that we may continue to influence other souls and change the darkness of this world into the glorious light of heaven on earth with the truth/light/glory of Jesus Christ abiding within us. Since you have surrendered your lordship and have declared your obedience to Jesus Christ – as your Lord and your God, now therefore… your unique individuality now abides in oneness with Jesus Christ to flavor the earth with the uniqueness of divine salt and light radiating through you as an ambassador for Jesus to change this world for the sake of Christ.

Sadly, it seems, we have forfeited our heavenly birthright every Sunday for a bowl of carnal-satisfaction stew to hear messages that make us feel good rather than producing an increase of glory that causes demons to tremble.

The Lord Jesus abides in Oneness – and dwells in oneness <u>with</u> you! We need to own this truth! Oneness – is what the Lord desires. This is the example that Jesus taught: God is in you, God is with you… walk in oneness with the Father abiding within you… and the glory which you had "before this world was" will be returned to you in the new earth, including your great reward – if you remain faithful to do all that Christ commands during this season of eternity on earth.

Understand this: Jesus wants us to live "in" revelation with Him every day as our natural response to living as saints according to the kingdom of God within you – whereby everything you do gives all glory and honor to God in the process. We are a kingdom of prophets, priests, teachers and kings who follow Christ the King to build His kingdom and establish His dominion over the earth… until He establishes it "anew again" at the regeneration of all things. Jesus our Creator is not making *all new things* in the regeneration… He is "making *all things new*" again (Rev. 21:5)… including you and me, and heaven and earth. And when the new heavens and the new earth come down "from out of" heaven, He will reward His faithful obedient saints with honor and glory as their inheritance accounted to them according to works of righteousness done in the name of Christ.

> "And has made us kings and priests to His God and Father, to Him be glory and dominion forever and ever. Amen" (Rev. 1:6)… "And the nations of those who are saved shall walk in its light, and the kings of the earth bring their glory and honor into it" (Rev. 21:24).

An entirely new season of eternity upon the earth in the age to come is about to begin, and the saints who were martyred on account of their faith in Christ will experience the first resurrection to rule and reign with Jesus for a millennium (Rev. 20:4-6), then the end of the ages will happen followed by the second resurrection with judgment (John 5:29) and then the regeneration. But… before the first resurrection happens, the great tribulation must occur.

Life is not about you… it is about He who dwells within you… and He has invited you to the wedding feast of the Lamb… but perhaps you will count yourself unworthy to attain the resurrection of life because you have chosen to live according to your purpose and plans. Eternity happens… but are you ready… even now… if your life were required of you?

Magnify Jesus. Exalt His name! Hear His Voice and do what He tells you.

It's all about Jesus – and God gets the glory!. Amen and amen!

The Big Picture

We are covenant sojourners under assignment from heaven sent to bring the atmosphere of heaven to earth, to establish the dominion of Christ over this world and to assist in its redemption through obedience to Jesus Christ. We are not the object of this story, but rather, the faithfulness of God is on trial by His enemies to see how He responds to rebellion by free will servants.

There was a rebellion in the kingdom of God in which Lucifer broke covenant with God, planted seeds of doubt in the minds of many angels and led 1/3 of heaven away captive with his lies and deception. The Lord cast Lucifer out of the kingdom onto earth where Lucifer (now Satan) set up his own kingdom that awaits judgment. In this moment, the kingdom of God was bifurcated into the kingdom of heaven and the kingdom of darkness upon the earth where, once and for all eternity, creation is being divided according to either sheep who will stand together with Jesus Christ – or goats that stand against. Once all souls have been offered the opportunity to bow allegiance to Christ on earth, then the enemies of God will be banished into a pit of eternal torment and darkness – and then Christ will restore the kingdom.

We are spiritual beings that are having a human experience. Once we understand this core concept as our true identity, we can comprehend why we are here and what we are supposed to be doing, but we must be wary, because there are some here who are not of His fold that follow the father of lies (Satan). All the inhabitants of earth are being tested one way or another to see the manner in which we choose to live. Since God does not condemn us, the flesh is the means whereby we will bear witness to our manner of living – and judge ourselves in the process. We are here for three reasons:

1. To be sanctified and thereby remove all seeds of doubt
2. To have dominion and to disregard the enemy

3. To inhabit the earth and fill the earth with the glory of the Lord

The earth is a giant dragnet that ensnares all in order to entrap those apart from faith who are not of the Lord's dominion. Satan will continue to deceive as many as possible with lies, doubt and fear resulting in unbelief, but for those who remain faithful to the end, the Lord Jesus will be their salvation and rescue them from the net of destruction.

In the meantime, man has been sent to live for one season of eternity upon the earth. We were with the Lord in the kingdom as sons of God, we were sent to earth as sons of men, and, when we finish our mission to have dominion, then we will return to the Father as sons of God, which "the earnest expectation of the creation eagerly waits for the revealing of the sons of God" (Rom. 8:19).

Jesus came with a multifaceted mission, as the Way, the Truth and the Life. The Life mission came as a result of our disobedience in the Garden of Eden, whereby the penalty of sin is death, but God knew all along that mankind was too weak in our human estate to withstand the powerful attacks of the enemy. Indeed, and that was the whole point; we were created in weakness without the ability to save or protect ourselves. The weak things of God would be put on display for all the enemies and principalities and powers of God to see, not only to watch the faithfulness of the Lord's unyielding love toward His creation unfold, but to also watch His servants obediently follow Christ with the faithfulness of Job.

The earth is the place where the proofing of our faith and obedience to Christ is being tested and approved; earth is the place where souls are sanctified unto good works to burn away the dross and chaff; earth is the place where we must be willing to surrender ourselves and reckon ourselves dead in order to gain life eternal; earth is the transitional place between covenant agreements and kingdoms whereby we were given dominion in order that we may give God all the glory according to His increase through our yielded lives.

We were sent to earth to stand with Christ; we were sent to be born anew by the Spirit, to be filled with the Spirit, to be sanctified by the Spirit, to be transformed by the renewing of our mind by the Spirit, and to be guided by the Spirit, so that we may attain the promises of God afforded by the Spirit, including the hope of resurrection by the power of the Spirit, so that we may be finished and complete, lacking nothing of God, and… being found without iniquity or sin, we are able to remain standing in His holy presence on the day of judgment.

Our life on earth is in preparation for eternity on the new earth without sin, doubt or fear. Apart from the Spirit, we know nothing – and we cannot attain anything… and without Christ abiding in us or the Holy Spirit dwelling within us, there is no hope of salvation.

Remember the promises. Remember the mighty works and deeds of the Lord. Remember, acknowledge, declare, proclaim; imitate with fervent obedience and always let your yes be yes.

Jesus came to show us the Way to live so that we imitate His example and be saved through the testing of faith. Jesus conquered sin and death by living a sinless life and He, for our benefit, overcame the penalty of sin (death) in the resurrection as a working of the Spirit's power that is available to all those whom the Holy Spirit has sealed for redemption.

Jesus showed us the Way – and then He sent the Holy Spirit to come alongside us, fill us with dunamis power and to help us stand together with Christ. Once we acknowledge Jesus as Lord, yet never doubting, the Holy Spirit will help us complete the journey of transformation from the chrysalis old man into the glorious redemption that waits to be revealed in the new man.

We were sent to earth to be sanctified; Jesus showed us how to live in His likeness as a man, and the Holy Spirit enables and empowers us to fulfill our original mission: to have dominion.

We are sons of light that have been living within an open heaven for 2,000 years. The glory of God was hidden in earthen vessels and we, having been filled with the Holy Spirit, are becoming "manifestations of God" upon the earth in the exact similitude of Jesus Christ, our Lord, to continue His works upon the earth against the kingdom of Satan by establishing the dominion of Jesus, the King of heaven, upon the earth – against which the gates of Hades shall not prevail!

The new earth is waiting on the sons of God to be awakened – now let's get going!

It's all about Jesus – and God gets the glory!. Forever and ever – Amen and Amen!

[page left blank for notes]

Read the entire Image Bearer series!

Grace and peace be yours in abundance, paul.

Made in the USA
Middletown, DE
12 November 2018